AUSTRALIAN RIPPING YARNS II

Editor's Note

The stories in this book happened before Australia changed from Britain's Imperial weights and measures to the metric system. For authenticity, and to avoid incongruity, the weights and measures are given as they were at the time. See the Conversion Table below.

CONVERSION TABLE
One inch = 2.54 cm
One foot = c. 30.5 cm
One yard = 0.914 metres
One mile = 1.61 km

One ounce = 28.3 grams
One pound = 0.454 kg
One ton = 1.02 tonnes

The Five Mile Press

The Five Mile Press Pty Ltd
950 Stud Road
Rowville Victoria 3178 Australia

Email: publishing@fivemile.com.au
Website: www.fivemile.com.au

First published 2005

Text © Paul Taylor

All rights reserved

Designed by SBR Productions Olinda

Printed in Australia by Griffin Press

National Library of Australia Cataloguing-in-Publication data
Taylor, Paul
Australian Ripping Yarns II: pirates & poisoners, scoundrels & screen stars, ratbags & rogues.

ISBN 1 74124 862 0.

1. Tales – Australia. 2. Folklore – Australia.
3. Australia – History – Miscellanea. I. Title.

AUSTRALIAN RIPPING YARNS II

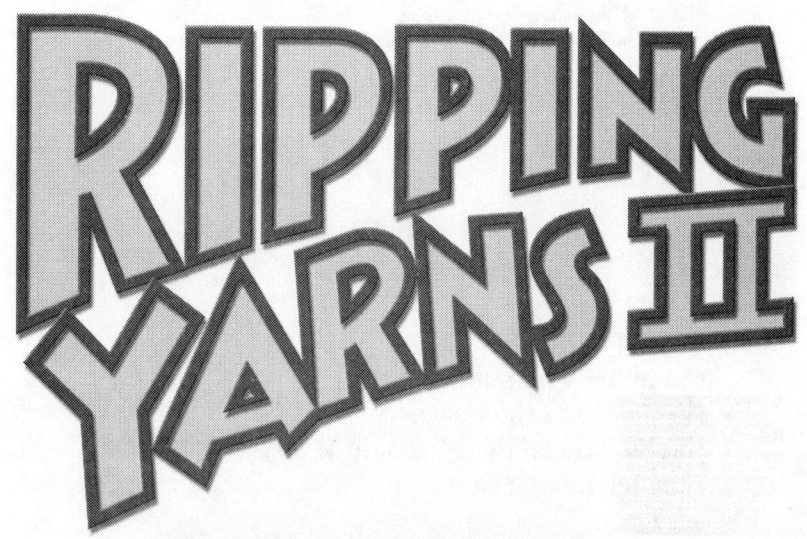

PIRATES & POISONERS
SCOUNDRELS & SCREEN STARS
RATBAGS & ROGUES

PAUL TAYLOR

The Five Mile Press

Contents

Preface	6
1 Buccaneers, cut-throats and castaways	9
The pirate who put us on the map	10
The *Trial* and the treachery	28
The fat lady on the good ship *Venus*	33
They fell among cannibals	36
2 Our dark story	43
'I'm not dead! For God's sake, don't cover me up!'	44
Black pearls and the butchered bishop	48
The man King Lash couldn't tame	52
3 What's in a bushranger's name?	61
Captain Moonlite's walk on the wild side	62
Did Thunderbolt go to his own funeral?	71
Give a dog a bad name	79
4 The Foreign Legion	87
The world's most perfect woman	88
Just a very naughty boy	92
Our star turns at the Vigilantes' necktie party	116
The *Boys' Own* adventures of the most influential Australian who ever lived	124
5 Good sports, bad sports	143
A chip off the young block	144
Black day at Rushcutters Bay	147
The look that lost the race of the century	156

6 Mad, bad and dangerous to know 165
The gold pirates of Port Melbourne 166
The *Monty Python* murder 171
The husband who murdered her wife 178
The Desperate Housewife of Frogs Hollow 184
The witch who danced with the devil 188

7 Beating the cruel sea 195
The soul survivors 196
'A man on the rocks! There he is!' 203

8 Deep secrets 209
HMAS *Sydney* and the riddle that remains 210
The bathtub revelation of Claude Sawyer 216
The canine clue to the Bogle–Chandler riddle 219

9 Ratbags and rogues 239
The comet who crashed 240
The obscene end of Eugene Goossens 246
The spy who never was ... was he? 254

10 Hats off to the unsung heroes 263
The man with the Nelson touch 264
How Horrie the Wog Dog hoaxed us all 268

Preface

When the first *Australian Ripping Yarns* was published people asked, are there other stories like this, and how do you choose them? This second book of Ripping Yarns answers the first question and for the second – how they were chosen – the answer lies on the cinema screen. My measure of a Ripping Yarn is the movies. Could you make a movie from this or that story? Every one of the stories in this anthology could be the basis of an internationally successful feature movie, from the first, the pirate Dampier's epic of bloodshed and discovery, to the last, Horrie the Wog Dog, the mongrel war hero who hoodwinked the nation.

There are horror stories. The ghastly fate of the 70 passengers and crew of the *Boyd* – most of them roasted and eaten – might open on the thwack of the 'cat' and flying bits of flesh as the Maori chief's son took his flogging. The tragic and puzzling sinking of HMAS *Sydney* with every one of her heroic 645 officers and crew aboard, might fade to black with the great, doomed, cruiser a glow on the horizon. The Eugene Goossens affair – a maestro ruined by his fascination with pornography and a rather nasty King's Cross witch – was a sensational news story that today, half a century later, we see clearly as a horror story.

There are comedy movies here. *The Monty Python murder* is a natural for Wes Anderson's quirky direction, and the Francis James conundrum cries out for Geoffrey Rush doing his Peter Sellers act as *The spy who never was*. Or was he *The imposter who never was*? An amusing question to mull over, but not one to compare with one of the 20th century's most baffling whodunits: the Bogle–Chandler killings in a Sydney Lovers' Lane early on New Year's Day, 1963.

There are the 'Westerns' – the bushrangers, as fascinating and as murderous as any in America's Wild West. Almost all of them died violently, but the three in this anthology, though each came to a brutal end, were very different characters whose pseudonyms echo their personalities. Captain Moonlite was probably homosexual. Captain Thunderbolt, thoroughly heterosexual, was often accompanied by his beautiful part-Aboriginal wife. And Mad Dan Morgan's savage and sad story was made into a movie with Dennis Hopper as the psychopathic killer.

The movies themselves play a role in this book. Annette Kellerman was that rarity – an Australian woman whose life inspired a Hollywood movie, *Million Dollar Mermaid* with Esther Williams as the Australian wondergirl swimmer who became a Hollywood movie star.

55 Days at Peking starred Charlton Heston in the role of a gung-ho American marine sorting out the insurgents in the Boxer Rebellion. But the tale of the real-life star of the bloody Peking siege is recounted in *The* Boys Own *adventures of the most influential Australian who ever lived* – Chinese Morrison.

The ideal Hollywood star to play Morrison would have been another handsome Australian adventurer, Errol Flynn – *Just a very naughty boy* – whose life, from his schooldays to his times dodging death at the hands of cannibals to his pathetic end in the arms of his under-age mistress, was one endless Ripping Yarn.

The sporting sagas – our first Test triumph; unassuming John Landy losing and yet winning; Jack Johnson changing the course of sport with a callous and brutal thrashing of Tommy Burns – are thrilling. The dramatic shipwrecks of the *Dunbar* and the *Loch Ard* are amazing and moving stories of survival.

Eccentrics like the enigmatic genius, Jorgen Jorgenson, will always intrigue us. And the first-hand accounts of the incredible savagery of our convict past still chill the blood.

Dramatic, mysterious, comic, blood-curdling and romantic, they are

Australian Ripping Yarns II

all riveting and true stories from our past, part of our tribal memory that should be preserved and celebrated for what they are: *Australian Ripping Yarns.*

Paul Taylor

1 Buccaneers, cut-throats and castaways

The pirate who put us on the map

William Dampier, exhausted, was sprawled with the other pirates in a steaming jungle clearing on the Isthmus of Panama. It was raining, as it had been day after day. Relentless rain punctuated by rumbling thunder that drowned out all other sounds. They were running for their lives.

Behind, back at the smoking fort, the Spaniards were triumphantly parading the impaled head of the pirate captain and busy mutilating his dead crewmen. The attack on the fort had been a disaster and the Spaniards, when they tired of rearranging corpses, could be expected to come after the survivors, hunt them down in the tangled undergrowth and swollen rivers and the swamps swarming with mosquitoes and leeches.

In the jungle the pirates had made a pact: those who couldn't keep up would be shot to save them from falling into the hands of the Spaniards. Now, in the clearing, the ship's surgeon and Dampier's close friend, Lionel Wafer, was sitting 'on the ground near one of our men, who was drying off gunpowder in a silver plate, but not managing it as he should, blew it up'. The explosion shredded Wafer's knee and shin and sent powder burns scorching up his thigh. He was in a bad way.

Would Dampier fight to save his friend? Or would he stay true to his pirate code?

William Dampier is an enigma. If he was an incompetent drunken coward, as some of the buccaneers who served under him claimed, he had an odd way of showing it. For more than 40 years and in the course of sailing three times round the world, Dampier did the things that pirates do: looting, pillaging and murdering from South America to Sumatra. But he was much more than a pirate. William Dampier was one of the greatest explorers, a man who had seen more of the world than any man ever had – he was the first man to visit five of the seven continents – and whose scientific records of those extraordinary journeys were felt for two centuries and more. Few have led a life more crowded with adventure.

Dampier followed in the bloodied footsteps of another and far more famous Englishman, the privateer Sir Francis Drake, who stormed Portobello on the Spanish Main a century before him. And in turn Dampier was followed a century later by another and far more famous Englishman, the navigator–explorer, Captain James Cook, who like Dampier turned England's eyes to the unknown continent of Australia.

Both men overshadow him. Yet neither could compare with Dampier's legacy of three books recording his experiences and his scientific observations. Cook relied on Dampier's observations when voyaging around the world; Darwin had his books on board the *Beagle* and Dampier's theory of 'sub-species' influenced Darwin's theory of evolution. Dampier's description of the breadfruit of the South Seas was the impetus for Captain Bligh's voyage on the *Bounty*. And his account of his life as a pirate has strong resonance in three classics of English literature: Robert Louis Stevenson's *Treasure Island*, Daniel Defoe's *Robinson Crusoe* and Jonathan Swift's *Gulliver's Travels*.

The Royal Navy's Admiral Burney wrote of Dampier in 1803, 88 years after his death, 'It is not easy to name another voyager or traveller who has given more useful information to the world; to whom the merchant and the mariner are so much indebted, or who has communicated his information in a more unembarrassed and intelligible manner.'

Yet generations of Australians have been taught to think that Dampier's part in our history – he was the first Englishman to set foot on the Australian mainland – is dry stuff, hardly worth mentioning.

'He seemed a more modest man than one would imagine by the relation of the crew he had assorted with. He brought a map ...' wrote the diarist John Evelyn who, with his fellow diarist Samuel Pepys, dined in London with Dampier in August 1698. His portrait shows the man who was the first to sail thrice around the world: a big-nosed, lean man, assured, sensitive ... and yet there is something secretive and melancholy in his black eyes, as if he knew his place in history would never be acknowledged because of his bloody past. Once a celebrated social lion, today he is little more than a footnote in history.

The son of a Somerset farmer, Dampier was born in 1652, went to sea as a boy and before he was 20 had sailed to Java on an East Indiaman. At 21, then in the navy and at war with the Dutch, he had his first taste of battle, was wounded and invalided out of the service and went home to recuperate. It would be four decades before this restless man took time to draw breath.

Within a year he had worked his passage to Jamaica to manage a plantation for a neighbouring Somerset family. There he got to know the pirates and privateers who flourished in those Caribbean waters. 'Privateers' – English sailors permitted by the Crown to plunder enemies in time of war – was the term Dampier used throughout his journals whenever he referred to the seamen he sailed with. The truth was they were mostly licensed pirates, whether or not England was at war.

Privateers, pirates, freebooters, buccaneers – whatever they styled themselves – these cut-throats were thickest where the richest booty was to be won, in the Spanish colonies of the new world: the northern regions of South America; the islands of the Caribbean and the Isthmus of Panama that joins North and South America, an area famous throughout the then known world as the Spanish Main.

Rich in gold, silver, and precious gems, particularly on the Isthmus, the Spanish Main might have been designed for piracy and plunder. On land, by mule, the Spaniards transported silver and gold from the mines to fortified ports set up along the coast, forts only the foolhardy attempted to attack.

Pirates, however, were nothing if not foolhardy. But if the fort repulsed them there was the option of ambushing the treasure trains, easy enough in the dense jungle with its narrow, twisting trails. By sea the great Spanish galleons were also vulnerable to audacious attacks by mosquito fleets of smaller, faster ships manned by cut-throats. And pirates were nothing if not audacious.

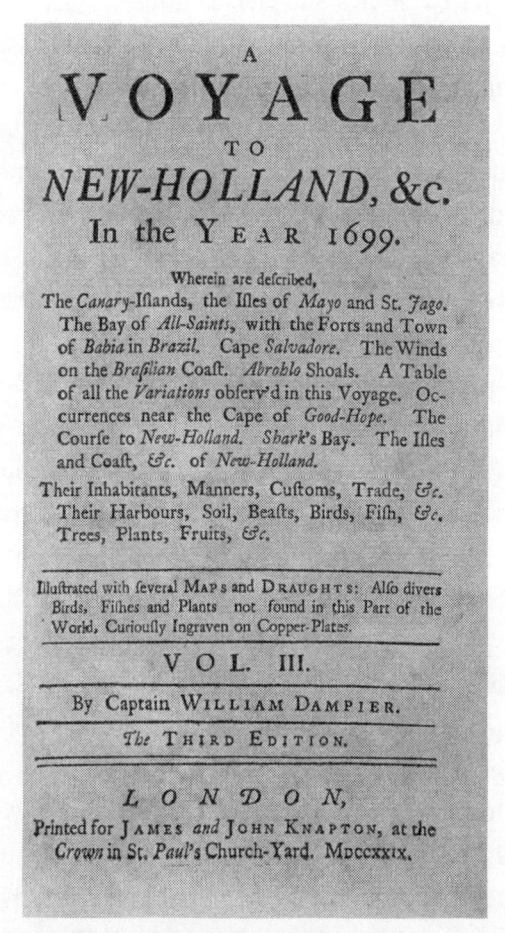

> A
> # VOYAGE
> TO
> ## NEW-HOLLAND, &c.
> In the YEAR 1699.
>
> Wherein are described,
> The *Canary*-Islands, the Isles of *Mayo* and St. *Jago*. The Bay of *All-Saints*, with the Forts and Town of *Babia* in *Brazil*. Cape *Salvadore*. The Winds on the *Brasilian* Coast. *Abroblo* Shoals. A Table of all the *Variations* observ'd in this Voyage. Occurrences near the Cape of *Good-Hope*. The Course to *New-Holland*. *Shark*'s Bay. The Isles and Coast, &c. of *New-Holland*.
> Their Inhabitants, Manners, Customs, Trade, &c. Their Harbours, Soil, Beasts, Birds, Fish, &c. Trees, Plants, Fruits, &c.
>
> Illustrated with several MAPS and DRAUGHTS: Also divers Birds, Fishes and Plants not found in this Part of the World, Curiously Ingraven on Copper-Plates.
>
> VOL. III.
>
> By Captain WILLIAM DAMPIER.
>
> *The* THIRD EDITION.
>
> LONDON,
> Printed for JAMES *and* JOHN KNAPTON, at the *Crown* in St. *Paul's* Church-Yard. MDCCXXIX.

The first travel book, a sensational best-seller. Dampier's jaundiced view of New Holland nevertheless led Charles II to send him back to discover more of the unknown land.

Dampier spent two years in Jamaica. He quit the plantation after six months and went to the Bay of Campeachy to join 250 men cutting logwood used to make ink and furniture, and much prized in Europe. But in June 1676 a hurricane ruined Dampier's logwood store, he lost his tools and, he tells us, he decided 'to seek a subsistence in the company of some privateers'.

He took part in a number of raids, but recounted only one: the attack on a fort guarding the town of Alvarado near Vera Cruz that cost the lives of 12 of the 60 pirates and yielded little.

Dispirited, Dampier went home, forced to work his passage. He meant to settle down; he bought land and married Judith, about whom he tells us very little. But marriage wasn't for him. Despite his best intentions he was a restless, 'rambling man'. (In Jamaica, the plantation manager had written that Dampier 'was given to rambling and could not settle himself to stay long in any place'.) William left Judith soon after the wedding to return to his true love – adventure and the pursuit of a fortune. In 1680, that meant the Spanish Main.

Dampier arrived in the Caribbean just in time to desert from his merchant ship and join a fleet of nine privateers in an attack on Portobello. Drake had tried and failed to take Portobello in 1572 and instead had raided the lightly guarded Spanish silver trains, returned to England a hero, and – when he gave Queen Elizabeth half the booty – her man of the month.

A century on, in 1679, Portobello fell when Dampier and more than 300 pirates swarmed into the town and took it with ease. Dampier got 100 pieces of eight for his part and whetted his appetite for life under the Jolly Roger.

In 1680 the pirates split into seven companies and walked through the rainforest to the fort of Santa Maria. Once again they had little trouble taking it, but found as they had at Vera Cruz, that the traders and the Spanish noblemen in the town had fled before them, taking with them their treasures and the hopes of ransom money. Frustrated, the pirates turned to Panama Bay where in one bloody day they burned half a dozen ships and slaughtered scores. But while capturing the 400-ton *Santissima Trinidad*, Captain Peter Harris, their leader, was peppered with musket shots as he jumped aboard. He and 18 shipmates died and another 42 were wounded.

Harris's death began a series of events that were straight from the 'How to be a Pirate' manual: bickering, fighting and fostering resentment over what they should do next, who should lead them, and how they should be treated; convening rambunctious councils of war; guzzling rum like there was no tomorrow – with good reason – and in quieter times going about their bloody business, marauding and murdering.

Richard Sawkins replaced the late Captain Harris, and for a heady while they captured 50,000 pieces of eight and 1,000 jars of wine and brandy. Off the coast of Chile the freebooters captured the *San Pedro* carrying 37,000 pieces of eight and invaluable sea charts that won them a free pardon when presented to Charles II.

But then Sawkins was killed in a raid on Pueblo Nuevo and things came to a head. Bartholomew Sharp, the new Captain, led an attack on a ship off the Isla de Plata. Below deck were 3,276 pieces of eight, and among the passengers and crew above deck, a priest. Sharp shot the priest and then fed the corpse to the sharks. This was frowned upon. Some of the men believed it would bring bad luck. Captain Sharp, too, had an irritating and suspicious habit of living up to his name. Too often for the pirates' liking he won their savings at gambling. So when their ship hove to and they celebrated Christmas 1680 on a desert island with heartfelt Yo-Ho-Hos and many bottles of rum, the pirates had a council, voted to strip Sharp of his command and threw him in the brig.

John Watling, the new captain, got the freebooters' spirits up again with an attack on another fort, this one guarding the port of Arica. Like all ports on the Spanish Main, Arica was fortified with high, thick walls and shore batteries that out-gunned the biggest cannons the pirate ships carried. Things didn't go smoothly. They were routed. Boulders thudded down on the buccaneers; snipers picked off those who fled; cutlasses and daggers finished those who couldn't run. As the sun set half of them lay dead on the beach and Watling's head was dancing around Arica's plaza, hoist high on a halberd.

The survivors split up, most following Bartholomew Sharp, now restored to command. Dampier and his friend Lionel Wafer and 42 others under Captain John Cook elected to make for the Isthmus in three open boats. There, in the steaming, sticky heat and rain of the wet season, Wafer was accidentally wounded. In agony from the gunpowder wounds to the leg, the surgeon stumbled after his shipmates.

Should he have been shot, as they had agreed?

' ... he was not able to march;' Dampier recounted in *A New Voyage Around the World*, 'wherefore we allowed him a Slave to carry his things being all the more concern'd at the Accident because liable our selves every Moment to Misfortune, and none to look after us but him'. The Spaniards had performed their own indelicate operations on three of Wafer's fellow surgeons left behind at Arica, and Lionel Wafer, as Dampier sensibly said, was all they had.

Six days out, during a tremendous thunderstorm, all but one of the Indian 'slaves' slipped away into the forest and the buccaneers, crossing a swollen river almost lost Wafer as he was carried downstream by a violent current and left behind two stragglers, Robert Spratman and William Bowman, who were reluctant to attempt the crossing. A third man, George Gainy, trying to get a rope across became entangled and was flipped over and swept away. In his knapsack he had 300 pieces of eight that sent him to the bottom.

Wafer kept up with them for nine days until at last he sank to the ground. He could go no further. He asked to be left to the uncertain mercy of the Kuni Indians. With him stayed two others, Richard Gopson, who always carried with him a copy of the Old Testament, in Greek, which he delighted in reciting, and John Hingson. Dampier and his shipmates pushed on for the coast. Starving, limping and in rags, they walked out on the Caribbean side of the continent on 24 May 1681, six weeks after they began the crossing of the Isthmus. Wafer followed them out three months later. Dampier, by now sailing in a new pirate fleet, saw a canoe approaching with five men aboard. He recognised four of them – the two left behind with Wafer and two others thought to have drowned in the scramble to escape. The fifth man, Dampier presumed, was a tattooed Indian. He was wrong. 'Mr Wafer wore a Clout about him, and was painted like an Indian and he was some time aboard before I knew him.'

A year later, after sailing to Virginia aboard the *Revenge*, Dampier and Lionel Wafer were off the coast of Africa in a captured 40-gun ship insensitively renamed, since some like Dampier were married, *Bachelor's Delight*. For the next three years he crisscrossed the oceans cruising off Peru, Guam, the Philippines, the Mekong Delta, the Gulf of Thailand, the South China Sea and Timor. Dampier recorded the course, distance, latitude, wind, and weather for every day. He told, too, of the mutinies, the savagery and the endless dangers the pirates contrived to put themselves in.

Sailing to Guam from Sana Pecaque they spent 51 tedious days at sea, rationed to half a pint of maize a day for each man, dog and cat.

'There was not any occasion to call men to victuals being made ready at noon, all hands were aloft to see the quartermaster share it, wherein he had need to be exact, having so many eyes to observe him. We had two dogs and two cats aboard, they likewise lived on what was given them, and waited with as much eagerness to see it shared as we did.' One sailor caught stealing rations was flogged: 'Captain Swan began first, and struck with a good will, whose example was followed by all of us.'

Then on 20 May, they sighted land. 'It was well for Captain Swan that we got sight of it before our provision was spent, of which we had enough for three days more, for, as I was afterwards informed, the men had contrived to kill first Captain Swan and eat him when the victuals was gone, and after him all of us who were accessory in promoting the undertaking this voyage. This made Captain Swan say to me after our arrival at Guam, Ah! Dampier, you would have made them but a poor meal; for I was as lean as the captain was lusty and fleshy.'

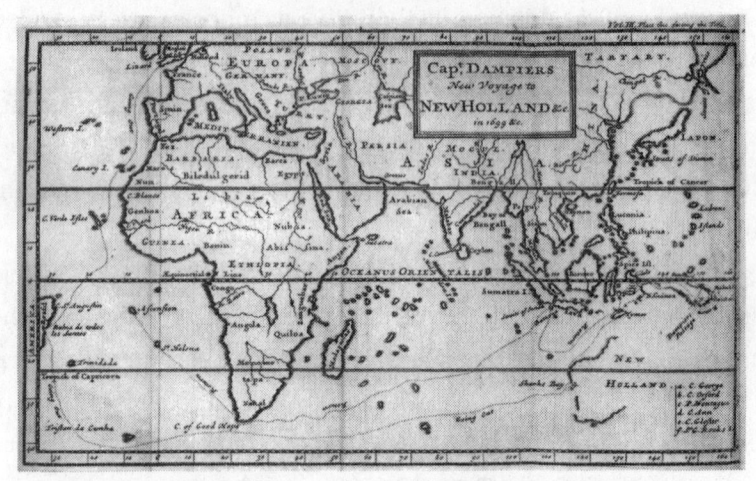

The first man to visit five of the seven continents, Dampier recorded, 'New Holland is a very large tract of Land. It is not yet determined whether it is an Island or a main Continent.'

At Guam Dampier ate breadfruit: 'The Bread-fruit grows on a large Tree ... when the fruit is ripe it is yellow and soft; and the taste is sweet and pleasant. The Natives use it for Bread; they gather it when full grown, while it is green and hard; then they bake it in an Oven, which scorcheth the rind and makes it black: but they scrape off the outside black crust, and there remains a tender thin crust, and the inside is soft, tender and white, like the Crumb of a Penny Loaf.'

Then, on 4 January 1688, after a mutiny – Captain Swan was deposed by John Reid – and a succession of desultory raids in the Philippines, the China Sea and the East Indies, the *Cygnet*, with Dampier navigating, ran into a typhoon that sent it willy-nilly down the north-west coast of Australia. 'Being now clear of all the islands,' Dampier wrote, 'we stood off south, intending to touch at New Holland, a part of *Terra Australis Incognito*, to see what that country could afford us.'

The hypothetical existence of *Terra Australis*, the Great South Land, had been mooted for more than a thousand years and had been proven by the Portuguese, first, and then the Dutch, in the 16th century. The English, however, had shown little interest in the land the Dutch called New Holland, and Dampier's distinct lack of enthusiasm, once he had set foot on it, reinforced this.

> *4th January, 1688, we fell in with the land of New Holland having made our course due south. New Holland is a very large tract of land. It is not yet determined whether it is an island or a main continent; but I am certain that it joins neither to Asia, Africa nor America ... The land is of a dry sandy soil, destitute of water except you make Wells ... The inhabitants of this country are the miserablest people in this world ... They are tall, straight-bodied and thin. They have great heads, round foreheads and great brows.*

Dampier stepped ashore at a point near the present-day Buccaneer Archipelago and was welcomed by Aborigines waving spears. A gun shot scattered them and then Dampier, having frightened the women and children into flight, offered the men clothing and ordered them to carry water to the boats. They declined both. The *Cygnet* was careened and its hull scraped at low tide and despite the men's fears that troglodytes walked the land – men whose heads grew under their shoulders and whose feet were so large that they served as sunshades when they lay down in the sun – the crew lived ashore for nine weeks, sleeping in huts and hunting turtles and manatees.

Dampier left the *Cygnet* at the Nicobar Islands and with seven others set off in a canoe for Sumatra. In 1691, 12 years after he had left, he returned to England, accompanied by a Filipino whom he told London was a member of Philippines royalty, 'Prince Job'.

He remained ashore for two years until in 1693 he sailed for the West Indies with a group of adventurers looking to recover treasure from sunken Spanish ships.

One of them was Henry Avery who, in May 1694, with 84 others, seized one of the ships, the *Charles II*, renamed her *Fancy*, and sailed off to become pirates. Marauding in the Red Sea Avery and his crew captured the Great Mogul's treasure ship, *Gang-I-Sawai*. They took the ship with ease but then, as one of them later confessed, committed 'the most horrible barbarities', raping all the women – among them a close relative of the Great Mogul – and torturing and slaughtering men and women. The pirates took away gorgeous jewels. There was a saddle entirely encrusted with diamonds, gold coins and trinkets worth at least £350,000 – more than any of them could dream of earning as a buccaneer.

Dampier's expedition, on the other hand, was a spectacular failure. It never reached the Caribbean, and Dampier returned to England in February 1695. Dampier, desolate, wrote, '[I made] very sad reflections on my former life and looked back with horror and detestation on actions which before I disliked, but now I trembled at the remembrance of.'

Dampier's written repentance was published in 1697 in a work that astonished all: *A New Voyage Round the World.* The Admiralty and the Royal Society began to show interest in the Pacific and particularly in the Great Southern Continent, New Holland. The diarist John Evelyn noted in August 1698: 'I dined with Mr Pepys, where was Captain Dampier, who had been a famous Buccaneer [and] had brought hither the painted Prince Job, and printed a relation of his very strange adventures, and his observations. He was now going abroad again by the King's encouragement, who furnished a ship of 290 tons.'

What Evelyn didn't note, and what became quickly apparent once the *Roebuck* set sail, was that the ship was barely able to stay afloat, the crew was poor and the master, the man responsible for carrying out the captain's orders, a drunk who almost put the ship aground on their first night out. Worse, the *Roebuck*'s first lieutenant, George Fisher, was outraged to find himself serving under a former pirate.

They fought from the start, Fisher insulting Dampier – 'old dog, old villain, old dissembling, cheating rogue,' and Dampier replying by thrashing Fisher with a cane and consigning him to a Brazilian jail.

Dampier intended to discover the east coast of Australia and sailed 900 miles around the western and northern coasts. He landed at Shark Bay and went ashore at Roebuck Bay, south of Broome. He wanted to capture an Aborigine but when the situation got out of hand he fired

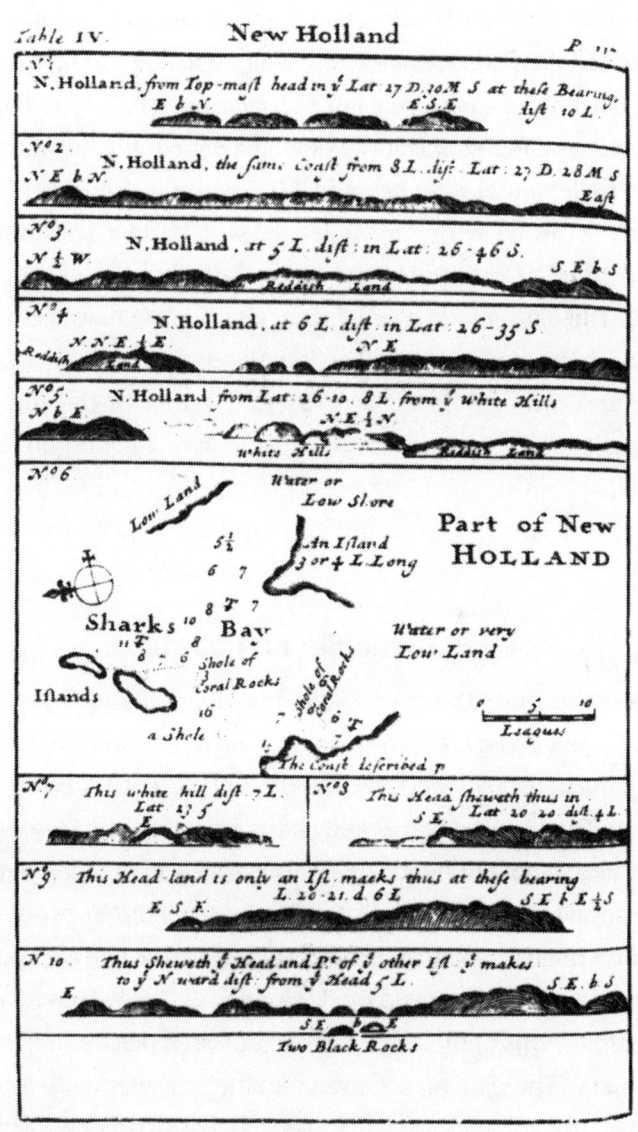

A diagram from William Dampier's *A voyage to New Holland*, published in 1699.

his gun into the air. When the Aborigines noticed that the noise had no discernible effect they charged and Dampier was forced to wound one of them, something he regretted.

He was tired, feeling his age, now. He fell sick but brought the rotting *Roebuck* as far as the Atlantic before it sprang a leak and went down off Ascension Island. He was picked up and came home to face a court-martial. Fisher had escaped from jail and made his way back to England and Dampier was found unfit to command a ship of the Royal Navy.

Undeterred, he took ship again in 1707 with the privateer Woodes Roger and returned with Alexander Selkirk, a man Dampier had marooned three years before, and booty valued at a clear profit of £200,000. The old sea-dog was 57 now, and his last days were spent quietly and fairly comfortably in London. His second book, *A Voyage to New Holland*, was published in 1709 and again, in the course of recounting his extraordinary adventures, was disparaging about Australia.

He died in March 1715. It is not known where he is buried.

A day in the life of a pirate

In September 1684 Dampier joined an old friend Basil Ringrose on the *Cygnet* under Captain Swan, and the pirates went in search of the Lima treasure fleet. They found it, but were outfoxed by the Spanish. The treasure had already been offloaded and they were duped and almost done for by a mischievous light in the night. Dampier tells the tale: 'The Spanish admiral and the rest of his squadron began to play at us, and we at them, as fast we could. They might have laid us aboard if they would; but they came not within small-arms shot, intending to maul us in pieces with their great guns.' The pirates, however, had the advantage: 'Being to windward of the enemy, we had it at our choice, whether we would fight or not. It was three o'clock in the afternoon when we weighed, and being all under sail, we bore down right afore the wind on our enemies, who kept close on a wind to come to us; but night came on without anything except the exchanging of a few shots on each side.'

In the blackness of the night the *Cygnet* kept windward of an intermittent light believed to come from the Spanish flagship. At dawn they discovered their mistake. The Spaniards had planted a decoy light on a small barque and under cover of night come around to windward: 'In the Morning, therefore, contrary to our expectation, we found they had got the Weather-gage of us, and were coming upon us with full Sail, so we ran for it, and after a running Fight all day, and having taken a turn almost round the Bay of Panama, we came to Anchor again at the Isle of Pacheque, in the very same place from whence we set out in the Morning. Thus ended this day's Work, and with it all that we had been projecting for five or six Months; when instead of making our selves Masters of the Spanish Fleet and Treasure, we were glad to escape them; and owed that too, in a great measure, to their want of Courage to pursue their Advantage.'

Basil Ringrose, like most pirates, came to a nasty end shortly after. Dampier was ill and missed the action when the buccaneers overran the silver-mining town of Santa Pecaque. Captain Swan, alerted that Spanish soldiers were hurrying to the rescue, ordered his men to drop their plunder and run for the longboats. The pirates brushed him aside and continued plundering. Then they left, weighed down with treasure – only to be ambushed, massacred and mutilated. Behind, they left 54 dead and Swan told Dampier they were 'stript, and so cut and mangl'd, that he scarcely knew one man'. Among the bodies was Dampier's 'ingenious friend Mr Ringrose [who] had no mind to this voyage; but was necessitated to engage in it or starve'.

The man who was Robinson Crusoe

The original depiction of Robinson Crusoe. The novel was inspired by Dampier's books and Alexander Selkirk, the fiery pirate Dampier marooned.

Alexander Selkirk, a quarrelsome Scot with a quick-fire temper, was First Mate on the *Cinque Ports*, a 16-gun 90-ton privateer commanded by Dampier. Dampier was a scientist, a brilliant navigator and pilot, but he seems to have been an inept captain. Selkirk, 27, violently fell out with Dampier, who was in his fifties and on his third voyage around the world. In atrocious weather and against common sense, Dampier had tried to take the ship round the notorious Cape Horn at the southern tip of South America. Three times he tried and three times he failed. And each time the ship and the crew took a heavy beating.

Dampier insisted the *Cinque Ports* would make it on the fourth attempt and set off in search of spoils in the Pacific. Selkirk had

had enough. He demanded to be put ashore on the next island they came to. Pirates had the right to jump ship or be put off whenever they wished and Dampier didn't demur. In September 1704 the *Cinque Ports* sighted the uninhabited island of Juan Fernandez, 400 miles off the West Coast of Chile. Selkirk was rowed ashore, given clothing, bedding, a firelock rifle, bullets and powder, a hatchet, a knife, a kettle, tobacco, some books, his mathematical instruments and a Bible, and watched as the *Cinque Ports* slipped over the horizon. He expected he'd be picked up by a passing ship in a matter of weeks.

Weeks passed. Months passed. Years passed. Four years and four months later, on 1 February 1709, two privateer ships, the *Duke*, navigated and piloted by Dampier, and the *Duchess*, sailed into the island's bay, dropped anchor and sent a longboat to investigate a 'wildman' seen running along the shore. Dampier recognised the hairy man in the goatskin as the hot-blooded Scot who had insisted on being marooned – an insistence, Selkirk was to learn, that almost certainly saved his life. *Cinque Ports* had sunk with the loss of most of the crew, and the few survivors were now rotting in a Peruvian jail.

Selkirk immediately resumed his career as a privateer and within a year he was master of the *Duke*, the ship that rescued him. Seven years since he had stormed from his home after a violent row with his brother – a practical joke had backfired – he returned to Scotland. He was £800 richer than when his family had last seen him, and, dressed in fine silk and lace announced his arrival by walking in on them as they were worshipping in the village kirk.

Like Dampier, however, Selkirk could not resist the call of the sea and in 1720 he joined the Royal Navy only to die of fever off the coast of Africa.

Richard Steele met him and wrote Selkirk's castaway story

and Daniel Defoe used Selkirk as inspiration for his character, Robinson Crusoe. But Defoe undoubtedly also borrowed much from Dampier's *A New Voyage Round the World*.

Here is Dampier describing an incident echoed in one of the most memorable passages in literature, when Robinson Crusoe saves the life of the native he is to call Man Friday, and Friday falls at his feet.

> March the 22nd 1684, we came in sight of the Island, and the next Day got in and anchored in a Bay at the South-end of the island, 25 fathoms Water and not two Cables length from the shore.
>
> We presently got out our Canoe, and went ashore to see for a Moskito Indian, whom we left here when we were chased hence by three Spanish Ships in the year 1681, a little before we went to Arica with Captain Watlin being then our Commander, after Capt. Sharp had been turn'd out.
>
> This Indian had lived here alone above three years, and altho' he was several Times sought after by the Spaniards, who knew he was left on the Island, yet they could never find him. He was in the Woods, hunting for Goats, when Captain Watlin drew off his Men, and the Ship was under sail before he came back to shore. He had with him his Gun and a Knife, with a small Horn of Powder, and a few Shot; which being spent, he contrived a way by notching his Knife, to saw the Barrel of his Gun into small Pieces, wherewith he made Harpoons, Lances, Hooks and a long Knife; heating the pieces first in the fire, which he struck with his Gunflint, and a piece of the Barrel of his Gun, which he hardened; having learnt to do that among the English. The hot pieces of Iron he would hammer out and bend as he pleased with Stones, and saw them with his jagged Knife, or grind them to an Edge by long labour, and harden them to a good temper as there was occasion. All this may

seem strange to those that are not acquainted with the sagacity of the Indians; but it is no more than these Moskito Men are accustomed to in their own Country, where they make their own Fishing and striking Instruments, without either Forge or Anvil; tho' they spend a great deal of Time about them.

. . . With such Instruments as he made in that manner, he got such Provision as the Island afforded; either Goats or Fish. He told us that at first he was forced to eat Seal, which is very ordinary Meat, before he had made hooks: but afterwards he never killed any Seals but to make Lines, cutting their Skins into Thongs. He had a little House or Hut half a mile from the Sea, which was lined with Goats Skin; his Couch or Barbecu of Sticks lying along about 2 foot distant from the Ground, was spread with the same, and was all his Bedding. He had no Cloaths left, having worn out those he brought from Watlin's Ship, but only a Skin about his Waste. He saw our Ship the day before we came to an Anchor, and did believe we were English, and therefore kill'd 3 Goats in the Morning, before we came to an Anchor, and drest them with Cabbage, to treat us when we came ashore. He came then to the Sea side to congratulate our safe arrival. And when we landed, a Moskito Indian, named Robin, first leap'd ashore, and running to his Brother Moskito Man, threw himself flat on his face at his feet, who helping him up, and embracing him, fell flat with his face on the Ground at Robin's feet, and was by him taken up also. We stood with pleasure to behold the suprise and tenderness, and solemnity of this interview, which was exceedingly affectionate on both sides; and when their Ceremonies of Civility were over, we also that stood gazing at them drew near, each of us embracing him we had found here, who was overjoyed to see so many of his old Friends come hither as he thought purposely to fetch him.

The Trial *and the treachery*

'*I*t is a truth universally acknowledged,' as Jane Austen's father might have told her, 'that a ship in possession of a good fortune must be in want of plundering'.

The *Trial* was such a ship. It carried a treasure in gold spangles and doubloons destined for the King of Siam when it struck a rock off the west coast of Australia on the night of 25 May 1622 and went down with the loss of 93 men.

The *Trial* was the first English ship to sight Australia, and the first ship known to be wrecked off the Australian coast. But what followed was an old story: a dark and despicable story of greed and treachery that was echoed 350 years later, deep in the *Trial*'s Indian Ocean tomb.

The *Trial*'s captain, John Brookes, was acknowledged to have behaved in a cowardly way when his ship struck: he left most of his crew to die and sailed to safety in Java. But in 1934 a woman researching the wreck turned the shipwreck tragedy into a detective story that revealed Brookes was much more than a coward: he was one of the great villains of maritime history.

The *Trial*, owned by the British East India Company and captained by Brookes, sailed from Plymouth on 4 September 1621 with a crew of 143 'good men' and a chart based on the 'Brouwer Route' to the East Indies.

Ten years before, Brouwer, a Dutch seaman, had shown that the best way to the Indies and the Javanese capital of Batavia (Djakarta) was to sail due east in the lower latitudes from the Cape of Good Hope, before turning north some several hundred nautical miles before the Great South Land was reached. This route gave his ship favourable and reliable winds – the Roaring Forties – and was considerably faster and healthier than following Vasco Da Gama's diagonal route up the east coast of Africa and across the Indian Ocean, which often left ships becalmed under the searing tropical heat, their crews rotting from disease. Following the new route too far east, however, meant encountering what Dirk Hartog called 'a large land mass' – the west coast of Australia. He became the first man to do so, at Cape Inscription on 25 October 1616.

In 1620 an English ship captained by Humphrey Fitzherbert had followed the Brouwer route and when, the following year, the merchant ship the *Trial* set out for the Indies the Company instructed Brookes to set its course from Fitzherbert's log. The British East India Company was bent on wresting the lucrative spice trade from the Dutch United East India Company, and the *Trial* was well named.

Brookes was a poor navigator. He sailed too far east and on 1 May sighted the Australian mainland in the vicinity of North West Cape. For weeks strong winds prevented the *Trial* from heading north for Java, but on 24 May the winds changed, allowing for progress north past Barrow Island and the Monte Bello Islands. On 25 May 1622, eight weeks after the *Trial* left the Cape, Captain Brookes had his ship, as he later reported to the British East India Company, steering 'north east thinking to fall in with the western part of Java'.

Instead the *Trial* fell in on a pinnacle of rock, an uncharted reef. 'At 11 o'clock at night, fair weather and smooth the ship struck,' Brookes wrote. 'I cried to them to bear up and tack to the westwards. They did their best, but the rock being sharp the ship was presently full of water ... The wind began suddenly to freshen and to blow. I struck round my sails and got out my skiff and ... made all the way I could to get out my long boat and by two o'clock I had gotten her out and hanged her in the tackles on the side.

'Seeing the ship full of water and the wind to increase [I] made all the means I could to save my life and as many of my company as I could. The boat put off at four in the morning and half an hour after the fore part of the ship fell in pieces! Ten men were saved in the skiff and 36 in the longboat.'

That left 93 men on board the disintegrating *Trial*. (Four men had died on the voyage.) And Captain Brookes' account also left out most of the truth of what happened when the *Trial* struck – and where and why.

The truth about Captain Brookes was disclosed by a man named Thomas Bright who sailed on the ship and whose letter detailing the events that followed the shipwreck was filed and forgotten for three centuries. Bright was the British East India Company's agent on board the *Trial*. His unsigned letter to a senior officer of the company tells how the captain wrecked his ship, abandoned most of his crew to certain death and, with the treasure, escaped on a skiff with his cabin boy and a chosen few.

> *May the 25th, about ten o'clock at night, fair weather and little wind, the ship Tryall, by carelessness for want of looking out, struck upon the rocks ... her hold full of water in an instant ... [Brookes'] crew and fellow and consorts providing provisions and saving his things, bearing Mr Jackson and myself with fair words, promising us faithfully to take us along.*

Then, 'like a Judas' while Bright had his back to him in the captain's cabin, Brookes slipped way and lowered himself into the skiff 'only with nine men and his boy. [He] stood for the Straits of Sunda that instant, without care and without seeing the lamentable end of the ship, the time she split, or respect of any man's life.'

Bright and 35 others got the long boat out with difficulty and stood off until dawn when the men remaining alive on the ship were left to their doom, the waters now crashing over the remains of the *Trial* and the sharks busy.

Brookes' skiff had a keg of water, two cases of bottles of wine and a little bread and 1500 kilometres of water between it and Java, but they made it to Batavia. So too did the 36 men on Bright's longboat, surviving on six kegs of water, a little wine and some bread.

In Batavia, Brookes wrote his official report on the disaster. To escape all blame he falsified the ship's position and said that the Trial Rocks as they were soon known, were many kilometres west – a lie that led seamen from Dampier to Flinders to search fruitlessly for the reef for the next 200 years.

Brookes also told the company that he had transferred the ship's treasure to Bright in the longboat. Bright's report disagreed: '... for two hours [he did] nothing but convey from his cabin to his skiff to my knowledge both letters, money and spangles in his trunk ...'

Despite this damning letter, Brookes' story was believed. The following year he was given command of the *Moone* and wrecked it off the coast of England. He and the master were imprisoned, charged with deliberately wrecking the ship and stealing the jewels and diamonds in the chest of a company official who had died during the voyage. Once again, Brookes' story was believed: he was given a reward of £10 plus wages for his cabin boy, who had stolen the jewels but then returned them to the company.

But he never returned the treasure of the King of Siam.

It took almost 350 years to discover the true site of the wreck of the *Trial*. In 1969 a group of Perth divers travelled 1500 kilometres north to attempt to find it. The wreck, they believed, had been pinpointed by brilliant research done in 1934 that uncovered Bright's damning private letter.

'Ida Leigh Marriott did the original research,' Jeremy Green, head of the Western Australian Museum's Department of Maritime Archaeology told the ABC in 2003.

'She looked at Brookes' journal and Bright's journal and put the story together and said this is clearly the Monte Bellos and this is clearly

Barrow Island, and the Trial Rocks by that point had been charted halfway between the Monte Bellos and Barrow Island and she spotted it as being these rocks up in the north which we actually called Ritchie's Reef, so these guys went up there – a very difficult place to dive – and were lucky enough to get on the site and found the cannon and anchors.'

Green himself did the dive two years later. He found there had been an attempt to plunder the *Trial*, just as there had been three centuries before.

'The first museum dive on the site – when we got there – we found it had been blown up. There were explosives all over the place, and there were detonator cords and pieces of gelignite. Somebody had got in there, and it was in fact Alan Robinson.'

Ellis Alfred 'Alan' Robinson was one of the team that found the *Trial*. A violent man, he is believed to have carried out the blasting some time shortly before Green's dive, working from a trawler. He was charged but, like Brookes, acquitted. Robinson is thought to have plundered other famous wrecks along the coast, among them the notorious *Batavia*, the 700 ton *Zuytdorp*, and the flagship of the Dutch fleet, the *Vergulde Draek* (*Golden Dragon*), sunk with 78,000 gold guilders.

In 1983, on trial for conspiring to murder a de facto, using explosives and acid, he died, probably by his own hand.

The fat lady on the good ship *Venus*

Was Charlotte Badger the fat lady of the Friendly Islands? Or had Charlotte, too, been eaten on the less friendly islands of New Zealand? The fate of the fat lady may hold the clue to the mysterious disappearance of the *Venus*, seized in a convict mutiny and sailed from Van Diemen's Land into the unknown.

By the winter of 1806 settlers and convicts alike in Hobart Town were close to starvation. The convicts' rations had been cut to two pounds 10 ounces of salt pork and four pounds of bread a week, hardly enough for two days in normal times. And the situation was worsened when Sydney's food supply was threatened by floods that destroyed crops along the Hawkesbury.

The situation was dire when, to their aid came the brigantine *Venus*, sent by Governor King with a cargo of essentials: five tons of salt pork and two and a half tons of meat and flour. An American, Samuel Rodman Chace captained her and, like his first mate, another American, Barnet Kelly, he was a sealer. Her pilot was a former gunner's mate, David Evans, a deserter transported to Botany Bay for 14 years. On board too, were three convicts, John Lancashire, Catharine Hagarty and Charlotte Badger and her infant, and their guard Private Richard Thomas of the New South Wales Corp.

Lancashire was unprepossessing: short, sallow and pockmarked, he was described by Governor King as a man 'possessed of every art and cunning that human invention could turn to the worst of purposes'. Catharine Hagarty's penal record describes her as a woman with a hoarse voice who was 'much calculated to smile' – this clearly being a mark of distinction in Sydney in 1806. Charlotte was 'very corpulent, with full face and thick lips'.

Lancashire was a forger – he'd narrowly escaped the gallows – and he had a skill which might have given him a comfortable living as a ship and tavern sign maker. But not so deep down he was a duplicitous rogue, as he demonstrated when his mistress was found disseminating forged bills. Lancashire gave evidence against her and once again ducked paying the supreme penalty.

Two years later he was at it again, caught forging, and this time there was no passing the blame. He made a run for it, stowing away with another convict, but they were recaptured, given 100 lashes, and sent to Van Diemen's Land to serve three years at hard labour.

So far, so bad. But now things, and the weather, took a turn for the worse. The *Venus* was forced to put in to Twofold Bay on the south coast of NSW where it stayed for more than a month while the wind – and the crew – raged. In a very short time the eternally cheerful Catharine and Barnet Kelly were sharing his bunk. Lancashire, Evans and the guard Private Thompson, spent their time tucking into the food store and broaching the port barrels. Captain Chace, who had lost virtually all control over the ship, breathed easier when, at last, the wind died and he could sail the good ship *Venus* into Port Dalrymple, on 16 June.

There, at the entrance to the harbour, the brig struck anchor and Captain Chace and the port's Naval Officer, Mr House, went ashore to deliver despatches from Governor King to Colonel William Paterson, the Lieutenant-Governor of Port Dalrymple.

Paterson's house was 10 miles from the harbour and when the pair reined their horses and presented their dispatches, and Chace gave his account of the last few weeks, Paterson was aghast to learn that they had left the *Venus* in the hands of Barnet Kelly. He ordered the pair to remount and immediately get back on board the *Venus*. Chase and House made their hurried farewells and promptly spent the rest of the night carousing aboard a schooner in the harbour. When dawn broke Chace decided it was time to call it a day and staggered out on deck just in time to see the *Venus* sailing for the horizon. Lancashire and Kelly had led a mutiny on board the brig, locked the second mate Richard Evans in a cabin and kicked off the ship those who refused to join.

That was the last reliable record of the *Venus*'s whereabouts. In April 1807, 10 months after she anchored at Port Dalrymple, the skipper of the *Commerce* sailed into Botany Bay with reports that she had been seen meandering up and down the coast of New Zealand's North Island. Kelly and Lancashire, he'd been told, had left her at the Bay of Islands where they had stayed with the Maori chief Te Pahi – the same Te Pahi who three years later, was to lead the massacre of the crew and passengers of the *Boyd*. (See *They fell among cannibals*, page 36.)

What was the fate of the *Venus*? The *Sydney Gazette* put things in vivid perspective: 'She [the *Venus*] is supposed to be still wandering about the New Zealand coast, but as she had no navigator on board no possible prospect can present itself to those who remain in her but to perish by the hands of the natives or fall into the hands of justice.'

Unfortunately, it seems those on the *Venus* fell into the wrong hands. It was thought that they were killed and eaten: the two women convicts, the baby, a mulatto seaman, a Malay cook, and Private Thompson. The *Venus*, like the *Boyd*, was burned and her iron used to make weapons and fish hooks.

That, it seemed, was that. Then, nine years on, in 1816, an American whaler reported that he had seen a fat white woman and her child on one of the Friendly Islands. If it was Charlotte Badger, the chances are that the *Venus* and her complement avoided the only two – awful – prospects that the *Sydney Gazette* foresaw for her, and instead all on board continued to have a jolly time cruising the South Seas on the good ship *Venus*.

They fell among cannibals

From where they were, high in the riggings, the six seamen had a perfect, bird's eye view of the passengers on the deck below, screaming as they were hacked apart for the cannibal feast that was to follow.

In the riggings the men looked at each other as the Maoris shouted to them, telling them that their lives would be spared if they cut the sails loose.

What were their thoughts? It's reasonable to assume that through their terror they one and all cursed Captain Thompson for flogging Te Ara, the Maori prince.

The six cut away the rigging and came crashing to the deck among the sails and the spars and the cordage. Their lives were not spared: they were seized, thrown over the side into canoes and taken ashore. There, still alive, they were dismembered, roasted and eaten – as were all but four of the 70 men, women and children on the brigantine convict ship, the *Boyd*.

The *Boyd* had sailed to New Zealand from Port Jackson in December 1809. She was dropping off New Zealanders going home and she was to take on timber from Whangaroa, the northern-most harbour in New Zealand. Captain Cook, 32 years earlier, had sailed into the harbour and noted that the kauri tree stands inland would make fine ships' spars.

Now, fresh from transporting to Australia a detachment of Her Majesty's 73rd Regiment and 137 convicts, the *Boyd*, under Captain John Thompson, had sailed out of Port Jackson with a cargo of 2000 salted seal skins and barrels of seal oil, nails, axes, gunpowder and muskets, along with 70 passengers and crew.

Among the passengers was Elizabeth Heathorn, who had been transported for seven years in 1792, and become the mistress of William Broughton, a servant to the colony's Surgeon General. She bore Broughton five children. Now, with other paying passengers, she was going home to England accompanied by the youngest of the children, two-year-old Elizabeth Isabella Broughton – Betsy.

Also on board, working his passage home to New Zealand, was the son of one of the Maori chiefs of the Kaeo tribe of Whangaroa, a man who was called George by the white 'pakehas'. Soon after the *Boyd* put to sea Captain Thompson, who was in the southern hemisphere for the first time and regarded the Maoris as savages barely able to speak English, ordered George to take his turn with the other crew. He refused. He was Te Ara, the son of a chief, a prince. He was ill and besides it was beneath his dignity. Captain Thompson again ordered him to get to work and again he refused.

Thompson ordered the bo'sun to have the man dragged to the capstan, trussed face down across it, and flogged with the 'cat'. A prince's blood sprinkled the deck of the *Boyd*. When it was over George showed no resentment and when the brig arrived off the coast of New Zealand he pointed out to the captain the best course for entering the harbour of Whangaroa and where best to drop anchor. Then he went ashore and showed his father, Piopio, his lacerated back.

Three days after dropping anchor, Captain Thompson, guided by Maoris, took a party of sailors up the Kaeo River to the kauri stands. The timber cutters were scarcely out of sight of the ship when the Maoris drew weapons from beneath their cloaks and massacred them. They stripped the clothes from their still warm victims, and put on their jackets, trousers, hats and frock coats, and carried the corpses to their village for a cannibal feast. Then they rowed the *Boyd*'s longboat back to the brig.

It was dark when the longboat, shadowed by canoes bristling with warriors led by Te Pahi, Chief of the Bay of Islands, drew alongside and passengers and the remaining crew prepared to welcome the captain and his party. Instead they heard a shell-trumpet wail from Te Pahi's war canoe and saw Maoris, dressed in European clothing and swinging clubs and battle-axes, swarming up the ship's sides.

Six seamen had time to scuttle into the rigging where the morning light found them. Elizabeth Heathorn and her baby Betsy were discovered hiding in a cabin. Elizabeth was killed immediately. Thomas Davis, the ship's 14-year-old club-footed cabin boy was found quivering in the hold. Te Ara ordered that Davis, another mother, Anne Morley and her baby and little Betsy Broughton be spared and taken ashore. The second mate was also let live. For two terrifying weeks he bought time showing how to make fish hooks from barrel hoops but then he too was killed and eaten.

The *Boyd* was towed up the harbour towards the tribe's pa, the Maori village. But in the shallows it heeled over and for the next week the tribe ransacked it for its muskets and powder. Piopio was trying to get one of the muskets to fire when a flint spark flew into an open barrel of gunpowder and he and nine others were blown high.

As masts crashed down into the water the fire that followed the explosion was fed by the seal oil in the hold. Soon burned to her copper sheathing, the *Boyd* sank into the harbour and the Maoris put a 'tapu' (taboo) on her.

The news of the slaughter and of the spectacular explosion on the *Boyd* reached the Bay of Islands where *The City of Edinburgh* was loading cargo for Australia. Alexander Berry, the ship's commander, gathered a party of men and sailed for Whangaroa. On board he took a trusted Maori chief, Metenangah.

When *The City of Edinburgh* sailed into the harbour three longboats of heavily armed men went ashore with Metenangah at their head. He came back with two of the chiefs and several warriors dressed in sail canvas and European clothes. They had clearly taken part in the massacre. On shore women were walking around in dresses. And on the landing place ashore there were the remains of a cannibal feast: teeth marks still evident on roasted human flesh.

Te Pahi. Not long before he led the gruesome 'utu' – revenge killings – Te Pahi had been so admired that Governor King himself farewelled him.

Berry demanded that the survivors be brought to him. Little Betsy Broughton appeared dressed in a white shirt that had once belonged to Captain Thompson. The cabin boy, Davis, too, was handed over, along with Anne Morley and her child.

Berry ordered that the chiefs be held in irons but any thoughts he had of hanging or shooting them were dismissed when Metenangah pointed out that the tribes would certainly overrun and once again massacre the pakehas. For the time being, Berry agreed, revenge had to wait.

Some time later five English ships sailed into the harbour to capture Te Pahi and bring him before an English court of justice to be tried and executed. Te Pahi and his warriors were ready and gave battle. When it seemed as if he was about to be taken the Maoris took to their war canoes and paddled to safety. He was never captured.

Wisely, the English let the matter lie.

Te Pahi's horrible revenge stunned those Europeans who knew him. He was well disposed towards Europeans, at ease in their company and enjoyed their highest respect. Three years before the massacre Te Pahi is thought to have befriended the convicts who had seized and sailed away on the *Venus* (see page 33) and he and his four sons had also spent a year in Port Jackson as guests of Governor King. An imposing, heavily tattooed man, he had successfully interceded with King when the Governor was considering the sentence of two men found to have stolen provisions. Te Pahi persuaded the governor to pardon the men. And when he left Sydney in the *Lady Nelson* the Governor was there to farewell him with generous gifts.

So why did he turn?

One explanation for the *Boyd* massacre has it that Te Pahi was enraged by the treatment given to his daughter. On the *Lady Nelson* he had fallen ill and was nursed by a seaman, George Bruce. Te Pahi adopted Bruce, who left the ship at the Bay of Islands and lived with the Maoris for three years, tattooing his face and marrying Te Pahi's 16-year-old daughter, Princess Aetockoe.

Bruce had left New Zealand and took a ship with Aetockoe to the northern-most part of New Zealand to look for gold. Years later he claimed that he and his bride had been forcibly taken instead to India.

Governor Macquarie scoffed at this story. Writing to the Under-Secretary for the Colonies he said Bruce had indeed sailed to Bengal, where he managed to raise a considerable amount of money by describing himself as a prince of New Zealand. He and his real life princess, Te Pahi's daughter, sailed to Sydney, where she died giving birth to a daughter. Bruce, Macquarie said, left the infant at the Female Orphans School and went back to England. He was a drunken rogue, Macquarie advised, and he should never be allowed to return to the colonies.

Five years later the Reverend Samuel Marsden, the flogging parson of Sydney and a man every bit as bloodthirsty as the cannibals of New Zealand, went to the Bay of Islands on behalf of Macquarie and spoke to the warriors who had taken part in the massacre. They told him that it was sparked by the flogging of Te Ara, the man the pakehas called George.

But the horrific slaughter could also have been Te Pahi's bitter revenge for the loss of his daughter and the abandonment of his grand-daughter by George Bruce.

Whatever the trigger for the butchery of the passengers and crew of the *Boyd*, Samuel Marsden was right to caution Macquarie, perhaps unnecessarily: 'The New Zealanders will not be insulted with impunity.'

2 | Our dark story

'I'm not dead! For God's sake, don't cover me up!'

'As I passed along the road about eleven o'clock in the morning, there issued out of the prisoners' barracks a party consisting of four men, who bore on their shoulders (two supporting the head and the two the feet) a miserable convict, writhing in an agony of pain – his voice piercing the air with terrific screams. Astonished at the sight, I inquired what this meant, and was told it was "only a prisoner who had been flogged, and was on his way to the hospital"! ... I soon learned that what I had seen was at that period an ordinary occurrence.'

— Roger Therry, Reminiscences

Few of us have ever seen a flogging. Once or twice a decade the newspapers carry a photograph and caption of a Middle Eastern or Pakistani man being caned. Video footage of the incident is almost never screened. It would shock and outrage adults, television channels know, and severely traumatise the young viewer.

A century ago, in Australia, floggings were administered not by a cane, but by the cat-o'-nine tails, and children were entirely at ease with it. A new arrival, Alexander Harris, was told, 'Flogging in this country is such a common thing that nobody thinks anything about it. I have seen young children practising on a tree, as children in England play at horses.'

It may have been common, but for newcomers like Harris it was something that could never be erased from their memories. 'I was sent to the Bathurst court house ... I had to go past the triangles where they had been flogging incessantly for hours. I saw a man walk across the yard with the blood that ran from his lacerated flesh squashing out his shoes at every step he took. A dog was licking the blood off the triangles, and the ants were carrying away great pieces of human flesh that the lash had scattered about the ground.

Watercolour depiction of a Van Diemen's Land convict

'The scourger's foot had worn a deep hole in the ground by the violence with which he whirled himself round on it to strike the quivering and wealed back, out of which stuck the sinews, white, ragged and swollen. The infliction was a hundred lashes, at about half-minute time, so as to extend the punishment through nearly an hour.'

Robert Jones, in *Recollections of Thirteen Years on Norfolk Island* described one such flagellator – a brute who took sadistic delight in his task. 'The flogger was a County of Clare man a very powerful man and took great pleasure in inflicting as much bodily punishment as possible, using such expressions as, "Another half pound, mate, off the beggar's ribs". His face and clothes usually presented an appearance of a mincemeat chopper, being covered in flesh from the victim's body.'

Sometimes there was no flesh to flog. One Norfolk island prisoner, Jones wrote, had 2000 lashes over three years and his back was 'quite bare of flesh and his collarere [sic] bones were exposed looking very much like Ivory Polished horns. It was with some difficulty that we could find another place to flog him. Tony [Chandler, the overseer whose job it was to supervise the floggings] suggested to me that we had better [flog] the soles of his feet next time.'

An American lawyer, Lines W. Miller, watched floggings at the Hobart Town Prisoners Barrack.

'A flagellator was appointed for the express purpose of inflicting corporeal punishment, and the scenes enacted at the triangles were most revolting. Two dozen lashes, which was considered a light sentence, always left the victim's back a complete jelly of bruised flesh and congealed blood. A pool of blood and pieces of flesh are no uncommon sight at the triangles after a dozen have been flogged.

'The cry of "Murder!" and "Oh, my God!" were not infrequently repeated by the sufferer during the infliction of the punishment, loud enough to have been heard a mile, while others of more nerve would clench their teeth and endure all without a groan.

'Some idea of this inhuman punishment may be formed from the fact that the sound of the blows upon the naked back of the sufferer may be heard at the distance of one hundred rods. Many faint while undergoing the torture and some are carried from the triangles to the hospital.'

The torture, of course, was not confined to the flogging triangles. Prisoners condemned to work on the road gangs suffered appallingly. One of them, Joseph Smith, recounted years later, 'I knew a man so weak, he was thrown into the grave, when he said, "Don't cover me up. I'm not dead! for God's sake don't cover me up!" The overseer answered, "Damn your eyes, you'll die tonight, and we shall have the trouble to come back again!"

'They used to have a large hole for the dead; once a day men were sent down to collect the corpses of the prisoners, and throw them in without any ceremony or service. The native dogs used to come down at night and fight and howl in packs, gnawing at the poor dead bodies.'

Joseph Smith served seven years on the road gang. 'We used to be taken in large parties to raise [lift] a tree; when the body of the tree was raised, Old Jones would call some of the men away – then more; the men were bent double – they could not bear it – they fell – the tree on one or two, killed on the spot ... Many a time I have been yoked like a bullock with twenty or thirty others to drag along timber. About eight hundred died in six-months at a place called Toongabbie, or Constitution Hill.'

Black pearls and the butchered bishop

Sometimes you have to butcher a bishop to get attention. When in 1871 the body of Bishop J.C. Patteson was discovered, shot through with arrows and bludgeoned, it followed a few weeks after the slaughter of around 70 men, trapped below a ship's decks. There was a common link in both killings and it forced governments in Australia and in England to look at that link: blackbirding, a whimsical name for a very nasty business.

The combination of the death of the godly – the bishop – and the killings by the ungodly – blackbirders – brought things to a head and the British Government passed a Kidnapping Act which gave its navy greatly increased legal powers to clamp down on the trade as it had successfully done on the slave trade. Three years before, the Queensland Government had made some attempt to control things with the regulations intended to improve the conditions of Kanakas working in the State, and laws that required recruiters to be licensed.

The law that most blackbirders respected, however, was the law of the gun. The men who lived and often died by it, or by war clubs or spears, kidnapped and lured Pacific island natives to work for fixed terms and low wages in the sugar cane fields of Queensland (usually at a wage of £18 for three years), the cotton plantations of Fiji, and the notorious nickel mines of Noumea. 'An islander decoyed to Noumea has a harder lot than his brother in Queensland,' 'Chinese' Morrison wrote in his exposé of blackbirding for the Melbourne *Age*. 'He is set to work in the nickel mines, he is badly paid and poorly fed; indeed his condition is a bad form of slavery. A Noumea schooner cannot get boys except by kidnapping them and by representing herself to be in the Queensland labour trade.'

Germans, Americans, Frenchmen, Englishmen and Australians, the slavers – as most of them were – included men such as Henry Ross Lewin who recruited the first Kanakas (the word meant boy) for the Queensland cane fields, lived in a fortress-like house in the New Hebrides and went everywhere with an armed guard because of his habit of killing out of hand. Lewin's habit eventually caught up with him when he shot a native dead for stealing a bunch of bananas and three days later a relative of the man ambushed and shot him when his back was turned and his armed guard was occupied.

Lewin was loathed and feared almost as much as the infamous American, Bully Hayes, a hulking brute; a murderer, pirate, bigamist and blackbirder. Hayes smuggled cargoes of Chinese into Australia during the 1850s gold rushes and co-owned a blackbirding brig the *Water Lily*, armed with 14 guns and with holes in the bulkhead so that troublesome natives below could be fired on. Bully didn't let sentiment stand in the way when it came to killing. Ben Pease, Bully's partner, disappeared – believed killed and eaten by cannibals. Bully had sent him ashore on a dangerous kidnapping mission, but had taken fright and sailed away without him.

Whichever hell Pease found himself in, Bully followed. In 1876, the cook of his yacht *Lotus* settled an argument by crashing a belaying pin down on Bully's head while his back was turned. Stunned, Bully reeled unbalanced and the cook quickly upended him overboard.

Blackbirding was a risky business. The captain of the Melbourne-owned schooner *Anna* would lure natives aboard, suddenly surround them with armed sailors, compel them to go below and then batten the hatches. This was a common tactic, but when he sold a cargo of 130 Kanakas to the captain of the *Moorea*, things went badly wrong. The islanders rose, killed the captain, the supercargo and the deckhands and barricaded the rest of the crew below. They cut the cable, planning to let the *Moorea* drift on to a reef where they would deal with the remainder of the crew and plunder its cargo. The mate of the *Moorea*, however, made a hasty bomb from a cask and gunpowder. The explosion blew a way out for the crew and killed and wounded the Kanakas on deck.

Attempted revolts by Kanakas, trapped below with little food and water, were not unusual. In 1871 HMS *Basilisk* found the *Peri* drifting out of control inside the Great Barrier Reef. Thirteen Kanakas were on board, the survivors of an original complement of 80 Solomon Islanders who had killed the European and Fiji crew, and then looted the ship. Without a navigator they drifted for about five weeks until, when the water ran out, they began to fight. The survivors lived off the flesh of those who died in the fighting. The thirteen found on the *Peri*, the captain of the *Basilisk* wrote, were 'living skeletons, creatures dazed with fear'.

A few months later Dr James Murray, part-owner of the brig *Carl*, sailed from Melbourne allegedly to trade its cargo of goods in Fiji. This, too, was a common ruse. Once in Fiji the skippers of the cargo vessels would sell their goods, change the name of the ship, and go blackbirding. Murray and the ship's mate Armstrong, dressed as missionaries (another old favourite) and lured natives aboard the *Carl* or rammed their canoes and dragged dazed and half drowned men on board. They had 70 men from the New Hebrides and 80 from the Solomons together in the hold when tribal fighting started a riot. To quell it, Murray and his crew fired on them for several hours until almost half had been killed. Those badly wounded were thrown overboard, bound at the wrists and ankles.

HMS *Rosario* stopped the *Carl* for inspection and found the hold cleaned of all signs of the slaughter but Murray, fearing the inevitable – it's impossible to keep secret the slaughter of 70 men – decided to save his neck by turning Queen's Evidence. At the trial in Sydney, Armstrong and another were sentenced to death, later commuted to life imprisonment, and five others were given two years.

A short time later Bishop Patteson and another missionary were murdered when they went ashore seeking missionary volunteers on one of the Swallow Islands. It was not uncommon for missionaries to be murdered. In the New Hebrides 'Chinese' Morrison had visited 'the only island in the South Seas where the complete Bible has been given to the natives in their own tongue ... a more delightful home for a missionary lies not under heaven.' He quickly learned of his error. On a nearby island he discovered that two missionaries had recently been murdered, that the Minister who succeeded them had also been 'brutally butchered' and that his brother, who came from England to bring back the body had suffered the same fate. Bishop Patteson and his colleague, however, were murdered in revenge for kidnappings by blackbirders and it's to be hoped that they died in the spirit of Christian forgiveness and understanding.

The man King Lash couldn't tame

The whistle of the cat-o'-nine-tails and the awful thwack as it hacked pieces from a man's back was, Alexander Harris wrote in the 1820s, 'such a common thing [in Australia] that nobody thinks anything of it'.

Well, nobody, perhaps, except the wretch being flogged.

Laurence Frayne was such a wretch. But what a man!

Frayne was an Irishman sentenced to transportation for theft who came to Sydney in 1829. His *Memoir of Norfolk Island*, a handwritten account held in the Mitchell Library tells a riveting story of the private war he waged with one of the most frightful of all the monsters who ruled Australia's penal settlements.

Read today, the punishment Frayne suffered defies belief. Yet there are many instances of men like Frayne who were flogged, literally, to within an inch of their lives – men like Charles Maher whose back, after a flogging on Norfolk Island 'was quite bare of skin and flesh', and who yet refused to bow.

The man Frayne refused to kowtow to was James Thomas Morisset, Lieutenant Colonel of the 80th Regiment.

An army man from his late teens, Morisset had been promoted through the ranks in Spain and Egypt until, as a captain during the Napoleonic Wars, he was hideously wounded in Spain. A mine explosion left him, Robert Hughes writes in *The Fatal Shore*, 'with the mask of an ogre. His mouth ran diagonally upward and made peculiar whistling noises when he spoke. One eye was normal. But the other protruded like a staring pebble and seemed never to move. The cheekbone and jaw on one side had been smashed to fragments and, without cosmetic surgery, had re-knit to form a swollen mass like "a large yellow over-ripe melon"; he would thrust this cheek forward in conversation as though daring his interlocutor to look away.'

Painted before his hideous disfigurement, Morisset's portrait belies his monstrous nature. He once had six men in a line, each flogging the man in front. Morisset was last in line

Morisset was 37 when, in 1817, he was posted to New South Wales and given command of the Newcastle penal settlement. The settlement had grown from its beginnings in 1804 when 37 convicts, Irish insurgents from the failed uprising at Castle Hill, were sent there to work in the mines. By the time Morisset arrived there were 1000 convicts enslaved in the settlement. Deep underground, working naked, miners hewed the coal and carried it back in baskets. At Fullarton Cove, across the river, more convicts burned oyster shells for lime and humped sacks of them to barges moored a hundred metres out.

He quickly won a nickname: King Lash. His practice was to order the convicts to be lined up and for every second or third man to be given 50 lashes for the sake of concentrating the minds of all on parade.

Men found guilty of the slightest 'offence' were marched with double leg-irons to the triangle where, to the beat of a kettledrum, and while convicts and the regiment looked on, two floggers, alternating, scourged the man.

King Lash would not stomach a flagellator giving less than his all. In those cases the cat was brought out for the slacker. One bizarre day a soldier was flogging a boy for stealing milk when Morisset, unhappy at the man's enthusiasm, ordered another flogger to lash the soldier. The second flogger also failed Morisset's high standards, and a third man stepped up to flog him. Finally there were six men flogging and being flogged with Morisset, at the rear, thrashing the back of the sixth man with his riding crop.

Raw lime and bleeding backs are a fearsome combination. Exacerbated by salt water – as it was when the limeburners waded to the barges with their bags – the effect was too painful for some. They would sink into the water and deliberately drown themselves, gulping water deep into their lungs, cutting off oxygen and accumulating carbon dioxide so that they sank in a mist of unconsciousness.

Morisset, you would suspect, derived some satisfaction from the suicides of these men who could take no more, some ghastly pleasure from the power he had over the life and death of the convicts. But in Laurence Frayne he met his match.

Frayne had come to Norfolk Island in 1830, less than a year after

Morisset's arrival as Commandant. He had been sent there from Moreton Bay, his punishment for 'repeatedly absconding'. Five years before, Governor Brisbane had dictated: Port Macquarie for first grave offences; Moreton Bay for runaways from the former; and Norfolk Island as the *ne plus ultra*, the ultimate.

When Frayne again tried repeatedly to escape from Moreton Bay he was sent to Sydney, sentenced to hang and then, with his sentence commuted, was sent to the *ne plus ultra*.

Waiting for transportation to Norfolk Island on the *Lucy Ann*, he was put on the *Phoenix*, a hulk, where he almost succeeded in breaking out. He was discovered as he slipped over the rails of the *Phoenix* and given 200 lashes.

In October the *Lucy Ann* set sail with Frayne, his back in ribbons, crawling with maggots. 'My shoulders were actually in a state of decomposition, the stench of which I could not bear myself, how offensive then must I appear and smell to my companions in misery. In this state immediately after my landing I was sent to carry Salt Beef on my back with the Salt Brine as well as pressure stinging my mutilated & mortified flesh up to Longridge. I really longed for instant death.'

In this state he arrived in the kingdom of King Lash.

In the quarry Frayne broke a flagstone – a flogging offence that earned him 100 lashes. He began the first of a series of exchanges with Morisset that are breathtaking in their audacity and courage.

'After the sentence I plainly told the Commandant in the Court that he was a Tyrant. He replied that no man had ever said that about him before. I said they knew the consequences too well to tell him so. But I tell you in stark naked plain English that you are as great a tyrant as Nero ever was.

'The moment I expressed these words I was sentenced to an additional 100 & to be kept in irons down in a cell for Life and never to see daylight again.'

Morisset ruled that the flagellation be made as drawn out and as painful as possible. First, he was given 50 lashes on his back. He was given four days for the wounds to form scabs and then was given another 50. Four days later he was given 50 on the buttocks and finally, four days later, the remaining 50.

Morisset oversaw the lashings and as usual took pains to ensure that every effort was made to get maximum efficiency.

'New and heavier Cats were procured purposely for my punishment,' Frayne wrote, '& the flagellator threatened to be flogged himself if he did not give it to me more severe. He replied that he did his utmost and really could do no more ... The Super[intendent] who witnessed the Punishment swore when I was taken down that I was a Brickmaster, meaning that I was like an Iron man past all feelings of the punishment. Alas, delusive idea! – I felt all too acutely the full weight, scourge and sting of every lash but I had resolution enough accompanied by inflexible Obstinacy not to give any satisfaction ... I knew my real innocence and bore up against it.'

Less than three months later the two met again. This time Frayne was charged with assaulting a convict named Harper, an informant. Morisset used informers as Stalin did, to ensure that no man felt safe conspiring to mutiny or escape, and as a way of keeping the convicts dehumanised and isolated. The Norfolk Island convicts constantly denounced one another to curry favour with the Commandant – and to avoid suspicion themselves, for once denounced, a man could be flogged merely on suspicion.

When Morisset, no doubt thrusting his gruesome cheek at Frayne, asked, 'What have you to say for yourself?' Frayne replied 'that I would leave it to you to judge whether I am guilty or innocent, you know the character & conduct of the informer; you also know mine. It is useless for me to gainsay anything ... If you actually knew my innocence yourself I well know that you would punish me ... If you acquit me for assault you will flog me for what I have now said to you, but I disregard both you and all the punishment you can give me.'

'His very next expression was, 'I will give you 300 at different whippings, you damned Scoundrel.'

'I said, 'I am no Scoundrel no more than yourself, but I don't think I can take that punishment.' This I said out of derision and ironically, with a sneer at the Colonel.

'I and the other man was taken out and we received our first 100 in slow time and with heavy cats. The flagellators were almost as much besmeared with blood as even we were ... When I was taken down an overseer who assisted to loosen the cords said, giving me a Fig of tobacco, 'You are a Steel man not a Flesh-and-Blood Man at all, you can stand to be sawn asunder after all that skinning and mangling.'

Once again Morisset ordered that Frayne and his fellow convict be given time for their wounds to scab over and after a week had them sent to the surgeon to see if they were ready for their next 100. Frayne told Gamack, 'I am ready to be scarified alive again.'

Gamack said, 'Do you wish to expire under the lash?' I said, 'I want to get it over and have done with it & all thought of it, being here injures me more than the flogging.'

He was sent to solitary after his second flogging. There, he poured his ration of water on the stone floor of his cell, pissed in the pool and lay in it to alleviate his agony.

'With my sore shoulders on the exact spot where the water lay ... I was literally alive with Maggots and Vermin, nor could I keep them down; to such a wretched and truly miserable state was I reduced, that I even hated the look & appearance of myself ... The trifle of soap allowed me to wash out persons & shirts was stopped from me, as I thought to spur me to abuse the Gaol authorities and thereby again subject myself to more cruelty ... knowing as they all did my hasty temper.'

Now Frayne had two pieces of 'luck'. Before he could have his final 100 lashes, the colonial secretary ordered that henceforth no flogging could exceed 100 lashes. Morisset responded to this irksome executive order by putting Frayne in the dumb cell: total isolation, light and sound deprivation of the type still popular in today's torture manuals.

On his release Frayne saw through jail bars two convict women, servants at Morisset's house, walking in the yard. One of them came from the same town as Frayne. He had contrived to be put in the jail for the purpose of meeting and, possibly, sleeping with them.

'I showed myself through the bars ... I told them they might expect me to pay them a visit at all hazard, & I would put up with the consequences if it was 300.'

That night he slept with them both.

When Morisset found out, Frayne was as brazen and defiant as ever:

I plainly told the Commandant that it was the only opportunity I had ever had or perhaps ever would have of spending a night in Womens company; it was a very natural offence in a twofold degree. 'How do you mean twofold?' asked the Commandant. 'The first,' I said, 'is too obvious to need explanation, the second is that they are both your servants – now you can do as you please, that is all I have to say.'

'Well then,' said the Commandant, 'I will give you 100 lashes in slow time so that you shall pay for your creeping into the women's cell.'

I said, 'I hope you will send me back to gaol right after it, and you can give me another 100 tomorrow for the same offence if that will gratify you or give you pleasure.'

Frayne dreamed of revenge, of course: 'I should certainly have taken his life ... & many a time I prayed, if I knew what prayer was, that the heaviest curses that ever Almighty God let fall on blighted men might reach him, for blood will have blood, and in no depth of earth or sea can we bury it, and the blood of several of my fellow-Prisoners cryed aloud & often to heaven to let fall its vengeance on this wholesale Murderer and despicable White Savage.'

Vengeance – almost – came on 15 January 1834.

Laurence Frayne, soon after the reveille bell rang at 5 a.m., was helping empty a night tub of urine when he called out to the convicts in the sawpits, 'Are you ready?' and, as a downpour of rain swept the settlement, the rebellion broke out.

The 1835 mutiny on Norfolk Island lasted seven hours before it was put down. It was not well planned and, when it was over, five convicts were dead and 50 wounded. Two soldiers died, mistakenly shot by their fellows.

The retribution was appalling. Morisset was too ill to deal it out. He had been sinking for some time, in increasing pain from his head wound and praying, like the men he ruled, to get off the island. For weeks he had dismissed the fears of his underling, Foster 'Flogger' Fyans that a mutiny was brewing.

When it was over, the Master's Apprentice proved every bit as cruel. The floggings literally wore out the cats – and they stopped only when Judge William Burton came to dispense justice. He gave the death sentence to 13 men and spared 16 – one of whom complained: 'We thought we should have been executed, and prepared to die, and wish we had been executed then ... I do not want to be spared on condition of remaining here: life is not worth having on such terms.'

Three months later a Catholic priest, Father Ullathorne, visited the condemned in their last week.

'I have to record the most heart-rending scene that I ever witnessed. The turnkey unlocked the cell door and said, "Stand aside, Sir." Then came fourth a yellow exhalation, the produce of the bodies of the men confined therein ... I announced to them who were reprieved from death and which of them were to die ...

'It is a literal fact that each man who heard of his reprieve wept bitterly, and each man who heard his condemnation of death went down on his knees, and with dry eyes, thanked God they were to be delivered from this horrid place.'

By then, six months after the mutiny, Morisset had gone. He went back to the mainland, sold his commission and invested it in a bank that collapsed. Forced to take a position as a police magistrate in Bathurst, his salary garnisheed to pay his creditors, he died in obscurity in 1852 leaving his 10 children and his wife penniless.

Laurence Frayne's end is not known. It is believed, however, that he wrote his memoirs after the arrival of the remarkable Alexander Maconochie as Commandant of Norfolk Island. Maconochie's vision was to change the focus on the island from punishment to reform and culturally and morally he transformed the island and the men on it. Frayne and other men were encouraged to write their memoirs and his is one of at least nine that survive today.

Whatever his end, however, we can be certain that Frayne faced it with courage.

3 | What's in a bushranger's name?

Captain Moonlite's walk on the wild side

Captain Moonlite. It's a name redolent of gallantry, mystery and romantic adventure.

But is there a hint, too, of the love that dared not speak its name; and that in adopting the name Captain Moonlite, the enigmatic bushranger Andrew George Scott was trying to tell us something?

Two young men died in a blaze of gunfire trying to give Scott time to escape. A third went to the gallows with him as Scott stretched out his hand and bade him goodbye. And an hour before he hanged, Scott asked to be buried beside one of the young men who followed him to death.

Blue-eyed, darkly handsome, charming and charismatic, Andrew Scott drew young men, and even boys, to ride with him. The son of an Irish Anglican clergyman, well educated and intelligent, he was a man who had the politician's gift of apparently believing his own lies. Of all the bushrangers, he is the most complex and the only truly enigmatic figure. The truth about Captain Moonlite, like his name, is somewhere in the shadows.

Andrew Scott's life was a kaleidoscope. In turn he was a lay preacher, a bank robber, a notable Sydney socialite, a forger, a convict, a jail-breaker, a lecturer on prison reform, and a bushranger. The central question of his life is what made him lay down the Bible and take up crime. The answer, probably, lies in his disturbed mind. He was an egomaniac who liked to walk on the wild side.

So much of Andrew Scott's life was befuddled by fantasy. He said he fought with Garibaldi in 1859 in Italy's heroic War of Independence, with the Union Army in the American Civil War of 1861–1865, and with the British in the bloody Maori Wars of 1861–1867, where, he said he was wounded at Waikato. It was true that he limped from wounds in his leg, but if he had fought in three national wars halfway round the world from one another he would hardly have had time to draw breath, let alone immerse himself in engineering, his ostensible occupation, when he came to Melbourne in April 1868.

There, the minister's son soon ingratiated himself with the Anglican bishop. The bishop recommended him to the parish of the Church of the Holy Trinity, Bacchus Marsh, where he took up the position of stipendiary lay reader. His first brush with the law came when he became friends with the son of a wealthy landowner in the district. When the youth was arrested on a charge of cattle duffing Scott took the stand and provided him with an alibi. The prosecution hinted that Scott himself was involved in the cattle thefts.

The bishop soon after transferred him to the gold mining town of Mount Egerton, near Ballarat, where it was expected that he would quickly become a minister. Scott was soon one of the community's most valued citizens. Despite his years at war in Italy, the United States and New Zealand, he was clearly a man of peace, a devout Christian. And what a friend he was to so many – particularly the town's young men. With his Irish charm and his adventurous past the young bucks of Mount Egerton saw Scott as a romantic figure. For some, he may have been in more ways than one.

Scott's church was on a hill overlooking the Mount Egerton branch of the London Chartered Bank and it was there, on 8 May 1869, on 'a dark night with a Scotch mist', as Ludwig Brunn later told a court, 'a man caught hold of me by the left shoulder and said be quiet or I will kill you.' Brunn, an 18-year-old friend of Scott's, was opening the door to the bank when he felt the barrel of a gun between his shoulder blades.

'Andrew!' said young Brunn, recognising his friend's familiar Irish brogue as he was shoved through the open door. Andrew, he saw, was wearing a black cloth mask and a felt hat and waving a pistol. Brunn was chuckling now at the practical joke. 'This is no time for jokes,' the masked man snapped as he held the pistol on Brunn and ordered him to unlock the safe. The masked man stuffed notes, sovereigns, gold flakes and a distinctive, horseshoe-shaped gold bar into a bag and then, limping as Andrew Scott did, he took Brunn across the deserted street to the schoolhouse where another young admirer of his, James Simpson, taught.

He ordered Brunn to sit down with pen and paper and by the light of struck matches he dictated a ludicrous note to the authorities: 'I hereby certify that L.W. Brunn has done everything in his power to withstand our intrusion and the taking away of the money, which was done with firearms.' Scott signed the note, 'Captain Moonlite, Sworn.' He gagged Brunn and tied him to a chair, placed the note on a table beside him, and took his leave. He had got away with cash and gold worth £1195.

Andrew Scott, or Captain Moonlite, either way the man was clearly mentally unbalanced. But the dashing pseudonym served him well. The idea that the god-fearing Andrew Scott might be a bandit by the name of Captain Moonlite was preposterous, and the police brushed aside Brunn's claims that he had indeed been held up by Moonlite and that he was sure Andrew Scott was the man calling himself such. Scott had an alibi, in any case: he had been in Melbourne when the robbery was committed, he said, and he produced a tattered train ticket to prove it. He also intimated that the handwriting on the note might have been the schoolteacher's, James Simpson's.

The police, taking their cue from the lay preacher, charged Brunn and Simpson with the robbery. The charges failed through lack of evidence, but both lost their jobs and their reputations. Devastated, Brunn determined to clear his name.

Scott, for his part, took the advice of the church's authorities and stayed out of the pulpit until things settled down. No doubt realising that Mount Egerton was not where his future lay, he took their suggestion

William Dampier's slightly melancholy portrait, by Thomas Murray, suggests he knew his piratical past would always overshadow his memory as a great explorer. Or perhaps it reflects his frustration at not getting more of the Spanish Main treasures he helped plunder. Dampier was a dinner guest at Samuel Pepys' home, where he entertained the diarist with accounts of his 'very extraordinary' adventures. At the table he could out-top the best of them with tales of bloody plunder, mutinies, terror and triumphs in his life as a buccaneer. He could talk, too, of the strange and hostile natives of the unknown New Holland and the weird species of the New World. *NewsPix*

ABOVE: The Wantabadgery siege in which Captain Moonlite – Andrew Scott – shot dead a policeman, and two of his gang were killed trying to give him a chance to get away.
Wood engraving from the Australasian Sketcher

LEFT: Moonlite's wild eyes are disturbing and he often exhibited signs of being mentally unbalanced. But the Superintendent of the Parramatta Lunatic Asylum, who observed him over four months, was under no illusions: 'I never considered him insane, but an artful, designing, unprincipled criminal ready to join in any scheme of fraud or ruffianly violence … his associates in the yard are the very lowest and hardened of criminals.' Scott's charisma attracted many young men inside and outside gaol.
Police Records Victoria Collection

OPPOSITE: Andrew Scott and Tom Rogan, with only seconds to live. Just before the hangman dropped the white caps over their heads the enigmatic bushranger stretched out his hand to his young accomplice and said, 'Goodbye Tom'. The poignant farewell would have been scant comfort for Rogan who went to the gallows 'in a dazed state'.
Reproduced from the Bulletin, *1880*

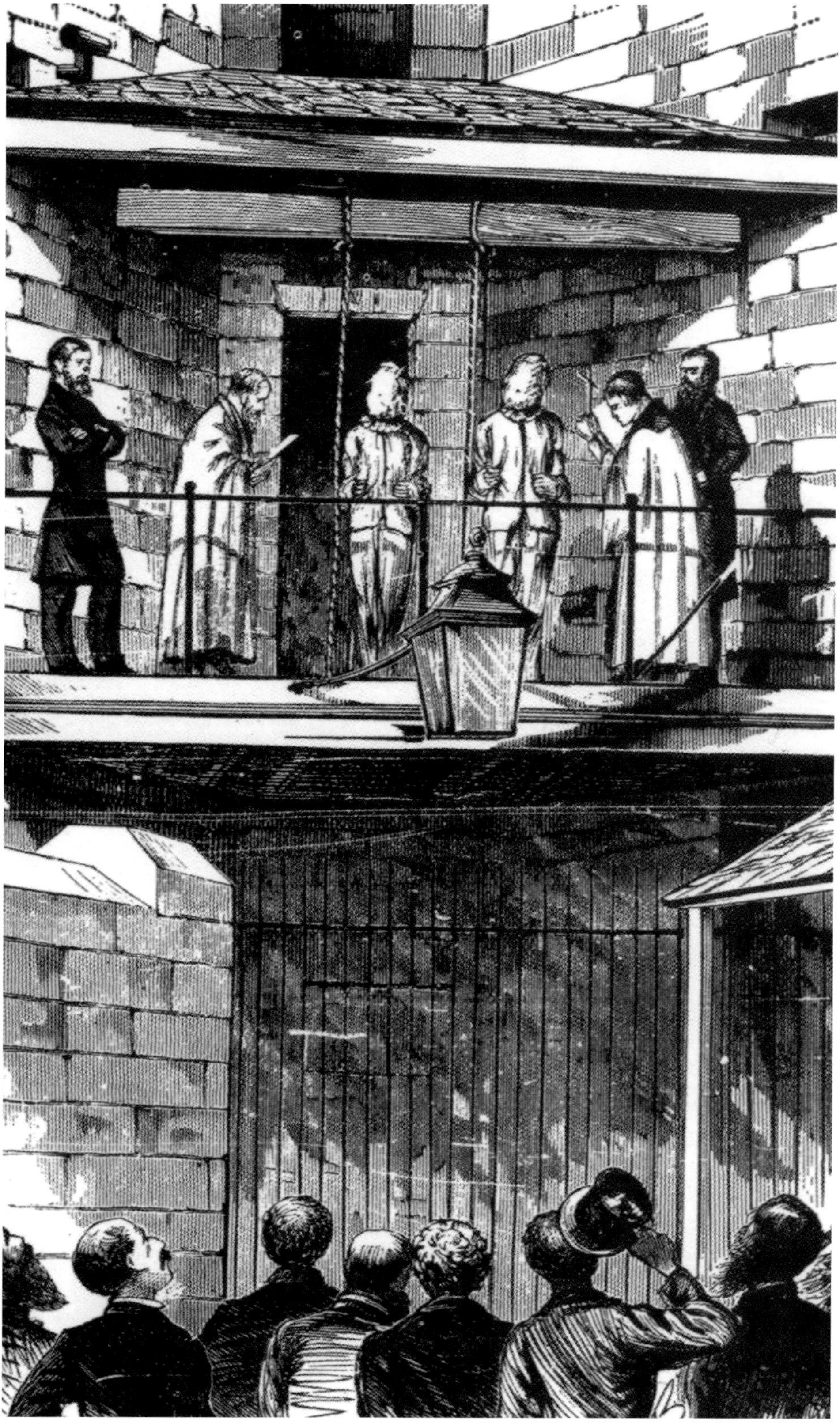

ABOVE: 'Poor leedle Tahmmy, your wife won't know you when you get home!' Jack Johnson, towering over Tommy Burns, taunted him from the moment his first-round uppercut lifted the white heavyweight champion of the world off his feet, dumped him on the canvas, and stunned 20,000 spectators at Rushcutters Bay. Johnson clinically and sadistically battered Burns until a policeman jumped into the ring and stopped the fight in the 14th. The referee Hugh D. McIntosh was also the fight promoter – and made a fortune from the historic encounter on Boxing Day, 1908. *NewsPix*

RIGHT: Was she sunk by a submarine – a Japanese submarine, perhaps, just weeks before Japan entered the war? If not, why didn't at least some of the cruiser's 645 crew abandon ship – and live to tell what happened? The mystery of the sinking of the 'invincible' HMAS *Sydney* remains unsolved. At the heart of it is the question of how *Sydney* was lured fatally close to the German raider, *Kormoran*.
NewsPix

Chic on a beach in France, Annette Kellerman exudes the confidence that was her biggest asset. Born out of her time, she had no illusions about her looks – whenever possible she posed in profile – but she gloried in her femininity and in 1918 wrote *Physical Beauty and How to Keep It*, extolling the virtues of diet and exercise. Stills from one of her films show long tresses failing to cover her nudity, and at the height of her popularity she was arrested on a Boston beach for indecency – she was wearing a revealing version of the one-piece swim suit she invented and popularised.

Mitchell Library, State Library of New South Wales

Could he possibly have foreseen what lay ahead? Young George Ernest Morrison had a clear ambition to become an adventurer and war correspondent like his hero, Stanley. But not even Morrison's boyhood fantasies could entertain his narrow escape from death in a New Guinea ambush, his heroic part in the 55-day siege of the Boxer Rebellion, his pivotal role in the fall of the Manchu Dynasty and the creation of the Chinese Republic. Extraordinarily brave, handsome and charming, he was nonetheless, as he wrote in his diary, 'oppressed by invincible shyness.' *Mitchell Library, State Library of New South Wales*

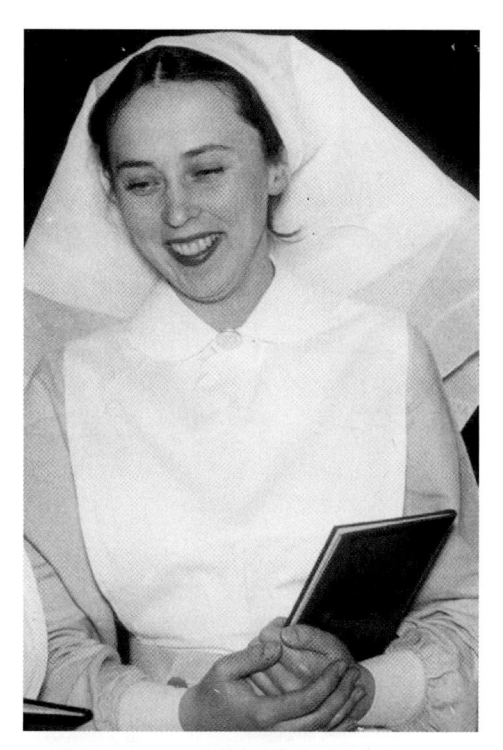

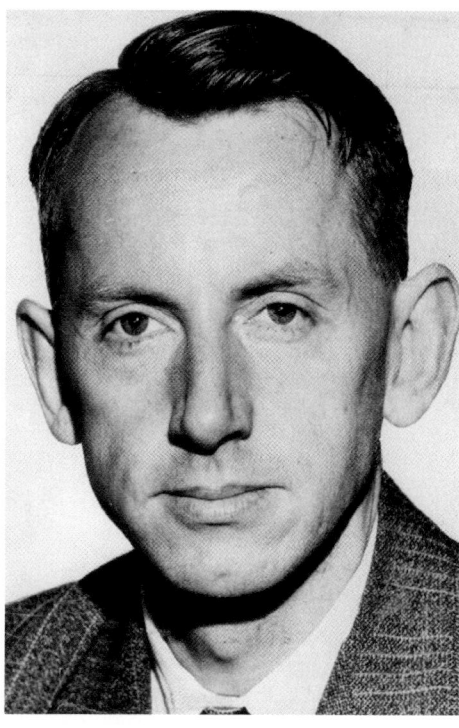

The fatal attraction between Margaret Chandler and her lover, Gib Bogle (above, right) led them to their deaths in a Lovers' Lane on New Year's Day, 1963. Geoffrey Chandler (left) wrote in his book, candidly titled, *So You Think I Did It*: 'I believe there was a third person concerned in the death of Gib and Margaret'. Chandler, a philanderer like Bogle, encouraged his wife's interest in having an affair. 'It was I who really forced the issue … She had been saying she was interested in Gib but really all she wanted was to get in the car and go home with me.'

All photographs on this page courtesy NewsPix

One hundred and twenty yards from the tape John Landy chose the precise moment Roger Bannister was at his right shoulder to look over his left shoulder. As 100 million television viewers and 35,000 spectators roared, Bannister, unseen and unheard by Landy, lengthened his gait and spurted past him in two huge strides. Bannister crossed the line with his head flung back in his customary Crucifixion attitude and Landy, five metres back, had the forlorn look of a man who had been dudded, once again. The Mile of the Century was the first sports event to be televised in the US coast to coast. *NewsPix*

and went to Sydney. With the proceeds of the robbery he quickly established a reputation as a wealthy squatter, a notable new Big Spender in town. He was fast going through the money when he bought a luxury yacht, the *Whynot*. He paid for it, however, with forged credit notes and a bouncing cheque and he was sailing for Fiji with a full crew and had almost cleared the Heads when the police in a steam launch caught up with and arrested him.

Scott was sentenced to 12 months in Maitland jail. He was released in 1872 and found some Victorian police waiting for him outside the gates. They wanted to talk to him about the Mount Egerton bank robbery. Ludwig Brunn had at last got his revenge and cleared the stigma from his name. Brunn had hired a Sydney solicitor, George Sly, to keep a close watch on Scott. Sly was so sympathetic towards Brunn's predicament that he gave his services free and had discovered that the Sydney socialite, widely admired for his dashing style and extravagant lifestyle, had sold a gold bar for £503. Easily recognisable, it was shaped like a horseshoe.

Captain Moonlite was extradited to the newly built Ballarat Gaol. There he was met by a large crowd, eager to see the man who had almost sailed to Fiji in a yacht called *Whynot*. That question, no doubt, reflected the sentiments of some in the crowd. Inside the prison with its 25-foot-high bluestone walls, Scott began at once to plan his escape. In the cell next to him was another Irishman, a man named Dermoodie. Scott cut his way through the wooden partition that separated them, picked the lock with Dermoodie's help and the pair then surprised and overpowered the warder. With his keys they opened the doors of four other cells and released the prisoners. Stripping their beds of blankets, tearing and tying them, the prisoners went to a point of the prison yard where the ground sloped up the walls, formed a human pyramid, and went over by the blanket-rope.

Captain Moonlite was at large once again. He had two weeks of freedom before, one by one, his fellow escapers were caught and he too was found, armed, in a bush hut near Bendigo. He had planned to rob a bank with Dermoodie.

In July, 1872, Captain Moonlite, now famous, went up before the feared Judge Redmond Barry. He insisted on conducting his own defence and for a week pleaded his case in a mixture of eloquence and high-flown nonsense that was summed up in his swearing: 'to the God of Heaven, as I pass from this dock to my living tomb, that I am not guilty.' Barry, who did his own line in rhetoric, and liked nothing more than lecturing the wicked before sending them down, gave him 11 years in Pentridge, Melbourne's new and formidable jail.

He was out in seven and found that Captain Moonlite was no longer news. The newspapers and all the talk was of the Kelly Gang. He missed the limelight. Then he was approached with an invitation to give a series of lectures on prison reform. He was delighted and for a while he was happy: full houses listening to his tales of the wretchedness and wickedness of the prison system. (Scott was an early conspiracy theorist. He claimed that his convictions were the result of The System trying to get him.)

Then interest waned. The Kellys had held up the Bank of New South Wales at Jerilderie and were defying a massive police hunt. The lectures attracted fewer and fewer. Captain Moonlite was yesterday's villain. In Pentridge he had made friends with a 24-year-old robber, James Nesbitt. And in the course of his lectures on the need for prison reform he had met four other feckless young men, all of whom were devoted to him. Thomas Rogan was 23, Graham Bennett, 20, Thomas Williams, 19, and Gus Wernicke, who had met Scott in a Melbourne brothel, just 15. Scott was more than twice his age – 37.

Scott told the gullible young men that he owned a spread at Wagga Wagga, and the six rode from Melbourne for their new life on Captain Moonlite's rural retreat. Only Scott and Nesbitt had handled a gun before, and at least one of the youths, Williams, could barely sit on a horse, but by the time they crossed the Murray and had reached the outskirts of the Wantabadgery Station between Gundagai and Wagga Wagga, they had realised that Scott did not own a property. They'd held up a store and stolen some horses and Scott's band of merry young men were now bushrangers – the Moonliters.

On Friday 14 November Scott went into the Wantabadgery homestead and asked about work for the six. The manager William Baynes told him there was no work and ordered him to clear off. Scott stormed back to his boys seething with rage.

The next day Captain Moonlite's gang surrounded the homestead and held everyone at gunpoint. For 36 hours the gang terrified more than 30 men, women and children, making wild threats to torture and kill them, holding mock trials and inviting William Baynes to choose the manner of his execution. At one stage Baynes was seated in a buggy, a noose around his neck, when pleading women stopped Scott from whipping the horse forward, using the buggy as the platform drop. Scott's mood was mercurial. When he tried to mount a horse that one of the hostages had ridden in on, it reared, and he shot it in the head. Then he was stricken with remorse.

On Saturday afternoon, unnoticed, Alexander Macdonald, one of the owners of Wantabadgery, slipped away and went for the Wagga Wagga police, 25 miles away. Four constables rode back with Macdonald and arrived at Wantabadgery at around four o'clock on Monday morning to be greeted by a volley of gunfire. Scott and the gang had discovered Macdonald's absence and, alerted by a barking dog, were waiting. The police fell back and retreated to a nearby homestead while one of them rode furiously for Gundagai to get more help.

Their way now clear, the gang rode off late in the morning and along the track encountered and held up a policeman and volunteers on their way to Wantabadgery. They took them with them until they stopped at a slab farmhouse on the slope of a hill owned by Edmund McGlede. They bailed up the McGlede's, told Mrs McGlede to make them breakfast and were just tucking in when a shout came from outside: 'Surrender in the Queen's name!' A bullet shattered the window.

Outside there were 11 policemen and volunteers from Wagga Wagga, Gundagai, and Wantabadgery, and around 300 spectators who had walked over the paddocks from Wantabadgery and seated themselves at vantage points on a nearby hill. It was a natural amphitheatre, a precursor to the ultimate reality television show. They enjoyed a thrilling 30 minutes.

The first to die was young Gus Wernicke. Drawing fire from Scott he rushed from the house, darted behind a tree and took aim just as a bullet smashed into his chest. The hillside spectators roared. Wernicke, writhing on the ground, cried, 'Oh God, I'm shot! And I'm only 15!', and a police sergeant fell on him. Bennett, shooting from a window, fell with a wound to his arm.

Then James Nesbitt charged out the front door, his gun blazing. Another cheer went up as he fell dead, shot in the temple by Constable Bowen. In return Bowen took a fatal bullet in the neck from Captain Moonlite. That left just three of the gang, and when police stormed the house they found Scott and Williams ready to surrender and Rogan, who had not fired a shot, too terrified to come out from under a bed.

Scott was charged with the murder of Bowen and defended himself eloquently on the grounds that he and his gang were retaliating after police opened fire on them. Moreover, he said, a fair trial was impossible because of the publicity he and his co-defendants had been exposed to. The newspapers had condemned him before the trial began, he said. It is a common argument today, but in 1880 it had no chance of succeeding. All four were sentenced to death, but Bennett and Williams, because of their age, had their sentences commuted to life imprisonment.

On the morning of 20 January 1880, at five minutes to nine, Rogan and Scott were led on to the hanging platform at 'Gallows Corner' at Darlinghurst Gaol. The *Bulletin*'s very first issue covered the double hanging and their man described Scott's 'fixed appearance of utter hopelessness and despair. The convict's wasted frame, his sunken eyes, his white face, the helpless, doubled-up appearance ...'

Captain Moonlite was long gone.

Poor Rogan, the young man who was never meant to be a bushranger, 'simply looked dazed.'

Andrew Scott stretched out his hand to Rogan just before the white cap was placed over his head. 'Goodbye, Tom,' he said and then the trapdoor slammed open.

Greater love hath no man

There was clearly a deep bond between Andrew Scott and James Nesbitt. 'We have a pure, real, true friendship,' he wrote to Nesbitt's mother while awaiting his execution. They had formed their friendship in Pentridge where Nesbitt, then still a teenager, had been serving four years hard labour for 'robbery in company'.

James Nesbitt met Andrew Scott in Pentridge and so idolised the older man that he sacrificed his life for him at the Wantabadgery siege.

After he had surrendered in the kitchen at McGlede's, Scott asked to see the body of his friend. Nesbitt had sacrificed himself to cover Scott's escape but he was shot down almost immediately. Police took Scott to where Nesbitt's body had been taken, a shed behind the slab house. 'He died trying to save me,' Scott said, looking down on the corpse, 'He had a heart of gold.'

Shortly before he was hanged, Scott wrote another letter – one of many he sent from Darlinghurst Gaol – asking that he be buried beside the grave of James Nesbitt: 'I am to die on the 20th instant, and hope that I may rest with my friend. The only thing I long for is the certainty that I may share his grave.'

Scott's request, of course, was denied, and his body was taken to what is now Rookwood Cemetery where it lay for 115 years. Then, in 1995, sympathisers paid to have his remains disinterred and taken in a horse-drawn hearse to Gundagai Cemetery. Today he lies, as he wished, within a few metres of the graves of James Nesbitt and Augustus Wernicke. Constable Bowen's grave is in the same cemetery but some distance away.

Did Thunderbolt go to his own funeral?

Captain Thunderbolt's name is less a soubriquet, more a brand. And, it appears, a franchise brand. Some of his descendants claim that there was more than one Captain Thunderbolt – perhaps as many as three – and that the man who was shot and clubbed to death at Kentucky Ponds in 1870 was not Captain Thunderbolt, but his half-brother, and that the real Thunderbolt, dressed as a woman, went to the funeral.

It's an intriguing story and entirely plausible. They say, too, that Thunderbolt was the first and only bushranger to give himself paternity leave. He was a devoted father of four who took time off from bushranging whenever his wife was expecting. The chronology of his career supports the claim.

Captain Thunderbolt's self-styled name anticipates one of the pioneer comic strip superheroes, Captain Marvel, who was born 80 years later and sported across his red skin-tight costume a yellow lightning flash on a barrel chest. Captain Thunderbolt, too, was all man. A tough bushman, a superb horse rider, courageous, a man who liked an ale and was loyal to the woman in his life, he remains an Aussie folk hero in the New England district of New South Wales where he spent much of his long, seven-year career.

There are those who claim he was an antipodean Robin Hood, taking from the rich to give to the poor. Sadly, this belief, common to many bushranging figures, has no substance. But Captain Thunderbolt had one redeeming feature unique among the bushranging fraternity: he was the loving husband of a part-Aboriginal woman, Mary Ann Bugg. Her pleasingly gentle and lyrical Aboriginal name was Yellilong. This, of course, was too difficult for colonial tongues and she was known as Yellow Long. Today we would contract this to Yello. Or Longo.

Captain Thunderbolt's real name was easier to pronounce and harder to contract. Fred Ward.

Born Frederick Wordsworth Ward in Windsor, New South Wales in 1836, the son of a farmhand, Fred Ward grew up around horses. By the time he was in his teens he had worked as a stockman, broken in horses, and rode as a jockey for a living. He rode so well and with such dash, 'like a bloody thunderbolt', someone said, that it was almost inevitable that his love of fast horses would lead him to stealing them. In 1854 his brother Michael drowned while droving horses from Tocal station to Maitland and in April 1856 in the Windsor saleyards young Fred was found in possession of 75 horses belonging to Tocal station. He was 'shelved' by an informer nicknamed Pelican and was sent for 10 years to the penal station on Cockatoo Island in Port Jackson, not far from where the Harbour Bridge would be built 76 years on.

Some say he was flogged and given solitary confinement often at Cockatoo Island, but whether or not, conditions there were hellish. Into a ward not much bigger than a contemporary inner city apartment – six metres by 15 metres – as many as 85 convicts were sardined, an arrangement guaranteed, as a visitor observed, to provide 'every facility and temptation to the commission of unnatural crime'.

After four years on the island Ward was given a ticket of leave and sent to the Mudgee district where he met Mary Ann Bugg – Yellilong. He lasted a year before he was back on Cockatoo Island; three years added to the remainder of his 10-year sentence, for being late for parole muster and stealing a horse. It was October 1861 and Ward was now looking at coming out of Cockatoo Island in 1870, middle aged and broken in health and spirit. On 11 September 1863, he escaped.

Fred Ward was a man with an incendiary – thunderbolt – temper.

When one of his mates was at the triangle, being flogged for malingering, Ward attacked the scourger and, with Frederick Britten, ran for it. They hid in a disused boiler until nightfall and then, in the dark, waded in to the cold waters of the harbour. Nearby, the colony's slaughterhouse made it a popular meeting place for sharks. But the two emerged intact at Balmain, stole two horses and rode to the Uralla district of New England.

Two months later Ward and Britten planned a mail coach hold-up at Split Rock, the giant boulder clump now renamed Thunderbolt's Rock that today can be seen beside the New England Highway. But on his way into Uralla the coach driver spotted the pair and alerted the police in town. When the coach returned it had a police escort and in the shoot-out Ward was wounded in the knee before he and Britten escaped. Britten went to Victoria, was arrested for robbery and escaped. The Police Gazette of 16 December 1866 had him back in NSW using the name John Clarke – but he may also have been using the name Captain Thunderbolt ...

Fred Ward went to the arms of Yellilong. For the remainder of her days Yellilong cherished and cared for her lover. She was his lookout, his intelligence officer, his quartermaster: when he and his men fancied something more than damper she'd steal and butcher a calf and take it to them. She rode with Ward, sometimes dressed as a man, while friends looked after their children. Fred Ward was at large for six years, five months and 23 days, an inordinately long career for a bushranger, and he could thank Yellilong for that.

On 21 December 1863 Ward emerged as Captain Thunderbolt, announcing that this was his name, in a hold-up of a tollbar house at Campbell's Hill. It was one of a series of hold-ups he carried out in the Bourke district with a man named McIntosh, a 17-year-old boy called 'the Bully' and a 14-year-old, John Thompson, and the beginning of a long line of bushranging activities with various companions that took him from the Hunter Valley, to New England, to Queensland and back again to where his career began and ended: Uralla.

Fred Ward tried never to harm. He had a number of battles with the police, fired at them and was wounded twice, but he is said to have disliked using firearms. He preferred whenever possible to outrun the police. A racehorse, he said, was better than a revolver. Invariably – with one fatal exception – he could outride any pursuer and he was almost always on a faster mount.

Though he himself escaped time and again, his various companions were not always so lucky. In one of the gang's clashes with police after robbing the mail north of Tamworth, John Thompson was shot from his horse and shot again as he lay, still firing, on the ground. Thompson got 15 years hard labour. Ward and the rest of the gang escaped, and Ward went over the border to lie low in Queensland. He returned in August 1865 and went back to highway robbery, bailing up mail coaches and robbing inns, and in yet another narrow escape was shot in the thigh by Port Macquarie police as his young apprentice, Thomas Mason, was captured.

Then Yellilong died of tuberculosis. On 11 November 1867 Ward had arrived at a station on the Goulburn west of Muswellbrook and asked that she be taken in to die peacefully. Her death seemed to spur him into a frenzied period of activity with another even younger apprentice, Billy Monckton, 13, who had fled from an unhappy home. The two carried out 13 robberies around Tamworth, Glen Innes, Tenterfield and other towns in the area in that year before Billy quit and tried to go straight. He succeeded for a while but then stole a horse and was sent to reform school. Seven decades on he would re-enter the Captain Thunderbolt story.

Now Thunderbolt was alone. Yellilong had gone and he must have felt his time was coming to an end. He had been on the road and on the run for more than five years now, there was rarely any rest and he, too, was suffering from tuberculosis. Bushrangers, he knew, had short, violent lives. His time was coming to an end.

In May 1870, on his favourite horse, Combo, a chestnut who came at his whistle, Thunderbolt arrived at a station. Combo was exhausted and he went looking for another horse. It was something he did often. A superb horseman he liked to steal racehorses for the pure pleasure of riding them at full tilt. He took a grey, but the horse, unknown to him, was also knocked up from recent hard riding. Ward was almost certainly at the Uralla races on 24 May 1870, and the following day held up an Italian hawker a few kilometres out of town. He told the man, Giovanni Cappusoto, he was free to go but he must go south, away from Uralla. Cappusoto did as he was told but once out of sight doubled back, uncoupled his horse from the dray, and spurred for Uralla.

Two policemen, Senior Constable Mulhall and Constable Alexander Walker, found Ward and his accomplice at Blanche's Inn and the bushrangers bolted for it. Walker, a fine horseman himself, went after Thunderbolt and, firing as they went, the two rode their horses to the point of dropping over five kilometres of rocky, rugged terrain. Finally, Ward's grey could go no further and the bushranger jumped from him at a junction in Kentucky Creek and waded into the stream. Walker rode up, shot the grey and faced Ward, now scrambling back up the creek bank five metres away.

Walker called on him to surrender and for a brief moment the pair had the sort of banal conversation that marks so many stories of the Australian bushrangers.

'Who are you?' Ward asked.

'Never mind, surrender!'

'Are you a policeman?'

'I am. You surrender!'

'What's your name?'

'My name is Walker.'

'Have you a wife and family?'

'I thought of that before I came here. You surrender.'

'No, I'll die first!' Thunderbolt shouted and Walker spurred his horse into the creek crying, 'You and I are for it!'

Walker's horse, plunging in, missed its footing and stumbled almost headfirst into the water. Thunderbolt took aim and pulled the trigger of his pistol but it misfired and Walker was on him. The two grappled and Walker, who had one bullet left, pressed his revolver against Ward's body and pulled the trigger. Thunderbolt staggered back. The bullet had gone clean through his right lung and smashed out of his back. But still he fought, clutching at Walker, who finished him with a blow to the head with the butt of his gun and dragged him to the bank. By the time they'd reached it, said Walker, Captain Thunderbolt gave his last gasps.

Some say that the body on the bank was not Frederick Ward's. They believe it was his half-brother, Harry, that Frederick Ward attended 'Thunderbolt's' funeral dressed as a woman and later escaped to Canada with the money – many thousands of pounds – that he had secreted in caves in the New England area. Others say it was his mate Fred Britten, and not Ward, who was Captain Thunderbolt. And still others believe he was a man named Michael Blake.

Captain Thunderbolt is credited with more than 70 hold-ups, robberies and thefts. He stole as many as 80 horses, many of them champion racehorses; he bailed up more than 25 mail coaches; and he raided dozens of inns, stations and stores. It defies belief that one man could run up such a tally. But more than one man, each introducing himself to his victims as Captain Thunderbolt, certainly could, and in the days before fingerprinting, identikits, DNA and The News at Six, it was likely more than one Thunderbolt was operating alongside Fred Ward and with his full knowledge.

Billy Monckton was one of many who identified Captain Thunderbolt. He arrived by train under police escort the day after the shootout and said, 'Oh, yes, that's him, right enough.' But did he mean that was Frederick Ward – or Captain Thunderbolt? In 1937 Monckton claimed that Captain Thunderbolt, the man he rode with for 15 months, was in fact Fred Britten.

The *Police Gazette* described 'Frederick Ward, alias Captain Thunderbolt, 30 years of age, five feet 8 inches high, pale sallow complexion, dark hazel eyes.' Whoever's body was dragged up 'the face looked haggard and careworn,' as the *Armidale Telegraph*, said, and as the posthumous photograph shows, it was the corpse of a man who was ready to die rather than go to prison. And that sounds like Frederick Ward.

Or Frederick Britten.

Yellilong, the woman he loved

Baptised Mary Ann at St John's Anglican Church in Stroud, NSW on 7 May 1834, Yellilong was the daughter of James Bugg and his Aboriginal wife, Elizabeth. Highly intelligent and resourceful, quite beautiful, petite, with a nose 'slightly cocked' she married a shepherd at the age of 14 and moved with him to the Mudgee district. When her husband died she met and married Frederick Ward in Stroud late in 1860 while he was on parole.

Yellilong is thought by some to have played a role in Ward and Britten's escape from Cockatoo Island but what is certain is that she rode with him on many of his sorties and she was an invaluable 'mate.' She could ride, she could track and hunt, she could cook, and she could give him what few bushrangers enjoyed, a love life with a woman he loved.

Yellilong was with Ward, their two children and his three gang members, McIntosh, the Bully and John Thompson, when police from Bourke tracked them to their camp and a gun battle broke out. The gang escaped but Yellilong and the children were taken to Willbie Willbie station while the police continued the hunt for Thunderbolt. Days later Thunderbolt and his gang rode into to the station, held it up, and left taking Yellilong and the children, gunpowder, station stores and food.

A little while later, in May 1865, pregnant with Fred Ward's third child, Yellilong was arrested as a vagrant and charged with consorting with a known criminal and sentenced to six months imprisonment. She was released three weeks later after Sir Henry Parkes agreed that she seemed to be the victim of police harassment.

On 25 March 1866 police galloped into Ward's camp just as he was mounting his horse. He got away but once again Yellilong and her children were taken. Once again she was given six months and once again the sentence was remitted, this time because of her health. By now she was showing the symptoms of tuberculosis.

Twenty months later Ward went to the house of the Bradfords near Musswellbrook on the Goulburn River, and begged Mrs Bradford to take in his wife. She was dying in a cave nearby. They found Yellilong and brought her back to the house where on 17 November, 1867 the Reverend White arrived just in time to give her the last rites.

Yellilong and Fred Ward's four children – Marina Emily, seven, Elizabeth Ann, three, Mary Ann, one, and Frederick Wordsworth, about six months – were adopted by sympathetic farmers.

Give a dog a bad name

Mad Dan Morgan's breath bubbled through the blood from his windpipe. 'Why did they not give me a chance?' he gasped. 'Why did they not challenge me?'

Morgan was dying, shot by a bullet that had smashed into his upper back and ripped up and out through his throat. But if he felt aggrieved at the way he'd been cut down he would have been enraged at what was to come. When the ghouls were finished with Morgan, and his remains were laid to rest, they were precisely that. Remains.

At the best of times Mad Dan Morgan was an unnerving and decidedly unattractive man. Tall, with malevolent eyes, an eagle-hooked nose and a mean mouth, the whole peering out from an eruption of black beard and shoulder-length tangled hair, Morgan was a fright. 'Expression of face ferocious,' a police report put it. When he appeared in a house without warning, as he sometimes did, the shock must have had hearts vaulting. In the Riverina and from Gundagai to Albury, he was feared as a sadist, a man who tortured a woman at a burning fireplace, trussed a man next to an inferno and killed half a dozen men on a whim. Is it any wonder that they didn't give him a chance?

Born in 1830, the illegitimate son of a prostitute, Kate Owen, and a father, 'Gypsy' Fuller, a costermonger around Sydney's Haymarket, little Daniel was deserted by his parents and taken care of, from the age of three, by Jack the Welshman, an eccentric herbalist of Campbelltown. He grew up with Jack until, in his late teens, he went to the Murrumbidgee where he worked as a stockman until 1854.

After that, Dan's various pseudonyms tell something of his character and his story. He was 'Down-the-hill Jack,' 'Bill the Native' and 'Bill the Jockey' before becoming 'Mad Dan the Murrumbidgee Terror'. In short, he was a frightening, expert bushman. At the climax of his career he became known as Mad Dan Morgan – he chose the name Morgan in honour of Henry Morgan the pirate – and when a stammering, frightened woman called him Mr Morgan he barked, 'Don't call me that! I'm Morgan!' Finally, a century after he was shot from ambush, he became Mad Dog Morgan in the Australian film of that name. Mad Dan apparently didn't sound terrifying enough for Hollywood, and Hollywood was right. Morgan was a mad dog: unpredictable, out of control, savage and deadly. Almost certainly he was a manic-depressive: suffering capricious mood swings that veered wildly from murder to remorse.

Mad Dog he may have become but in 1854 his name first appeared on a charge sheet as plain John Smith, accused of armed robbery of a hawker not far from Victoria's Castlemaine goldfields. It took three weeks but the Castlemaine police eventually tracked him down and found him hiding under a bed with a pistol in each hand. They were bringing him back to the jail, handcuffed to the saddle, when Morgan dug his spurs into his horse's flanks. In the short, brutal chase that followed he was knocked from the horse with a rifle butt and dragged along the ground for some distance.

John Smith aka Sydney Hill, came up before the ubiquitous judge Redmond Barry who gave him 12 years hard labour, the first two in irons. He began his term in the notorious hulk, *Success,* anchored off Williamstown. The experience of imprisonment on the hulk was enough to derange the mildest and most well balanced of men. 'The treatment received at the hands of the officers,' wrote the convict poet Owen Suffolk who spent time on a hulk, 'was so cruelly inhuman that it goaded them to madness ... scarcely a day passed without my being horrified by the shrieks of some poor wretch who was receiving a "neddying" from the warders.' In 1857, two years after Morgan had been transferred to

Pentridge prison from the *Success*, despairing and enraged prisoners from the hulk, working in the quarry at Williamstown beach, beat to death the Victorian Inspector-General of Prisons, the hated John Giles Price. Morgan was not the type to forgive and forget the experience of the *Success*.

Not surprisingly, when Morgan emerged from Pentridge after six years and got his ticket-of-leave for the Ovens and Yackandandah district he failed to report on the due date and, beginning with horse stealing, graduated to bushranging in 1863. It was to be a career punctuated by vengeful violence and murder. He opened it at Urana when he and a mate, Flash Clarke held up the Wagga police magistrate, Henry Bayliss. They robbed Bayliss of the money he had – then returned it when they learned who Bayliss was, asking him to 'go easy on us if we come up before you'. Bayliss, doing his best to make sure the pair did come before him, returned to the area with three troopers and tracked them to a bush hideaway. The police party was rummaging around the campsite when the bushrangers suddenly rose from the scrub and began firing. Bayliss was shot in the shoulder but not before he had got off a shot, which may have hit Clarke. Morgan escaped. Clarke's body was later found in the bush but the suspicion is that he was shot by Morgan to aid his getaway.

Now he had a price of £200 on his head, but few were willing to run the risk of turning him in. A few days after the Bayliss shoot-out, Morgan killed a shepherd he believed had informed on him. And a few weeks later he turned up at the Mittagong station where, he believed, the manager Isaac Vincent was helping the police track him down. He tied Vincent to a fence next to the woolshed and burned it down, cutting him loose just at the point where the terrified man seemed about to be roasted alive. He visited the home of another shepherd he suspected of being in league with the authorities and when he found the man, Haley, was not at home tied his wife with her back to the fireplace, burning her badly.

Morgan's robbery under arms specialty was mail coach hold-ups. He added his distinctive signature flourish when he was finished ransacking the mail. Morgan would lock the driver in the coach and stampede the horses, sending them and the coach careering out of control. He bore a grudge against squatters, saying that one of them had helped convict him and he liked to bail up stations and treat the hands to free grog and food from the stores. He forced the squatters or the station managers to serve them and dance jigs at the point of his revolvers. At Round Hill station, near Culcairn, he was supervising one of these impromptu knees-ups when the manager said something that fired his ire. Morgan, mounted on his horse, wrenched it around, drew both of his revolvers and began shooting wildly, putting a bullet through the hand of the manager when he instinctively flung it up to protect his head, The bullet went on to plough a furrow through the top of his skull. Another wild shot went through the leg of a young boy and hit a man standing behind him. Morgan, as was his wont, was immediately stricken with guilt and remorse and agreed to let the cattle overseer John McLean ride to Walla Walla for a doctor. McLean had hardly put his horse into a canter before Morgan, suddenly suspicious, swung on to his horse and galloped after him. Not far down the track he shot McLean in the back. He returned to the station with the dying man and sat with him for some time. It's never too late to say sorry.

Five days later he killed again. Sergeant David Maginnerty and Constable Churchley unexpectedly came upon Morgan riding ahead of them on the road near Coppabella. Maginnerty, not realising it was Morgan, trotted up alongside and found himself staring into the ferocious face of the man he was looking for. 'You're one of those bastards looking for bushrangers,' Morgan shouted, whipped out his Colt and shot McGinnerty in the heart. Down the track trooper Churchley spurred his horse and galloped hard in the opposite direction.

Three months later, Morgan ambushed a party of troopers camped near the Sydney Road and sent a volley of gunfire into their tent, wounding Sergeant Smyth, who died three weeks later in Albury hospital. And in mid-January 1864 he held up some Chinese navvies working on the road, ransacked and burned their tents and made them dance for him at gunpoint. He shot one of the Chinese and the navvy died later in Albury hospital. Then he stuck up the Albury mail coach. The newspapers, the Cobb & Co mail coach company and the station owners were shrill in their demands for his capture, but the police seemed incapable. Across the border, their Victorian counterparts jeered and publicly boasted that Morgan wouldn't last a week if he crossed the Murray.

On 2 April 1865, he took them up on their boast. He went looking for revenge – the motif of his life of crime – at Whitfield station, near Wangaratta. In 1860 he had stolen a prize horse that belonged to the station owners, the Evans family. They had trailed him to a cave and wounded him in the arm when he dashed to freedom. He had brooded over this for five years, long after the wound had healed. Now he announced he was 'on a raid upon Victoria' and intended 'to take the bloody flashness out of them [the Victorian people and the police].'

Morgan began in fine style, stealing a racehorse at Tallangatta and holding up a station at Little River. Arriving at the Whitfield station he found Evan Evans absent, set fire to the barn and granary and took two horses, and while the police hunted for him in the King River Valley, held up a succession of travellers on the road between Glenrowan and Benalla. At Warby's dairy station he strode into the kitchen and ordered Mrs Warby to fry up a hearty breakfast, exchanged one of his horses, asked the way to Connolly's, where a prize racehorse, Lockingarr was stabled, and told the groom he was off to hold up the inn at Glenrowan. (Fifteen years later the Kelly Gang had the same idea.) Superintendent Winch from Beechworth and three troopers had been on Morgan's trail and when they arrived at Warby's an hour after Morgan had rode off they reckoned the bushranger was on his way to Connolly's. Instead, Morgan had played a double bluff. He headed north to Peechelba station,

20 miles from Wangaratta on the Ovens River.

On 8 April he arrived at the station. It was around six on a wet and stormy Saturday night and the part-owners, the McPhersons, were entertaining. One of the girls was playing the piano when young Gideon McPherson answered a knock on the parlour door and found the barrel of a Colt revolver between his eyes. The wild man behind the gun hardly needed to introduce himself, but he did the honours. 'I'm Morgan.' There were four men and eight women at the station and Morgan herded them all into the one room. One of the women, Alice MacDonald, a nurse, told Morgan she needed to check on a sick baby in another room. It's said that when Morgan curtly refused she slapped his face and told him she was going anyway, and that this feisty and entirely unpredictable behaviour so impressed Morgan that he allowed her to go. Whatever the truth, brave Alice MacDonald did leave the room and at the back door whispered to a station hand about to come in to run to the Rutherfords just a quarter of a mile away. She returned and they all settled down, at gunpoint, to a pleasant Saturday night. Morgan, enjoying the warmth and the companionship of the ladies ordered all to be seated for dinner and 'tuck in.' After dinner he sat by the piano as one of the girls played. He shared a whisky with McPherson and told him he would be off early, taking a horse but paying for it. It was probably among the happiest and most contented nights of his life.

Outside a party of 14 armed men, station hands, townspeople from Wangaratta including the Presbyterian Minister, the Reverend Robertson, all under Senior Constable Evans, stealthily surrounded the house. At seven in the morning Detective Manwaring arrived from Beechworth with three troopers as Alice Keenan served Morgan his last meal. At 8.15 he got up from the table and prepared to leave. McPherson, his son Gideon, and two of the station hands went out first, Morgan following them with guns drawn. They were walking to the stockyard where Morgan was to choose a horse when McPherson caught a movement out of the corner of his eye. He stepped aside and the bushranger, suddenly apprehensive, was turning to see why when an Irish station hand, Quinlan, stepped out from behind the trunk of a tree. A renowned shot, Quinlan was 40 yards away when he took aim and fired. Morgan was in agony until he died, four and a half hours later.

Mad Dan's murderous rages were unpredictable. At Round Hill station he shot a boy, apologised, and then killed the man he sent to get a doctor.

The corpse was hardly cold when it was propped up on a mattress in the woolshed, eyelids held open with matchsticks, Colt revolver in hand. A photographer went to work as station hands and gawkers from Wangaratta began filing in. Quinlan posed beside Mad Dan with his gun, like a Big Game hunter and his trophy kill. Ghouls began cutting souvenir locks from the long black hair. Then the flowing beard was ripped from his face. 'Flayed,' the *Wangaratta Despatch* recorded: 'the lower part of the face hacked and the skin and portion of the flesh dragged round and over the chin, till the operator performed the task of taking from the corpse his massive beard. This disgusting task finished, the official departed with his trophy.' The official, Superintendent Cobham, the senior police officer for the district arrived two hours after

Morgan died but that didn't deter him from taking away the beard 'to peg it out and dry it like a possum skin' so he would always have a souvenir of his part in the death of Mad Dan Morgan.

Then the coroner, Dr Dobbyn, arrived at the scene. A phrenologist, he decided that he would like a plaster cast of the head for scientific study, and Morgan's corpse was decapitated. Some say his body suffered other indignities, but at last, on the following day, Sunday, they laid what was left of him to rest.

Mad Dan's grave can be seen today at Wangaratta. But it is an interesting comment on the sturdy good sense of the people of Wangaratta, and the lack of imagination of the area's tourist industry that in the 140 and more years since he was buried no one has ever reported seeing a headless horseman galloping through the morning mists of that picturesque countryside.

4 | The Foreign Legion

The world's most perfect woman

Professor Dudley Sargent of Harvard University, having completed his scientific research – running a measuring tape around 10,000 women – felt confident in his announcement that he had at last found the perfect female body.

It belonged, he reported, to 'a model for all young women for her beauty of outline and artistic proportions'. Sargent didn't have time to wait for the drum roll, and he had the good sense not to.

Who was she?

'I will say without qualification that Miss Kellerman embodies all the physical attributes that most of us demand in the Perfect Woman.'

Annette Kellerman was the most famous Australian of her day. She was Kylie, she was Elle, she was Germaine, she was Nicole. She was Cathy Freeman. And she was all of them in one: the world's most acclaimed female athlete and a show business superstar, Annette Kellerman was for a substantial period of the 20th century the most famous Australian woman the world had known. Yet, when she died three decades ago, Annette Kellerman was remembered perfunctorily as the Australian who had invented the women's one-piece swimsuit; and wasn't there something about her making movies?

She deserved better. Apart from being Australia's first movie star and a swimmer who could beat the best women – and some of the best men – in the world, Annette Kellerman was, unquestionably, a great pioneer of the women's movement, perhaps 70 years ahead of her time.

Of course that meant she came in for some sharp criticism. She may well have been pronounced 'The World's Most Perfect Woman' but there were many who thought her the World's *Wickedest* Woman.

Annette Marie Sarah Kellerman was born in Marrickville, Sydney, in 1886. She was the daughter of Frederick Kellerman, an Australian violinist, and Alice Charbonnet, his French wife, a pianist and music teacher. As a child, she was encouraged to take up swimming to strengthen her legs. Crippled by polio, she swam, as the cliché has it, like a fish: by the time she was 16, she was swimming among them twice daily at the Melbourne Aquarium and getting paid the considerable sum of £5 a week to do so.

Annette's father took her to London. They were going to make their fortune. She was a flop. No-one showed the least interest in a girl from the Antipodes who could swim. Then, as a publicity stunt, Annette swam 15 miles up the Thames River and the press and promoters from all over Europe scrambled. The *Daily Mail* sponsored her in an attempt to swim the English Channel, but a month later, in Paris, the only woman competitor, Annette made headlines when she competed in a 12-kilometre race down the Seine. Seventeen men started beside her, but there were only four swimmers who finished, and only two finished in front of her.

In June 1906 Annette tried a third time – and just failed – to swim the Channel, and the Prince of Wales, a man famously fascinated by the female form, asked her to give an exhibition of her swimming at the London Bath Club. Annette agreed – provided she could wear the costume she had used in her Channel attempt.

She was still a teenager, vibrant, fresh and attractive and her one-piece swimsuit – she stitched black stockings into a boy's costume – revealed her slim, athletic body, unusual for the time, when the measure of a desirable woman was her plumpness. The middle class was scandalised but the future King, whose mistresses included Lily Langtry and almost all the great courtesans of France, was delighted. Annette's fame was assured, and women's swimwear, which until then had consisted of smocks and stockings designed to obscure the female form, was about to change forever.

She did a brief season at the London Hippodrome – by now she had a vaudeville act that consisted of aquatic feats and was later to encompass acrobatics, wire walking, singing and ballet dancing before mirrors – and later that year went to America.

She was a sensation. For a huge fee, $1250 a week, the 20-year-old 'Australian Mermaid,' swam in a glass tank at the White City fairgrounds in Chicago, then Boston and New York. A year later she won priceless press coverage when she was arrested on Boston beach for wearing a brief one-piece swimsuit. She won the landmark case and changed the design of women's swimsuits irrevocably.

Annette took her show to the leading theatres in the US, Europe and Australia, married her agent in 1912 and then went, inevitably, to Hollywood.

She starred in several films. In one, she had to dive 28 metres from a cliff-top into the sea, a world record for a woman. In *Daughter of the Gods*, the first film with a $1 million budget, she had to dive 19 metres into a pool filled with crocodiles. A ladder was out of camera range and, Annette later recalled, 'I dived under those crocs and was up that ladder before you could say snap!'

When Harvard's Professor Sargent, encouraging healthy exercise, announced after a much-publicised search that Annette was 'the perfect woman', she became one of the world's best-known performers and in such demand from rival studios and theatrical promoters that she could afford to turn down a five-picture deal with 20th Century Fox. (The professor, using graphs and charts demonstrated that Annette Kellerman's dimensions approximated those of the Venus de Milo. She herself didn't fully agree with the professor. She was perfect, she said, 'only from the neck down'.)

Three decades later she was the subject of a Hollywood bio-pic very

Annette Kellerman was a lifelong advocate of exercise and diet. Her corset-free curves, a revelation in 1910, were a harbinger of the feminists' Burn the Bra call 60 years later.

loosely based on her life, *The Million Dollar Mermaid*, with Esther Williams. Although she was a consultant on the movie, she didn't care for it, calling it 'namby-pamby' and it clearly failed to capture the kaleidoscopic personality that was Annette Kellerman. She seemed to be able to do it all: a dazzling performer on the high-wire, a ballet dancer, a tough competitor on the tennis court, an accomplished linguist, a songwriter. Above all she was a propagandist for the joys of life: 'If only you could know what it is to walk and work and play and feel every inch of you rejoicing in glorious buoyant life.' A vegetarian, her attitudes to health and beauty anticipated today's attitudes and she was a forthright advocate for the cause of women left at home with children.

For more than 50 years she gave lecture tours on health and beauty and wrote books on the subject before she returned to Australia to live on the Gold Coast in 1970.

Annette Kellerman died aged 89 in Southport on 6 November 1975, in the week of the dismissal of the Whitlam government. For once in her life she couldn't grab the headlines.

Just a very naughty boy

All my life I have tried to find my mother, and I have never found her. My father has not been Theodore Flynn, exactly, but a will-o'-the-wisp just beyond, whom I have chased and hunted to see him smile upon me, and I shall never find my true father, for the father I wanted to find was what I might become, but this shall never be, because inside of me there is a young man of New Guinea, who had other things in mind for himself besides achieving phallic symbolism in human form.

— From *My Wicked, Wicked Ways*

If Errol Flynn had not existed, the devil would have had to invent him.

In fact, he *was* invented in the character of Flashman, the villain of one of Victorian literature's classic ripping yarns for boys, Thomas Hughes' *Tom Brown's Schooldays*. In it, Flashman, the sadist of the fifth form, roasts young Tom over the fire in his study. It may have been the late 18th century, and the school may have been Rugby, but it just wasn't cricket to toast your fag. Flashman – the rotter! – gets sent down for his sins. After that he's hardly heard from and *Tom Brown's Schooldays* becomes exceedingly boring.

Then, in the 1970s, George MacDonald Fraser resurrected Hughes' delicious villain and made Flashman the centrepiece of a dozen historical adventure novels. In all of them, whether rolling in the sweaty embrace of the cruel Queen of Madagascar, whimpering with fear in the fetid dungeons of the insane tyrant of Abyssinia, or inadvertently starting the Charge of the Light Brigade (with a thunderous and frightening fart induced by too much champagne the previous night), Flashman always has one eye for the ladies and the other for the main chance. He invariably behaves in a downright despicable way, only to emerge, skintight jodhpurs tattered, wrists still red raw from the ropes that bound them, with his reputation intact, unsullied – enhanced!

Flashman's attitude to women is always appalling. 'He's a monster,' says George MacDonald Fraser. 'You must remember he raped a girl in the first book; since then he's never needed to.'

Did George MacDonald Fraser have anyone in mind when he resurrected Flashman? 'David Niven was keen to play him,' MacDonald Fraser once said, 'He would have made a wonderful Flashman. Or his friend Errol Flynn, who had that shifty quality.'

He got it half right. David Niven would have been excellent acting in the role of Flashman and he was a fine actor. But Flynn, the actor, got his finest reviews in the last years of his life when he played himself. Flynn *was* Flashman.

Flynn himself said that 'few others alive in the present century have taken into their maw more of the world', and it's true that even Flashman, and the characters Flynn played on the screen – Robin Hood, Don Juan, Captain Blood or General Custer – might have bitten off more than they could chew when it came to playing the real life man, Errol Flynn.

Like Flashman, he was a devil with the women and a peerless cad. But even the fictional Flashman would be hard put to rival the remainder of Flynn's CV. Flynn was a man who beat a murder charge and three charges of the rape of underage girls. He was a con man, a brawler, a drunk, a drug addict, a gigolo, a congenital liar, a slave trader, a thief, a man who fought off cannibal headhunters, went to the Spanish Civil War – just to see it, not caring who won – and gave the world the wink, wink, nudge, nudge phrase, 'In like Flynn'.

In short, an absolute shower! But when you understand his

beginnings you realise Errol Flynn wasn't the devil incarnate: he was just a very naughty boy.

Once you get to that point of understanding it's hard to resist him. He was, at heart, a boy who grew up looking for trouble, an Australian larrikin who went on to become a deeply troubled man, racked by insecurity and his strong sense that he had wasted his life. It's true that Errol Flynn was, in the last decade of his life, a parody of himself – a man addicted to drugs, alcohol and sex. But it's also true that, right to his pathetic end, he retained an essential decency.

Many didn't see it that way of course. Among them, significantly, was his mother.

According to Marelle Flynn, he was a naughty boy almost from the day she gave birth to him, Errol Leslie Thomson Flynn, on 20 June 1909 in Hobart.

He was descended on her side from Richmond Young, a midshipman who joined the mutiny on Captain Bligh's HMS *Bounty*. Flynn, ironically, was to make his screen debut in the role of the man who led the mutiny, Richmond Young's friend, Fletcher Christian. Another of his ancestors, his mother said, was her uncle, Robert Young, a 'blackbirder' cooked and eaten by South Seas cannibals. (In New Guinea, Flynn dabbled in the form of slave trading euphemistically known as blackbirding and several times, he says, came across the horrific remains of cannibal feasts.)

His father's side was much more prosaic. The emigrant Flynn family had a history of poverty in Ireland: one was hanged for sheep stealing. Errol's father, Theodore Leslie Thomson Flynn, tall and straight in every way, was a highly respected boffin: a lecturer, and later Professor of Biology at Hobart's University of Tasmania, who went on to get an MBE and an entry in Britain's *Who's Who* for his work at Queen's University Belfast. There was nothing out of the ordinary about Theodore apart from a theatrical way of giving lectures to his students, and his international eminence in the field of marine biology.

Errol's mother, however, was altogether another fish. Lily Mary (Marelle) Young was beautiful – a stunner – who refused to breastfeed her baby because she didn't want to ruin the line of her bosom – an aesthetic concern that Errol, not so many years later, would perfectly understand. The apple didn't fall very far from the tree.

According to Errol, Marelle was unfaithful to Theodore, certainly later in her life in Paris. There, he implied, she had an affair with the Aga Khan among others. Professor Flynn spent much of his time from 1930 in Antarctica, England and Northern Ireland and Marelle preferred France. An intriguing cocktail of self-centred extrovert and uptight Anglican stirred with a dash of the disciplinary traditions of the 18th century British Navy and shaken with the jazz soundtrack of the Roaring Twenties, Marelle Young was probably not cut out to be anyone's mother, certainly not Errol's. The two fought from the time he could toddle. He was an intelligent, precocious child, articulate, questioning and stubborn. She was an adult. She punished Errol with slaps or, sometimes, thrashings. He hit back by his refusal to bend to her will or beg for her love.

'My young, beautiful, impatient mother, with the itch to live – perhaps too much like my own – was a tempest about my ears, as I about hers,' Errol wrote in his autobiography *My Wicked, Wicked Ways*, published shortly before his death in 1959.

'Our war deepened, so that a time came when it was a matter of indifference to me whether I saw her or not. These brawls with her, almost daily occurrences, did something to me. Mostly I wanted to get away from her, get away from home.'

Once, when he was six or seven, he did get away. Playing under a porch with Nerida, a neighbouring little girl, they were surprised by Nerida's mother. She saw the two small children examining each other's private parts – the first of many thousands of mutual examinations that Errol would subsequently share. (Twelve to fourteen thousand, was his estimate.)

She mustn't play that game, Nerida's mother told her little girl and left it at that. Errol's mother, on the other hand, became near hysterical with rage, screeched that he was a 'dirty little brute', gave him a hiding and demanded he tell his father what he'd done. Instead little Errol ran away from home.

'We suffered agonies of anxiety for three days and nights,' Marelle Flynn recalled in a letter. 'He was found miles away where he went and offered himself for work at a dairy farm. He asked only five shillings a week as wages, saying that would do him, as he "never intended to marry."'

(Flynn commented when told of this letter. 'That tells it. I never have married. [In fact he was married three times and had children with all three wives.] I have been tied up with women in one legal situation after another called marriage, but they somehow break up.')

Mother and son, they spent a lifetime warring. 'He was a nasty little boy,' she told reporters at the height of his fame. He had only one word for his mother, the four-letter word rarely used about one's mother. It was the word of a cad, but clearly much of the sins of Errol Flynn can be laid at Marelle's feet.

Errol Flynn's schooldays, unlike goody-goody Tom Brown's, were marked from beginning to end with rebellion and expulsion. He went to several Hobart schools and was asked to leave each of them after a short stay. At the Hobart High School's annual fete Errol and the head prefect, 'a hitherto earnest, dependable type', dropped ice-creams on to the heads of people below them in the hall and topped things off by smearing treacle on the steering wheel of the headmaster's car. He left Hobart High 'unexpectedly' immediately after, on 16 December 1925. Gone, but not forgotten.

'Naturally, we his class, followed his future career with great interest,' a school prefect recalled. 'His character was dominated by a contempt for convention and a desire to shock. He was the complete egotist. His extreme good looks were spoilt by an incredibly smug expression, plainly seen in his pictures.'

His father took the family to London and the pattern of being expelled from school after school continued. His parents were frequently away and Errol was something of a waif, largely left to fend for himself. But when Professor Flynn came back to Australia, this time to his home town Sydney, his name ensured Errol a place at Shore, one of the nation's top schools. Without Professor Flynn's credentials Errol could not possibly have passed the Shore admittance test and Mr Robson, the headmaster, formally cautioned him that he needed to pay attention to his studies. In other matters, however, Errol led the school. He was 16, bigger than almost all his classmates, skilled at tennis, swimming, diving and boxing – he relished a playground scrap – and he was far more worldly. But like boys in those days he was largely ignorant of the mysteries of sex. Here young Errol showed a high aptitude for learning. He gained a girlfriend he was later to become engaged to – 'Naomi was as naïve about sex as I' – but his sexual awakening led him to focus on another.

> In the index to Amy and Irving Wallace's *The Intimate Sex Lives of Famous People*, Errol Flynn gets star billing in a variety of roles: Men Who Enjoyed Girls 16 Years or Younger; Polygamists; Open Marriages; Sex Trials; Great Lovers & Satyrs; Caught in the Act; Busy Entertainers; Macho Chauvinists; They Paid for What They Got; Endurance and Staying Powers; Voyeurs; Peeping Toms; Practitioners of Oriental Techniques

Elsie, the school's attractive maid, a woman about 30, would meet Errol behind a hedge below his first floor dormitory window. Errol, naturally, would drop the five metres from the window to the hedge.

Nothing much happened, he says. 'She used to do a bit of grubbing, but I didn't know how to open my flies with a lady present.' Even so, as he pointed out, 'It was much more interesting than algebra.'

Inevitably he was kicked out of Shore. He was, Mr Robson told him, a disturbing influence on the rest of the scholars (not to mention Elsie). Once again Errol was on his own. His father was in England, his mother in France. He got work through a friend of his father, the manager of Dalgety and Company, the famous shipping and merchandising business and given a job in the mail room sticking stamps on letters. Young Errol enlivened the boredom of it by tickling the petty cash box. He and a workmate, Thomson, took the cash to go to Randwick racecourse, meaning to put the money back once they subtracted it from their winnings. It's seldom that easy. The likely lads were duly sacked and once again Errol found himself needing somewhere to live and a job.

Thomson introduced him to the Razor Gang – vicious muggers who operated around Kings Cross with a razor-blade embedded in a cork. Errol didn't fancy that life and when Thomson fell foul of the gang and had his throat slashed Errol thought it healthier to live with three other tramps in the Domain, the inner city park overlooking Sydney Harbour. Arranging his *Sydney Morning Herald* as he settled into bed one night he saw the front page headline: *Gold Strike in New Guinea. Hundreds on the trail.* Errol felt he was about to go north, young man.

(Well, that's how Flynn told it. A much more likely version of this epiphany is that Errol never really got involved in the Razor Gang, nor did he need to sleep in the park. The news that there was a fortune lying around to be picked up in the mountains of New Guinea probably came to him over toast and marmalade and a pot of Bushell's tea at Grandma's. In Sydney Errol had two adoring grandmothers, well-off aunts, uncles and cousins, and numerous influential friends of his father.) Whatever the truth, one of them gave him the fare to New Guinea.

In a journal he kept in New Guinea, Errol set out a young man's pompous but clear manifesto of how he intended to live his life. He had no intention of discovering as he lay dying that he had not lived, he said. Life was not a rehearsal and 'I shall know it by experience – and not make wistful conjecture about it conjured up by illustrated magazines.' Ironically, his life was to be the subject of illustrated magazines galore and enough gossip column inches to bury the island of New Britain, his first port of call in 1927.

He was just 18 when he sailed from Sydney to the island off the mainland of New Guinea. Still a teenager, still growing, still a little gawky, and entirely self-centred as he always would be, Errol spent some months there, mostly dancing the Charleston and the foxtrot to the *Tropical Troubadours* at the Kokopo Hotel in Rabaul and working when he had to in menial jobs. Then he went to the mainland, and got a job as trainee District Officer for the Australian Government. His first rung up this public service ladder was at the very bottom: government sanitation engineer. It lasted until he was found in bed with the Polynesian wife of one of his superiors and the next day he was ordered to accompany District Officer Taylor to Madang, where four prospectors had been killed.

> *I am going to front the essentials of life to see if I can learn what it has to teach and above all not to discover, when I come to die, that I have not lived.*
>
> *I am going to live deeply, to acknowledge not one of the so-called social forces which hold our lives in thrall and reduce us to economic dependency.*
>
> *I am going to live sturdily & Spartan-like, to drive life into a corner and reduce it to its lowest terms and if I find it mean then I shall know its meanness, and if I find it sublime I shall know it by experience – and not make wistful conjecture about it conjured up by illustrated magazines.*
>
> From Errol Flynn's New Guinea notebook, written as a 24-year-old, in 1933, and left behind when he had to skip town.

Flynn once said his mother 'could stretch a good story' and here, again, Errol took after her. He carried a copy of the short stories of Jack London with him when he went to New Guinea, and his father would post him books by such authors as Robert Louis Stevenson, R.M. Ballantyne and H.G. Wells; stories of derring-do in tropical islands, often based on fact. Flynn's account of his New Guinea years should be read in much the same way. It makes it difficult, however, to find the truth of his four and a half turbulent years in New Guinea.

Here, for instance, is Flynn chatting in his carefree, cavalier way, to a Melbourne *Argus* reporter on 12 September 1936 about 'The Only Time I Have Ever Been Scared.' (It's twice as amusing if you read the account in the drawl of W.C. Fields.)

'I was ambushed in New Guinea by a tribe of natives with a peeve, or something. They sprang from the jungle, bows and arrows ready. My boys dropped their loads and ran ... My gunbearer – he's usually the last one to stick – dropped my gun and left for parts unknown.

'Grabbing my trusty pistol I winged one of my attackers on my way out. My only scar is on my shin, and was put there by a poisoned arrow that struck me as I made tracks away from there.

'I kept on going until I came to a clearing. Pouring rain added to the jolly occasion. There I stayed all night, twisting my head to watch in all directions. The worst of it was that although I had cigarettes I had no matches. Miserable night! A smoke and no way to light it!

'Next morning my boys came back, sheepishly, finding me drenched and very, very, irritable. They backtracked and got the load – including the matches – and I smoked instantly.'

This colourful account, which might have described a scene from any one of the *Tarzan* movies then in vogue, is typical of Flynn's swashbuckling writing style. When famous, he wrote two novels. Precursors to the Mills & Boon school of novel writing, *Beam Ends* and *Showdown* are bodice-ripping yarns drenched with action and romance and a hero not a million miles removed from Errol Flynn himself.

In New Guinea he had a brief moment of madness: he considered becoming a lawyer. Errol wrote to his father asking the professor to pay for him to study law at Cambridge, but then, coming to his senses he toyed with the notion of making his living as a writer. He corresponded for the *Bulletin* from Port Moresby; at the height of his fame wrote his two novels and near the end of his life wrote his autobiography, *My Wicked, Wicked Ways*.

Mostly, the autobiography, written with Earl Conrad, is an amusing, wry and factual story, but the New Guinea chapters – the most obscure yet undoubtedly the most colourful of Flynn's life – are painted with a broad and melodramatic brush.

Here's our hero again, this time stumbling into a smoking, coastal village devastated by raiding mountain headhunters:

'There were charred bodies, guts were strewn all over. Children lay around decapitated. All had their skulls cracked open: the normal custom, for the brains were taken away and eaten. The worst sight of all was where a half-dozen tall pointed stakes had been driven into the earth. Pregnant women had been impaled on these points: the baby on top of the stake, on the sharp point, and the mother's body with the stake right through it. The flies were there in swarms working on the entrails.'

Nearby, hiding, he discovered a girl, 'a honey-coloured girl of exceeding femininity ... a perfect figure, and the most lovely little hollow, and then the line goes way up into the air and tattooed'.

What to do? Leave her? But then those headhunters might return. 'I took another sharp look at her breasts and made the decision. "She comes with us."'

Whatever the 'stretch' of this story, gruesome, erotic and humorous in turns, and whatever his co-writer's part in it, one thing is certain: Errol lusted for young girls then and for the rest of his life. Later, on a Port Moresby tobacco plantation he owned, his 'Boss Boy' introduced Errol to his daughter. Once again he mentally gawped at 'little up-pointing breasts so symmetrical and perfect as to have been attached by some means I didn't stop to explain to myself ... I had to buy her.'

Both girls were clearly very young. Flynn, unabashed, explained in *My Wicked, Wicked Ways* that '... there is no such thing as age in New Guinea. A girl generally matures about 12'. He cultivated a predilection for under-age sex in New Guinea and it stayed with him throughout his life. Under-age girls were the demons that lay in wait for Flynn. They brought him to the brink of disgrace and a long prison sentence and at the end he died in the arms of a 17-year-old.

The New Guinea years, as Flynn tells them, were a glorious cavalcade of lusty adventures in a Stone Age land. He tells of witnessing the hangings of New Guinea tribesmen for killing white men. He tells how he himself was charged with murder (A darker and deadlier variation of the yarn he retailed for the Melbourne *Argus*, this time it has one of his carriers fatally speared as Errol shoots a headhunter dead.) Flynn says he was acquitted when he was able to take the court to the ambush site where the body of his dead 'boy', skewered by a spear, still lay. He argued self-defence, and in any case there was no habeas corpus – the dead headhunter's body had been taken away.

He tells of being fired as assistant District Officer and getting a job as an overseer in a copra plantation. He tells of buying a joint interest in a schooner, the *Maski*, and then working on another boat, the *Matupi*, with a gold prospector, Ed Bowen. As a sideline, he and Bowen hunted the PNG national emblem, the glorious Bird-of-Paradise, whose plumage was highly coveted in the thirties.

They also went in for 'blackbirding'.

'If you could get into the hinterland and bamboozle the natives into coming back with you to a plantation or a coastal city, you would be in the chips. They were strong fellows, good workers, and you could sell them to plantations or at ports for use in the goldfields. I was a little young perhaps to go in for slave trading, but it was an acknowledged way to turn a penny.

'Recruiting was what they called this form of slave stealing and when you got a bunch of boys in your grasp they were called "indentured labourers." It was one of the main businesses of the rough-and-readies like myself who flocked into the New Guinea Territory.'

'Blackbirding' was one of Errol Flynn's shady occupations. 'I was a little young perhaps to go in for slave trading, but it was an acknowledged way to turn a penny.'

In New Guinea, in 1931, aside from the rough-and-readies – never mind the nubile smooth-and-readies – he met another, less attractive but charismatic figure, a man who was to play an important and intriguing role in the Flynn saga.

Dr Hermann Friedrich Erben was 36 when he met young Errol. A man after Errol's own heart, he was a con man, a sexual predator, a pioneer in the exotic field of tropical medicine, an explorer, an adventurer and a soldier of fortune. He was also a Nazi spy. Dr Erben hired Flynn and his schooner to sail up the dark and dangerously unhealthy Sepik River to find and film headhunters. Flynn readily agreed and they sailed on Flynn's schooner. (Flynn came out of New Guinea with malaria, an illness that, combined with a weak heart, stopped him from serving in the US military. He tried to volunteer, said his friend David Niven, but was classified 4-F: 'unfit for military duty'.)

Erben played a powerful role in Errol Flynn's life. Together, after New Guinea, they roared through the Philippines, China, Vietnam and India. In all these exotic locations they distinguished themselves. In brothels and bars, in scams and scandals, in sickness and in health (in Shanghai Flynn contracted what he called the Pearl of Great Price – gonorrhea) they demonstrated an unerring capacity to find themselves in and out of trouble but always one jump ahead of retribution and the people they swindled.

(Years later, when New Guinea debtors – there were many – wrote asking the now wealthy star for payment he would send them an autographed photograph of himself with a form letter explaining to the slower-witted that in years to come it would be worth considerably more than their puny outstanding invoice.)

Finally, in Marseilles in 1932, they parted: Erben to return to his native city, Vienna, where the Nazis were now a powerful force, and Flynn to England in search of fame and fortune. (They next met when Flynn had both – in 1937, in Paris. Erben persuaded Flynn, now the hottest movie star in the world, to go with him to Spain where, in the flimsy guise of a war correspondent, Flynn was, briefly, a spectator at the Civil War.)

Flynn never lost his adolescent veneration for the sinister Dr Erben. In 1980 Charles Higham wrote a book claiming that Erben recruited

Flynn as a Nazi spy. Norah Eddington, Flynn's second wife was infuriated by the claim.

'Errol was a wild spirit and about as unconventional as any man ever born,' she wrote in a letter to the *Los Angeles Times*. 'He hated authority, particularly policemen, and so the idea of him being attracted to the Nazis is absurd ... I would also like people to know that Sir William Stevenson, who was the Chief of British Intelligence, has said that Errol was not a German spy.'

The book's flavour and accuracy can be gauged from this excerpt:

'He and Erben had much in common. Errol inherited his anti-semitism from his mother, but she was not alone in hating Jews. Tasmania was as racist as Austria ... in Hobart, Jews were tortured at school, eliminated from businesses if found out. They were forbidden to work in politics or the police department, and their shops and offices were smashed by hoodlums. There were strange, militaristic clubs whose members donned uniforms and jackboots – almost like Nazis themselves ... filled with disgruntled Irish expatriates, the country, male-dominated, chauvinist, worshipping the male body, had an under-current of sadomasochistic repressed homosexuality to which Errol responded.'

And that was only on St Patrick's Day!

Still, Dr Hermann Erben undoubtedly exerted an influence on Flynn beyond that of any other man or woman. Here's Flynn's vivid description of him, on a boat taking them to India.

'Each morning he stood naked at the ship's stern, absorbing the sunshine – head thrown back, a vast Epstein-like sculpture, grossly misshapen, baring his gleaming teeth fang-like to the sun. He had a theory that sunlight was good for the gums and throat. He stood with his hairy blond legs, thighs stretched wide apart. His huge flabby belly undulated uneasily with each breath. His entire torso was covered with dense blonde hair. He was a heroic sight – except for the incongruously small phallic symbol between his legs.'

Erben's phallic symbol may have been small, but as things turned out within a few years Flynn was to complain bitterly, and for the remainder of his life, that he was seen as nothing more than 'a 6ft. 2in., walking phallic symbol'.

'What,' the District Attorney asked pretty Peggy Satterlee, 'was the next thing that happened?'

'Mr Flynn came into the room.'

'How was he dressed?'

'He had on pyjamas.'

'What was said?'

'I asked him what he wanted and he just said he wanted to talk to me. I asked what he was doing in a lady's bedroom ... he asked if he could get in bed. He said he would not hurt me, but would just get in bed with me. He got into bed with me and completed an act of sexual intercourse.'

On 11 January 1943, in the Los Angeles Hall of Justice, Errol Flynn's life went into the first phase of what was to become a tragic decline. He was at the peak of his career. Eleven years before he had been spotted on a Bondi beach and cast in the role of Fletcher Christian in the Australian producer/director Charles Chauvel's movie, *In the Wake of the Bounty*. Two years later he tried his hand at acting again, this time in England where he had bluffed his way into an acting job with Northampton Repertory Theatre before making his mark in a third-rate thriller called *Murder in Monte Carlo*, a dismal British movie that nonetheless came to the notice of Jack Warner, who invited him to come to Warner Bros' California studio for screen tests. Flynn took the next boat.

On board the *Paris*, he met his first wife, the woman he was to call 'Tiger Lil' – a gorgeous and fiery French movie star, Lila Damita, returning to Hollywood to co-star in a movie with Jimmy Cagney. There seemed to be little ahead – in the work sense – for her young bunk mate, the unknown Errol Flynn, but neither of them was concerned about his career at that stage.

> ## Catch a tiger
>
> Lila Damita and Errol Flynn were made for each other – intoxicated with passion, at least for the little time it took them to meet and get married. But Flynn was not made for marriage. 'Tiger Lil', David Niven recalled in his autobiography, *Bring on the Empty Horses*, 'taught him a great deal about living and living it up, but a quick marriage in Arizona in 1935 did nothing to dispel her pathological possessiveness and in the next few months during a spate of Herculean battles, Flynn drifted away from her'.
>
> Inevitably Flynn went to his playmate Niven and suggested they set up in a bachelor pad. 'Let's move in together, sport, I can't take that dame's self-centred stupidity another day.'
>
> The marriage may have been a quickie, and Flynn may have abandoned it soon after, but it took seven years of on-and-off relationships, numberless affairs and tempestuous knock-down-drag-out fights before they called it quits. They divorced in 1942. Damita won a tax-free alimony of $1500 a month plus a half interest in all his properties. In turn, in 1941, she gave him Sean, who inherited his father's looks but grew up loathing him. A photojournalist, Sean disappeared in Cambodia during the Vietnam war.

Then, in 1935, he got a dream break. Lounging around Hollywood, playing a lot of tennis, and playing up a whole lot more, he was unexpectedly thrust into the starring role designated for Robert Donat in Warner Brothers' pirate epic, *Captain Blood.*

He was an instant sensation. The world was dazzled by this new, improved, extra strength Hollywood leading man. Errol Flynn was 26 and radiated with a pure beauty seldom seen in men: laughing eyes, dazzling teeth, square jaw, broad shoulders, a slim but muscular 6 foot 2, and the whole informed by a zest and agile grace that was entirely unique. Above all Flynn had tremendous sex appeal.

Flynn got $1500 a week for *Captain Blood* and followed that landmark movie with *The Prince and the Pauper* and then an even bigger success, playing opposite Olivia de Havilland in the Technicolor classic, *The Adventures of Robin Hood*. The next year, 1939, another smash, *The Private Lives of Elizabeth and Essex*, with Bette Davis and the two having legendary off-camera battles. (Flynn was a noted boxer, bested by very few men, but Bette is said to have knocked him cold in one of their tiffs.) In 1940 came *The Sea Hawk* and then the roles of General Custer in *They Died With Their Boots On* and the heavyweight champion Jim Corbett in *Gentleman Jim*.

By January 1943 Errol Flynn was one of the Hollywood elite, the subject of international adoration, envy and endless salacious gossip. Unlike his movie peers – Clarke Gable, Humphrey Bogart, Gary Cooper, John Wayne and Cary Grant – Flynn's screen image and his private life were virtually identical. He was the same reckless, dashing, devilishly handsome hell raiser on screen and off. His love life was now legendary. It was accepted that he could have any and all the women he wanted.

So why did he want Betsy?

Betsy Hansen was a 17-year-old drugstore waitress, a girl Flynn described as he was being arrested as 'a frowsy little blonde', adding bitterly, and incriminatingly, 'I hardly touched her!' There is no denying that Betsy was a rather plain bubblehead, a girl with an overbite and a pasty complexion: a million miles from the woman Flynn was then living with, the dark beauty, Linda Christian.

On 27 September 1942, however, Betsy and some friends from Warner Bros. studio gate-crashed a lively Bel-Air party where, she said, Flynn, who had been playing tennis, chatted with her, sat her on his lap and, when she had drunk too much, took her upstairs and raped her.

Betsy didn't bother to report the incident and it came to light only when she was picked up by the police in a seedy hotel and Flynn's telephone number was found in her address book. Betsy told them Flynn had sex with her twice. Asked if she had resisted Flynn's advances Betsy said, 'No, why should I?'

A few days later another teenager, Peggy Satterlee, claimed that Flynn had twice made love to her on his yacht, the *Sirocco*.

Flynn held Peggy Satterlee, 17, a dancer, in high regard. A stunning and charming brunette, she had caught the eye of the movie idol as an extra on the set of his recent movie, *They Died With Their Boots On*. Later, at a nightclub, her sister introduced her to Flynn. Peggy Satterlee, he said, 'had sensational upholstery'.

To defend Flynn against charges of statutory rape (sex with an under-age girl) Warner Bros. hired the most famous trial lawyer in America, Jerry Geisler, a master of the honey trap technique of cross-examination. The two 17-year-olds were no match for him.

Both gave testimony that, if true, revealed the screen Casanova to have the seduction techniques of a schoolboy. Betsy told the court that once Flynn took her upstairs to lie down after drinking at the Bel-Air party she had allowed Flynn to undress her, saying as he did so, 'You don't think I would really let you go downstairs do you?'

She had said, 'Yes, I do.'

'So, he removed all your clothing?'

'Yes sir. Everything except my shoes.'

'What clothing did *he* remove?'

Betsy was blunt.

'He removed everything but his shoes.' The court erupted. (*They Died With Their Boots On* was playing in hundreds of movie houses across the country.)

Peggy Satterlee, for her part, said Flynn left his socks on when he forced himself on her, causing one wag to suggest that the title of Flynn's forthcoming movie *Gentleman Jim* should be retitled *Jim*.

Geisler got Betsy to admit that she had given oral sex to her boyfriend (then an offence) and had sex with two young men who had gone to the

Bel-Air party with her. And Peggy, who appeared in court in pigtails, flat shoes and a young girl's dress was forced to agree that she and her sister lived in an apartment paid for by a pilot and that she had once pranced around a mortuary with the pilot and – shades of Abu Ghraib – pressed their faces against those of the corpses. She'd also had an illegal abortion.

Most damning, because it was melodramatically shown to be false, was Peggy's testimony that Flynn had lured her below deck where together they had looked at the moon through a porthole of the *Sirocco*. Geisler demonstrated that the moon was showing on the other side of the moored yacht on that night. The jury – two men and nine women, came back with a not guilty verdict on both counts but Betsy and Peggy had done for Errol Flynn. He was never the same man.

'In those days Errol was a strange mixture,' David Niven wrote in *Bring on the Empty Horses*. 'A great athlete of immense charm and evident physical beauty, he stood, legs apart, arms folded defiantly and crowing lustily across the Hollywood dung heap, but he suffered, I think, from a deep inferiority complex; he also bit his nails. Women loved him passionately, but he treated them like toys to be discarded without warning for a new model, while for his men friends he preferred those who would give him least competition in any department.'

This innate insecurity, undoubtedly born of his mother's rejection of him, and the lonely life he led for much of his youth, had been concealed all his life under the cavalier swagger and charm that had swept all before him. Now he was shamed, humiliated, in the eyes of the world. Errol Flynn was a laughing stock, a walking phallus. (The Hollywood grapevine had it that Flynn was a man of ordinary sexuality, haunted and mocked by his reputation as a prodigious lover.)

During the trial a journalist had coined the phrase 'In like Flynn'. It stuck and he hated it. Despite his incorrigible bent he had always craved respect and now, he knew, he was never to get it. (There was another half-baked rape and indecent assault charge in Monaco in 1951.)

Exacerbating his humiliation was the universal ridicule and contempt for his role in *Operation Burma*, a war film that was perceived to show Errol Flynn – who had starred in the movie while missing war service – single-handedly defeating the all conquering Japanese in Burma. This was a surprise to the 180,000 troops of the 14th Army who had been in Burma and who had no recollection of running across him during the campaign.

In the post-war years as his star began to fade Flynn increasingly took refuge in morphine, cocaine and vodka. His face coarsened, his once slim body thickened. During the trial he had met a striking redhead, Norah Eddington, the 18-year-old daughter of the sheriff of LA County, who served behind the cigar counter at the Hall of Justice. Each day Flynn flashed his dazzling smile as he passed the cigar counter on his way to more humiliation. They married in 1943 but divorced five years later and Flynn quickly remarried. This time his bride was another film star, Patrice Wymore. Unlike 'Tiger Lil' Damita, both women remained fond of the old rascal to the end.

The Adventures of Don Juan, made in 1948, a tongue-in-cheek reminder of Flynn's golden years, was his last major film and for the next 10 years he was, in effect, committing suicide – painstakingly slowly.

His movie roles got smaller and fewer. In 1957, he won the critics' applause playing a character very similar to himself: a boozy burnt out case, in the film adaptation of Hemingway's *The Sun Also Rises*. It was the sort of dramatic performance he had always felt himself capable of, but time was running out for him to reinvent the character that he had crafted so carelessly over almost five decades.

In 1958 he met Beverley Aadland. A Las Vegas dancer at the Sahara from the age of 13, Beverley, 16, was the daughter of a one-legged former dancer. Beverley had been around the block quite a few times, but her mother Flo always insisted – a waste of breath surely – 'My baby was a virgin the day she met Errol Flynn!' (Flo may have had mixed feelings about Flynn. She once complained that in wintry Times

Square Errol had sent her hobbling from a cosy movie house where the three of them were enjoying a film, to hunt down a bottle of vodka.)

By that time, said Norah Eddington, who met him in New York with their two daughters, Flynn 'looked like a man with one foot in the grave'. On the brink of bursting into tears she 'just wanted to take him in my arms, to baby him, to take care of him. He had aged: he was enormously heavy; the weighty hand of dissipation was on his once beautiful features'.

On 9 October 1959, Flynn and Beverley Aadland flew to Vancouver, where Flynn was hoping to sell his yacht to a Canadian millionaire, George Caldough. On the way to the airport Flynn fell ill and Caldough stopped at the apartment of a friend, a doctor, who advised that Flynn should lie down in his bedroom.

When Beverley looked in, 30 minutes later, Flynn's face had turned blue and his lips were trembling. He died in her arms trying to speak.

What was he trying to say?

It's tempting to think his last words would have been along the lines of a Christmas message he broadcast to Australia and that concluded:

'If there's anyone listening to whom I owe money, I'm prepared to forget about it if you are.'

How he got the part. Takes 1,2,3,4

In 1931, Flynn returned to Sydney from New Guinea. Borrowing £300 from his mother, he bought an old yawl, *Sirocco*, and with four mates made a leisurely return trip up the Queensland coast, through the Great Barrier Reef, and on to Port Moresby where he managed a tobacco plantation. When he returned to Sydney the following year he found himself in the role of Fletcher Christian in Charles Chauvel's *In The Wake of the Bounty*, the Australian movie based on the mutiny on the *Bounty*.

Like almost everything in Errol Flynn's life there are a number of versions of how Chauvel discovered his star. It is said he was struck by a newspaper photograph of Errol, with a caption telling of how the young Australian had swum ashore from a shipwreck off New Guinea. Chauvel's wife Elsa is sometimes credited with seeing Flynn in a Sydney pub (a ring of truth here) and the movie's casting director may have spotted Errol sunbaking on Bondi beach. Another, more elaborate, amusing and implausible story has Flynn impersonating the chosen actor who Elsa Chauvel had seen only on stage.

Elsa saw the man, John Hampden, perform in Melbourne and went backstage to invite him to come to Sydney the following weekend to sign the contract. Flynn arranged for Hamden to be met at the station and tricked into going to a non-existent meeting. Meanwhile Flynn arrived at Elsa Chauvel's office.

'Who are you?' she asked and, falling on one knee, in a pose from the period play Hampden was starring in, Flynn replied, 'It's me, Hampden.'

'You look so different without your make-up!' Elsa said and then, when he signed 'Errol Flynn' to the contact, 'But you are John Hampden!'

'Just my stage name.'

Could it possibly be true?

Flynn himself said: 'However, despite good reviews (with the exception of the *Bulletin*) the film was overshadowed when Hollywood released its own version, *Mutiny on the Bounty*, with the world's biggest star, Clark Gable in the role of Fletcher Christian.'

Flynn and Flashie – spot the difference

The parallels between Errol Flynn and the fictional character Flashman can be seen in these two excerpts, one from Flynn's autobiography, *My Wicked, Wicked Ways* and the other from *Flashman on the March*. The two are interchangeable.

'Madge [in Sydney and broke, he had been picked up by a rich, older woman] was my first experience of what a real woman could mean. But there was no future for me in Madge either, and I am quite sure she knew it too.

At that moment my eyes lit on the dressing-room table. There, sparkling at me, were a few jewels, big ones, small ones. Some had gold or silver chains, and there were a couple of rings.

I looked back at the bed where she lay, a lovely picture, arms outspread, lovely full breasts.

This is criminal. Not the way to treat anybody. She has been so wonderful.'

He scooped up the jewels.

From *My Wicked, Wicked Ways*

'... in another moment both of us would be swept away into that thunderous white death in the mist. There was only one thing to be done, so I did it, drawing up my free leg and driving my foot down with all my force at Uliba's face, staring up at me open mouthed ... one glimpse I had of the white water foaming over those long beautiful legs, and then she was gone. Damnable altogether, cruel waste of good womanhood, but what would you do?'

Illustration and excerpt from *Flashman on the March*

In 1958 David Niven bumped into Flynn in London. Niven, who hadn't seen Flynn since the glory days, was shocked by his friend's disintegration. The once beautiful face was puffy and blotched, but there was an internal calm and compassion that had never been there during their roaring years. The pair went for a long lunch in a French restaurant in Soho.

Over the brandy and cigars Flynn told Niven, 'I've discovered a great book and I read it all the time – it's full of good stuff.' Then he warned, 'If I tell you what it is sport, I'll knock your goddamn teeth down your throat if you laugh.'

Niven promised to keep a straight face.

'It's the Bible,' Flynn said.

Our star turns at the Vigilantes' necktie party

John Jenkins didn't imagine for one moment that he was going to a necktie party. Jenkins was quietly going about his business – stealing safes – when he was seen by a passer-by. The man went hotfooting down the waterfront hollering for the Vigilantes. Jenkins had been manhandling the safe in the street at Long Wharf and he was cool enough – and greedy enough, there was $1500 inside its steel walls – to carry on and bundle it into his boat. He was leaving the scene of the crime just as the Vigilantes came galloping up.

Jenkins heard the horses thundering into Long Wharf before he saw the Vigilante posse and heaved the safe over the side. His heart sank with the safe: it lay there for all to see, sticking up in only a few feet of water.

At 10 p.m. Jenkins was bundled into the Vigilante committee rooms in Battery Street and his trial began. By midnight a bell rang summoning the citizens of San Francisco to a lynching.

Until he heard the bell Jenkins had affected a nonchalance born from his experience that the Sydney Ducks, again and again, could flout the law and escape without punishment in the Wild West town. If the worst came to the worst he'd be sprung from jail; or the snivelling, craven townsfolk, frightened of reprisals, would not dare pass sentence of death on him. Most likely he'd be run out of town and he'd come back in his own sweet time, meet up with the Ducks – Gentleman Jim, Singing Billy, Jack the Dandy and the rest of the boys, and it would be business as usual.

'Do you have anything to say?' the head of the jury asked him. Jenkins was a bully and a loudmouth but he wasted few words on them.

'I have nothing to say. I only wish to have a cigar.'

They gave him the cigar and told him that he would swing by morning.

Morning? Already some, like the Vigilantes leader Sam Brennan, felt there had been far too much palaver. Brennan's views on the Sydney Ducks and the best way to show them the error of their ways had appeared in black and white in his newspaper, the *California Star*.

'Where the guilt of the criminal is clear and unquestionable, the first law of nature demands that they be instantly shot, hung or buried alive,' he'd thundered.

Jenkins was clearly and unquestionably guilty and now he had to 'rise with the sun' – sooner if Captain Howard, impatient and getting to the nub of the matter – had his way. 'I thought we came here to hang somebody!' the captain said.

Sam Brennan sent a man out for a rope and another to fetch a parson. The Reverend Flavel Mines hurried in and spent 45 minutes in private with Jenkins preparing him to meet his maker until a Vigilante, exasperated at the delay, burst in:

'Mr Mines, you have taken about three-quarters of an hour, and I want you to bring this prayer business to a close. I am going to hang this man in half an hour!'

At 2 a.m., they dragged Jenkins, his hands tied behind him, outside and down the street while a couple of thousand ruffians, who had gathered to enjoy the spectacle of an impromptu floorless jig, jeered and cheered.

They slung the rope first over a flagpole. But the crowd, outraged, saw this as unpatriotic and Jenkins was hauled to the old Spanish Adobe. There, at the corner of the town square, they threw the rope over a beam, slipped a noose over Jenkins' head and about 20 men hauled him high. Legs kicking wildly, his body twisting in agony and desperation, he strangled. Now all the Vigilantes had to do was to string up the rest of the Sydney Ducks.

There was Palmer the Bird Stuffer; The Slasher; Wilson the Horse Thief; Bluey; Long Charlie; Little Charlie; there was James Stuart, known variously as 'English Jim' or Gentleman Jim,' a forger, gold robber, arsonist and murderer; Sam Whittaker, a man you didn't turn your back on; Singing Billy, Thomas Belcher Kay, a corrupt official; George Adams, 'Jack the Dandy', whose specialty was cutting duplicate keys, and a few score more vicious criminals – Sydney Ducks – who had come to seek their fortune in the wild gold rush town that was San Francisco in 1851.

The California gold rush began in 1848 when a carpenter discovered the yellow metal in Sierra Nevada. Just as it did in Melbourne, three years later, the magic of the word gold transformed San Francisco within weeks. In Australia, in the Old Barracks in Sydney, shipping agents mounted posters screaming 'Gold! Gold! Gold! In California' and the *Sydney Morning Herald* authenticated this with stories that prospectors could collect up to $1500 worth of gold in a week – a year's wages for the entire reporting room of the *Herald*.

'There are no poor men in California,' the *Herald* breathlessly asserted. 'The most indolent man can easily procure his ounce or two per diem and hundreds daily obtain two or three times that amount.'

Reports like that had thousands of Sydney men catching the first boat to San Francisco, and among them were those most indolent of men – criminals, ex-convicts mostly, who had served their time, and who knew that where there was gold there were easy pickings to be had.

In San Francisco, skulking in the quarter called Sydney-town, they were to become known as the Sydney Ducks – Americans, disparagingly said the Australian accent had a quack-like sound to their ears.

Once off the ship in San Francisco the soon-to-be Sydney Ducks went straight to Sydney-town. On the slope of Telegraph Hill, among the lowlife bars, the hovels and the whorehouses, they settled into a life of crime that allowed them far more liberty and far greater rewards than they had enjoyed back in Australia.

San Francisco was a town where gun law ruled. There were around 75 policemen to keep order among 20,000 mostly wild men. A hundred thousand gold seekers from around the world – wide-eyed optimists hoping to pick up a bag of nuggets and sail back to Sydney to retire; desperate, disappointed down-on-their-luck men; card sharps and confidence tricksters; bully boys and gunmen; men of God and gullible men and a few thousand women – mostly prostitutes – passed through San Francisco on their way to the Sierras between 1848 and 1851 and what law there was had no chance of keeping order.

'Horse stealing is common ... murders everyday occurrences, and everybody carries ... pistols for self defence,' said the *Sydney Morning Herald*, now singing a different tune.

On San Francisco's waterfront and at Sydney-town taverns, in The Noggin of Ale, the Jilly Waterman, the Port Phillip House, and in the Magpie, the Sydney Ducks plotted garrottings, forgeries, highway robberies, bank stick-ups and murders.

Some of the publicans themselves, old lags from Sydney, were known to be receivers of stolen property. And if any of the gang were caught, well, the Ducks were expert, too, at fixing trials, faking alibis, introducing fraudulent witnesses, corrupting court officials and intimidating witnesses.

There was no question that they were beyond the law. The question was what could be done about it?

The *California Courier* took it upon itself to supply the answer. The Sydney Ducks 'brought the city to a crisis where the fate of life and property are in immediate jeopardy,' it editorialised. 'There is no alternative now but to lay aside business and direct our whole energies as a people to seek out the abodes of these villains and execute summary vengeance upon them.'

That was the feeling, too, of the *Courier*'s readers. Leaflets went out reading:

> *Citizens of San Francisco, the series of murders and violence that have been committed in this city, without the least redress from the laws, seems to leave us entirely in a state of anarchy ... redress can be had for aggression through the never failing remedy so admirably laid down in the code of Judge Lynch.*

Judge Lynch was soon to be called upon.

In 1851, a storekeeper, Jansen, bent over his account books late one night was set upon, robbed and bashed almost to death. Marshall Fallon, San Francisco's chief law officer, arrested two men, Berdue and Windred, in the mistaken belief that they were 'Gentleman Jim' Stuart and his accomplice. The storekeeper was in a bad way and he could not positively identify the two – but he recognised the quack of their accent. They were Australians, it was true, and one of them, Windred, was a Sydney Duck. But they were both innocent. Fallon's hunch that the robbery was the work of Gentleman Jim and his partner was correct.

The two men's trial began at City Hall but by nightfall, with proceedings adjourned until the morning, there was a crowd of several thousand outside shouting for action, 'Bring 'em out! Lynch 'em! String 'em up!'

The following day the jury was wrestling with entirely reasonable doubts about the guilt of Berdue and Windred. This indecision enraged the lynch mob outside. They kicked in windows, crashed through doors and stormed the building. As the jury, with six shooters in hand, held off the insurgents, Berdue and Windred were hurriedly bundled out the back and taken to a safe place. Two weeks later they were found guilty as charged, of assault and robbery, and sentenced to long terms of imprisonment: 14 years for Berdue and 10 for Windred.

The Sydney Ducks were accustomed to springing men from jail. They did it again for Windred, using a duplicate key that Jack the Dandy had cut, and on 5 May 1851 Windred and his wife were smuggled aboard a ship for Sydney. Berdue they left in jail.

It was the last straw. Sam Brennan, a Mormon who was editor of the *California Star*, and a man with a not unblemished record himself, was all for forming the Vigilantes and getting to work on ridding San Francisco of the Ducks. A rival newspaper, the *Alta California*, weighed in with much the same idea: 'I propose then to establish a committee of safety whose business it shall be to board every vessel coming in from Sydney, and inform the passengers that they will not be allowed to land unless they can satisfy this committee that they are respectable and honest men, and let anyone transgressing this order be shot down without mercy.'

On 9 June 1851, the townspeople elected a Vigilante committee with Brennan at its head.

He got his chance the next night. And by the early hours of the following morning the Vigilantes were looking up at the Cuban-heeled boot soles of John Jenkins, the late Sydney Duck.

The next month they caught Gentleman Jim.

James Stuart, English Jim, Gentleman Jim, was an exceptional man who, as a 16-year-old had been transported to Australia for forgery and who now had established a formidable record in San Francisco as a villain who could be relied upon to do anything. He led a gang of highwaymen, he had a horse-stealing ring, and he robbed gold transports.

In Monterey he had the nerve to appear in court under an alias and give false evidence to swing a hung jury, and, while the jury deliberated on his fresh evidence, helped the accused escape custody. In 1850 he was imprisoned for his role in the theft of gold bars worth $5000. The jail couldn't hold him and he escaped to Maryville where he shot and killed a man, Charles Moore, and then had to flee back to the safety of Sydney-town when Moore's friends came looking for him.

An ice-cold killer, good-looking and ruthless, James Stuart's time was up a month after they got John Jenkins. He was unlucky. On 4 July, Independence Day, the Vigilantes picked him up in a round-up meant to catch a burglar. He passed himself off as a William Stephens, and was about to walk free when one of the Vigilantes recognised him: 'Hello, Jim. What are you doing here?' It was all up for Gentleman Jim. He did his best: he turned over more than 100 of his Sydney Duck mates – named them all and told them of his life as a thief and an arsonist. It was very helpful, but Gentleman Jim was always going to swing.

Australian badmen Sam Whittaker and Bob McKenzie left their hearts – and everything else – in San Francisco when Vigilantes slipped nooses over their necks and flung them from windows - Mitchell Library, State Library of New South Wales

The Committee of Vigilance considered all this, took a vote and 'Resolved: That prisoner Stuart be hung – unanimously carried.'

They took Gentlemen Jim down to the pier at the foot of Market Street and flung a rope over a derrick while a large crowd cheered. The Mayor, Charles Brenham and Judge Myron Norton rode up and appealed for a return to law and order.

Sam Brennan had an answer to that. 'We are the Mayor and the Recorder. The hangman and the laws! The law and the courts never yet hung a man in California,' and Brennan and his Vigilantes were about to rectify that. Stuart dangled at 3 p.m., but not before he had cleared the guiltless and still imprisoned Berdue.

A few weeks later, on 24 August, two of the Ducks Stuart had implicated in his crimes, Sam Whittaker and Bob McKenzie, were arrested and waiting for trial when a party of Vigilantes broke down the jail door and brushed past the guards. Sheriff Hayes was away that Saturday afternoon, at the bullfight.

The Vigilantes marched the struggling pair to their Battery Street committee rooms and, only seventeen minutes after they were taken from their cells, McKenzie and Whittaker, tightened nooses around their neck, were taken to the second floor where a double gallows had been rigged, and flung out the windows.

Sydney-town was deserted within days. That same month gold was discovered in Ballarat and the Sydney Ducks disappeared into history.

The Boys' Own *adventures of the most influential Australian who ever lived*

'Are you up for the Fu?' It was Strouts and raining. He had a cup of tea at the Customs mess while I slipped on my things, and I went over with him. We crossed by the deep cutting and stone barricade to the south of the Legation and in the Fu kept well under the wall while making our way to the outpost. The wall was pitted with shot and shell. It was difficult to image how I could have passed it unhurt yesterday amid that hail of bullets.

*I*t was 16 July 1900. The writer of the above, George Ernest Morrison, was now 'Chinese' Morrison, and about to become 'Morrison of Peking'. He was also about to be shot. Strouts, too. But Strouts would be shot dead. Morrison and Captain B. M. Strouts were on their way to the crowded, chaotic 'Fu', the compound where 3000 Christian Chinese had fled from the Boxers – fanatics who were hunting them down, house by house, to be slaughtered.

For a month they, and the 800 Europeans and Japanese in the embassy compound inside the imperial capital of Peking, had been under siege by the Boxers, supported by the Chinese army, and with the full blessing of the decadent and treacherous Empress of China. The situation was desperate. There was no hope of help arriving within the next month or more. Morrison must have been loving every minute of it.

An audacious, fearless adventurer who was carried from an ambush in New Guinea with spearheads deep in his head and stomach; a journalist – unquestionably Australia's greatest; a secret agent; a man who saved the lives of hundreds and emerged the hero from the tumultuous and bloody 55-day siege of Peking; a political strategist who helped bring down the last Chinese Emperor and became the close adviser to the president of the new Chinese republic; a pivotal figure in Japan's historic attack on Russia, George Ernest Morrison has been called the most influential Australian who ever lived. In Hong Kong 'Banjo' Paterson bumped into him and wrote that of the three great men of affairs that he had met up to that time – Morrison, Cecil Rhodes, the father of Rhodesia, and Winston Churchill, 'Morrison had perhaps the best record ... he outclassed the smartest political agents of the world.'

He was a legend in his own time. But his own time was too long ago for most of us.

Now, eight decades after he died, after clinically noting his imminent demise in his diary: 'Almost can believe death struggle began' – George Ernest Morrison is almost entirely forgotten in his native country.

> *I loafed about the town for an hour or two and in the afternoon went down to the Oval to see Jarvis play [cricket].*
>
> *As I seated myself in the grandstand a general titter passed through the crowd and everybody tried to be funny at my expense. Just because I had on a flannel cricketing shirt – perhaps a little dirty – old serge breeches, a green cap, leggings, old boots and a knapsack.*
>
> *One pertinacious old fool was very inquisitive and would have it that I had been down two years before with sheep and he had seen me.*
>
> *I have now finished my walk and my diary and I certainly have found the latter the more arduous of the two. I am now fairly done up with exhaustion so I'll shut up.*
>
> *By the way, Jarvis got run out first ball.*

Young George Morrison, as he says in this extract from his diary of 14 February 1880, had just finished his walk. What he doesn't say is that he'd walked 600 miles, from Geelong College, where his father was the headmaster, to Adelaide 'to while away my holidays'.

He had turned 18 just 10 days before, but already the clues to his character can be found in the pages of the diary. He is a sports lover, (a passionate follower of the Geelong Australian Football team). He is bashful around women. (In the Botanic Gardens, 'by the strangest coincidence in the world I met sweet Annie Evans,' but, unexpectedly, his father encounters them. 'I feel I am blushing up to my eyelids.'). He is attracted by danger: 'The whole country is in a state of alarm at the Kellys, the dead body of a constable has been found riddled with bullets.' He has a cutting but amusing wit. 'This elderly gal ... has got a squeaky miserable sort of voice, just such a voice as you would expect from a woman of 38 who has a bust like a deal board, a set of teeth bought in Colac (and second hand even then) and a mouth graced with a moustache a la Lord Harris.' And he is intrigued by journalism: '[Forbes] for his newspaper corresponding service in the Turko-Russian war was allowed £5000 expenses and when he got home received 2000 from the proprietors of the *Daily News*.'

Encouraged by his mother, to whom he was devoted all his life, he offered the Melbourne *Age* publication rights to his account of his walk to Adelaide and it was published in the *Leader*, the *Age's* weekly magazine, as *The Diary of a Tramp*. He was paid seven guineas. Small beer for Forbes perhaps, but a start.

With it he bought a canoe and prepared to paddle almost 1200 miles down the Murray, from Wodonga to the sea. He would be the first to do so. He named the canoe *Stanley*, in honour of his hero, Sir Henry Stanley, 'Special Correspondent to the New York *Herald*, the discoverer of Livingstone, the identifier of the Lualuba and Congo [Rivers], the greatest traveller of this or any age, the most extraordinary man, and the man for whom before all others in this world I admire most.' (In London 19 years on, and then himself famous, he was to meet Stanley.)

Young George Morrison doesn't say so, but clearly he dreamed of emulating his hero and making his name as an adventurer-explorer, the Special Correspondent for a great newspaper. The canoe expedition was part of his apprenticeship.

Once again the *Age* serialised his account, *Down the Murray in a Canoe*, and now David Syme, the proprietor of the trailblazing paper gave the teenager an extraordinary assignment. He wanted Morrison to expose the trade in 'black pearls' – the South Pacific islanders, men, women and boys whom 'blackbirders' lured or forced on to their ships and sold to Queensland sugar farmers. They did the exhausting, dirty work, clearing fields and cutting cane for a miserly wage before they were allowed home at the end of a specified period. The Queensland premier was just one of a number of influential figures profiting from the trade in human lives.

Morrison got a job as an ordinary seaman on a blackbirder, the *Lavinia*, taking 88 Kanakas back to their homes, 'bright, clean, strong intelligent fellows whose labour surely is cheap at £18 for three years'. Returning the natives could be a risky business. Though many went willingly to Queensland, others were seized and taken aboard ship to the feared nickel mines of French Noumea. Cannibalism was popular among the islanders and blackbirders notorious for the way they treated their human cargo needed to take great care not to fall into their hands. Some did.

Morrison's reports jolted Australia into a realisation that the trade had to stop, and the *Age*'s campaign played a powerful role in ending it. Morrison had made his name.

Next he decided to walk the length of the continent. Burke and Wills had attempted and failed the same trek only 21 years earlier, despite setting off with an expedition of 15 men, 21 tons of baggage and 54 camels and horses. Morrison, alone and with only a pack on his back, walked the 2,000 miles from the Gulf of Carpentaria to Melbourne in 124 days to the astonishment of the nation. The *Age* once again published his account of the walk and then commissioned him to take another walk – leading an expedition across New Guinea.

The New Guinea assignment – he was given the grandiose title of Special Commissioner by the *Age* – was exactly what he wanted. Tall, fair-haired and blue-eyed, 20-year-old George Morrison saw himself now, as he had a right to, as an explorer/journalist, an expedition leader in the mould of Stanley, venturing into a savage, unknown country.

David Syme, notoriously careful with his pennies, had such faith in the young man that he gave him, at first, an open cheque book to mount an expedition that came to rival that of Burke and Wills in size and in its tragi-comedic elements. The men Morrison chose to accompany him were a mixed and mostly comical lot. There were five white men, among them John Lyons, 'by repute one of the best bushmen in the north', and Ned Snow, 'remarkably short and of such eccentric confirmation that, whereas his body seemed longer than his legs, his head appeared more lengthy than either'. There was a Malay named Cheerful – possibly because he was an opium smoker – and another, Lively, who was 'curious'. All told, 25 men and boys and three native women set out from Port Moresby on 11 July, 1883 to cross the mysterious island. At the same time a rival expedition from the *Argus* also set out.

After 37 days on the track tribesmen attacked Morrison's party and escaped with all they could carry away. Morrison shot one of them. Lyons wrote later, 'He came and told us what he had done and said he felt like a murderer. That afternoon there was a great howling and crying among the savages.' The next morning the expedition encountered a blunt warning on the track: crossed spears and a shield. Lyons argued for them to turn back. Morrison, of course, pressed on.

It was the wrong decision. Lyons heard rather than saw what happened next. '... a most piercing scream after which a shot was fired', and discovered Morrison 'stretched on his back and covered with blood from head to foot'. He had two spears in his body: one, driven into his head near his right eye, the other deep in his stomach. Lyons snapped the shafts of the spears from Morrison's body and the expedition – what was left of it – turned for Port Moresby. Eleven days later, suffering excruciatingly, Morrison was carried into the town on a blanket. He owed his life, as he freely acknowledged, to Lyons.

On the ship taking him home he blew his nose and shot out a two centimetre splinter of wood. In Melbourne, 169 agonising days after the ambush, a surgeon removed the spearhead that was now wedged in the back of his throat. Without anaesthetic the surgeon took the tip of the spear – six centimetres long – through and up the throat and into and out of Morrison's right nostril.

So that was that; the second-last physical reminder of what Morrison saw as his failure in New Guinea. (He was still walking around with the second spearhead in his body.) Psychologically, however, he was undoubtedly scarred. He felt he'd let down the trust that Syme had put in him, had let down the *Age* in the race with the *Argus*. He decided to leave Australia and journalism and to complete his medical studies – theoretically he had been studying medicine at Melbourne University. He sailed for London on 27 March 1884, where he had the second spearhead cut from his abdomen. 'It was about the size of your second finger,' he wrote to his mother, and graduated, a doctor, from Edinburgh University two and a half years later.

In the early months of 1900, thousands of Chinese members of a secret society – the Boxers – had roamed the countryside, attacking Christian missions and slaughtering foreign missionaries and Chinese converts. Then they moved toward the cities, attracting more and more followers as they came and calling for the expulsion of all foreign devils from the Celestial Kingdom. Nervous foreign ministers in the legations in Peking demanded that the Chinese government stop the Boxers. But the Boxers were acting in connivance with the old and ruthless real ruler of China, the Dowager Empress Tzu-Hsi. From inside the Forbidden City, the Empress told the diplomats that her troops would soon crush the 'rebellion'. Meanwhile, she did nothing as 20,000 Boxers entered the capital.

In the intervening years since he graduated from Edinburgh, Dr George Morrison had roamed the world. Immediately after graduating he sailed for Canada and from there, in rapid succession, travelled and worked as a doctor in Philadelphia, Kingston, New York, Cardiff, Spain, Tangier, Ballarat, Hong Kong and Siam. In Siam, where the British and the French were vying, he worked as a British secret agent. 'I was to travel as an Australian doctor interested in the commercial development of Siam,' he wrote in *Reminiscences*, but in fact he was 'to report especially upon the truth of the alleged action of the French government in registering the Cambodians as French subjects'. Finally his travels took him to China. 'I went up the coast to Shanghai and then crossed over to Tientsin and Peking.'

He was 32. Time to take another walk. From Shanghai he walked 3,000 miles across China and wrote a book about it that led to him walking, finally, into the offices of Moberley Bell the manager of the *Times*, in Printing House Square, London. *The History of The Times* has this gushing but accurate description of the man Bell saw:

'Morrison was strikingly handsome, tall and well built – a magnificent specimen of Australian manhood. Morrison, moreover, was scientific in his observation, scrupulous in his thinking, and equipped with remarkable memory. He was expert with the gun and the canoe, uniquely self-reliant and invariably unaccompanied on his explorations. His mind was candid, his writing fluent and balanced.'

Perfect, in short, for the Peking correspondent Moberley Bell was looking for.

On 16 July 1900, he was in Peking and under siege. In the compound just outside the Forbidden City's walls there were 473 civilians, 409 Japanese and European soldiers and almost 3000 Chinese refugees, most of them Christian, 'secondary devils'. They had just four pieces of light artillery, rifles and small arms to defend themselves.

The uprising of the Boxers, and the siege was the subject of the film *55 Days at Peking*, with grim-jawed Charlton Heston playing a character inspired by the American marine, Jack Myers, who led an audacious and successful counter-attack on the Boxers. 'A seething, polyglot mass,' as Morrison described them, from the legations of Britain, Russia, Japan, Spain, America, Italy, France and Germany, the European diplomatic staff and their infantry could have come straight from Hollywood's Central Casting.

There was Sir Rupert Hart, 'after 40 years service, cooped up in the Legation, living on horse flesh and exposed to the bullets of Chinese soldiers'; Pichon, the despairing French minister (Morrison called him 'a craven-hearted cur'); Edmund Backhouse, the son of a baronet who wrung his hands over the burning of the homosexual quarter of Peking, and who took the opportunity, in the mayhem, to purloin a priceless 600-year-old Ming Dynasty encyclopedia. There was the tempestuous German Minister, Baron Klemens von Kettler, whose assassination in the street signalled the start of the siege; and from the Imperial Palace, literally overlooking them all in the legation compound, was the scheming and bloodthirsty Dowager Empress of China.

'Ministers show up badly,' Morrison wrote. 'Joostens and Pichon especially ... De Giers slouches around, squint eyed Posnaieff and swarthy Pokotiloff work despairingly ... American missionaries work splendidly. Catholic priests drink wine, eat, live and are happy ... Bredon is the picture of woe and misery.'

Morrison, on the other hand, showed up very well, as the American Polly Conduit Smith wrote: 'Not a foreign man on the place to protect us; a quantity of badly frightened Chinese servants to reassure; three children and ourselves to make plans for. We did what women always have to do – we waited; and our reward came when we saw down in the valley a dusty figure ambling along on a dusty Chinese pony, crossing from the direction of Fengtai ... It was Dr Morrison.'

Polly Conduit Smith recounted a narrow escape shortly before the siege of the embassy compound began. She had been with the Squiers, a family of Americans, staying in a villa in the hills outside Peking. Boxers were slaughtering, hacking and burning all foreigners they could find, when Morrison, on his way back to the city to file for *The Times*, remembered the family and realised the plight they would be in. He was preparing to barricade the balcony of their villa when help arrived. When the family settled in the compound Morrison stayed with them and Polly, clearly smitten, wrote, 'He is the most attractive man ... He works where a strong man is needed, and he is as dirty, happy and healthy a hero as one could find anywhere.' (Morrison, sadly, was less taken. 'Fat and gushing', he called Polly.)

On 15 June he was saving the lives of hundreds of 'rice Christians' – the Chinese converts to Christianity. Henry Savage Landor wrote: 'At two in the afternoon Dr Morrison, who has a nobler heart than many of the selfish refugees, on hearing that many Christian converts were still at the mercy of the Boxers near Nan-tang church, applied to Sir Claude MacDonald for guards to rescue them. Twenty British were given to him, and were joined by a force of Germans and Americans. Morrison guided them to the spot, and it will ever be a bright spot in the record of the doctor's life that he was the means of saving from atrocious tortures and death over a hundred helpless Chinese.'

And then, wrote The Reverend Roland Allen, 'Dr Morrison returned with a large convoy of Roman Catholic Christians and brought the most ghastly stories of the state of affairs ... He said it was the most horrible sight he had ever seen. They found the Boxers going about from house to house cutting down every Christian they could find and the place was running with blood. The rescue party marched through the streets, calling upon the Christians to come out and join them, and many did so. Among them many were wounded and some were sick. They were escorted over to the East City and placed in Prince Su's palace, commonly called the Fu, by the care of Dr Morrison and Mr Hubert James and there tended with the utmost care by these two men assisted by a few volunteers.'

The next day Morrison was in a party of 38 British, American and Japanese soldiers who stormed a temple where Boxers were in the act of massacring Christian Chinese. '45 killed – butchered; and Christian captives, with hands tied, being immolated ... All the Boxers were killed; only one dared face us. I myself killed at least six.'

On 16 July Morrison himself had the narrowest escape, making his way to the 'Fu' which was now sheltering thousands of Chinese Christians.

'Are you up for the Fu?' It was Strouts and raining. He had a cup of tea at the Customs mess while I slipped on my things, and I went over with him. We crossed by the deep cutting and stone barricade to the south of the Legation and in the Fu kept well under the wall while making our way to the outpost. The wall was pitted with shot and shell. It was difficult to image how I could have passed it unhurt yesterday amid that hail of bullets. At the outpost there was not much change. The cutting had been made a little deeper rendering access less dangerous, but I observed with alarm that no attempt had been made to heighten the barricade above what I had myself made the other day. Col. Shiba joined us; then he and I went alone and passed from the cutting along the direction of fire a short distance, then turned up over the brow of the slope into the Japanese trench. Shots were fired at us. We were evidently within view of the barricade not 35 yards away. There we waited, when Strouts came along. 'Come and see the Japanese line,' I said. He replied that he must go back to the Legation. 'Then I will go with you,' as I was bound to do, for I had accompanied him across. 'And I will go too,' said Shiba. We three then descended the few paces into the line of fire and were walking towards the barricade when suddenly I heard

some shots, how many I cannot tell, but I think three, and felt a cut in my right thigh. At the same moment, 'My God,' said Strouts, and he fell over into the arms of Shiba, who was on his left. Then I jumped forward and with Shiba dragged Strouts out of fire, though shots were still coming whizzing by us; and then he lay down while Shiba ran off for the surgeon. In the meantime I tried to slip my handkerchief round his thigh and stepped out to find a twig with which to use as a tourniquet. But the result was not good. I could see the fracture and the bone projecting against the trousers. Then Nakagawa came up and we two tried to staunch the bleeding by compressing the external iliac. The body was soaked in blood, but the poor fellow was conscious and asked me where I was hit. I said mine was unimportant. Then I fainted. In a little while the stretcher bearer came up and the captain was carried away. Then I started to walk, but was getting faint and was carried into the Legation, Caetani coming with me. Then it was found that another bullet had splintered and some of the fragments struck me. Poole cut this out and while he did so I fainted again and then vomited, the pain being intense, though I have no reason to think that it was one half as great as other pain I have suffered. In the ward Strouts was brought in. He was dying. He said nothing, but by and by he gave a few sobs of pain, then his breath came quickly, and then he sank away into his death.

That day, in London, *The Times* carried a story that was sent from Shanghai. Written by a rogue posing as a journalist, an American former gun runner named Sutterlee, it purported to be an account of a massacre of the Europeans in the compound.

Sutterlee reached for his jingoism dictionary and spared *The Times* readers nothing: 'When the last cartridge was gone their hour had come. They met it like men ... They died as we would have them die, fighting to the last for the helpless women and children who were to be butchered over their dead bodies ... Of the ladies ... their agony was long and cruel, but they bore it nobly and it is done ... All that remains is for us to mourn them and avenge them.'

The next day *The Times* printed its obituary of Morrison that said, among two reverent and adulatory columns, '... it is to Dr Morrison that the British public has looked from day to day for the earliest and most accurate intelligence ... important information of which the official confirmation used only to limp in with halting steps two or three days later.'

Almost a month later the world discovered that Morrison and the Europeans in Peking had not been overrun and slaughtered. On 14 August British and Allied troops entered the city and raised the siege. Looting and disgraceful reprisals began immediately, led by the Russians, who raped and pillaged, the Germans, who exterminated hundreds of Chinese without discrimination, and the French. Hundreds of Boxers were beheaded and the Chinese government made to pay reparations for the next 40 years.

Morrison was tired, almost spent. But there was still one more conflict to be part of. He desperately wanted and worked hard for a war between Japan and Russia. Russia's presence in Manchuria was a challenge to Britain's influence in China and, from there, to its reign in India. For the sake of the British Empire, which Morrison fervently believed in, Russia had to be driven from China. 'There must be war. There *shall* be war,' he wrote in his diary. 'May the Lord grant it that war shall come round between the alert, keen, active, prepared Japanese and the sodden, dull, stolid, unprepared Muscovite.'

Well, whether or not the Lord would grant it, war would happen if Morrison had anything to do with it.

When war came, just after midnight on 8 February 1904 with a surprise attack on the Russian navy at Port Arthur, China's warm water harbour on the Yellow Sea, Morrison had much to do with it. His part in encouraging and supporting the Japanese was such that, for a time, the Russo-Japanese War was known as Morrison's War. In military and diplomatic circles he was described as 'the author of the Russo-Japanese War.' During the war, in gratitude, the Japanese supplied him with progress reports, and when they triumphed, openly acknowledged the role Morrison had played by inviting him to accompany Commander Nogi on his entry into the great fort.

The traumatic defeat of a great European power by a country previously despised, sowed further seeds for the Russian Revolution and altered the international balance of power. It was the first time an Asian power had defeated a European power, and the success of their surprise attack encouraged the Japanese to repeat the strategy at Pearl Harbor in 1941. Morrison was wary of the Japanese, however, and warned two Australian prime ministers – Deakin in 1903 and Hughes in 1919 – that Japan's expansionism was a real danger. His about-face was such that in 1908 his foreign editor attacked him: 'I heard ... about your views concerning Japan and the necessity of smashing her as you had smashed Russia,' and urged him to follow the paper's and the British Government's policy on Japan

Morrison found himself once again at the centre of a tumultuous and historic moment. The death of the malevolent Dowager Empress led to a revolution that was resolved when Morrison outlined a plan to the warlord heading it that would lead to the abdication of the Manchus and the fall of the Dragon Throne. He left the *Times* and his legendary career in journalism and officially became the right-hand man to the President of the Republic of China. He was in effect the country's foreign secretary.

Was there anything he couldn't do?

Morrison was a magnetically attractive man. 'His features are very pleasant indeed, regular and clean-cut, eyes blue-grey and twinkling, and a strange wandering smile plays about the corners of his mouth. His hair is never brushed or at least, if it is, never looks it. He has a happy faculty of getting acquainted with everyone,' an admirer noted. Yet, handsome, heroic, man of action that he was, Morrison was nonetheless shy with women. He wondered why. He adored his mother and corresponded with her all his life and the clue undoubtedly lies there. He couldn't fall in love. He certainly tried hard and was capable of infatuation, but it was of the schoolboy variety.

In Spain, a 30-year-old doctor, he had been captivated by a young girl named, inevitably, Pepita. In Paris he spent all his savings on Noelle, who then moved on to a waiter. In Rangoon, he had an idyllic affair with a Eurasian, Mary. In London, aged 43, he had fallen heavily – and expensively – for a 22-year-old Hungarian, Toni, who soaked him for a string of costly gifts. In Peking, briefly, he lusted for Bessie, an Australian 'so sweet to look upon, so exquisitely formed'. There was a German actress in Sydney. And he had come close to an orgasmic swoon when May, an insatiable 24-year-old American heiress, had him in the shadow of the Great Wall. He was spellbound by her sexuality, and described her as 'the most thoroughly immoral woman'. This seems a reasonable assessment in the light of his diary account of her industrious and indefatigable love life:

Accustomed as long as she can remember to play with herself every morning even when unwell, even after passing the night in bed with a man. Seduced by Jack Fee, a doctor, in the French restaurant in San Francisco known as the Hen and Chickens or the Poultry or some such. Pregnant ... Went to Washington, got out of difficulty [had an abortion] ... slept constantly with Congressman Gaines ... Four miscarriages. 'Kissed' all the way over in the Siberia after leaving Honolulu by Captain Tremain Smith. Had for days in succession by Martin Egan. Mrs Goodnow had told her that once she was kissed by a woman she would never wish to be kissed by a man. Her desire now is to get a Japanese maid to accompany her back to America and to kiss her every morning ... In Tientsin she was kissed by Seppelin the Dutch consul ... In Shanghai she wired me Please come Japan be good ... That same evening she met C. R. Holcomb who had her 4 times in two hours ...

Morrison was dejected when May, too, dumped him, but at the age of 53, in 1912, he came to his senses and married his young assistant, Jennie Robin, a beautiful New Zealander who had answered his advertisement for a secretary in the *Times*. She was 23. For seven years they enjoyed a happy marriage and had three boys, Alistair, Colin and Ian. Alastair and Ian grew up to become successful authors and Colin, a teacher. But in Paris for the Peace Conference in 1919 he was struck down by a mystery illness – chronic pancreatitis – and on 27 May 1920 he wrote the last, brave, entry in the diary he had kept from his boyhood.

Almost can believe death struggle began ... Temperature 95, 4.10 a.m. Almost collapsing. If to die better die now so that arrangements can be made for Jennie in good time.

'Chinese' Morrison died the following day.

'George Ernest Morrison was the noble professional,' Peter Thompson and Robert Macklin wrote in *The Man Who Died Twice: The Life and Adventures of Morrison of Peking*, one of only two biographies of this outstanding Australian.

'He was to journalism what Don Bradman was to cricket ... Yet while Bradman's exploits on the cricket field resonate down the years and his reputation finds new lustre with each succeeding generation, Morrison has largely been forgotten ... Morrison's record is not perfect, but it is a quantum leap beyond today's insidious news management. His was a life so crowded with adventure and the reporting of great events that he not only wrote history, he made it.'

The great and the great and powerful were at his funeral in the little Sussex town where he had made his home. The President of the Republic of China sent a wreath. There was no wreath from the Commonwealth of Australia, and the Australian High Commissioner sent an underling in his place.

'Banjo' Paterson Meets Chinese Morrison

'Banjo' Paterson wrote that he 'had the luck to see ...such men as Lord Allenby, Winston Churchill, "Chinese" Morrison, Rudyard Kipling and Lords Roberts, French and Haig.'

China is a big place in which to find anybody, but by great good luck I ran against 'Chinese' Morrison, the *Times* correspondent in China ... I had a letter to Morrison from our Scotch engineer, who had known Morrison's father, as well as Morrison himself, in Victoria.

'Ah wuddent say that he'll be glad to see ye,' said the engineer. 'He's a nosty conceited jockass – a bit of a freak y'unnerstant. But in his own way he's the cleverest man I ever saw. The conceit of him! He's the only white man that unnerstands they Chinese. He learnt the language and, when he went to a meeting of mandarins, an' they all rigged out in jewels an' peacock feathers, there was a big seat at the top of the table for the boss mandarin. Morrison walks in and takes that seat an' not a Chow in the lot was game to call his bluff. An' him the son of a school-teacher in Victoria! Man, it'd cow ye! If they'd ha' known, they'd ha' stuck bamboo splinters in him till he wuz like a hedgehog. But he gets away wi' it, an' he never tells 'em a lie an' he has the *Times* at the back of him. So the Chows run to him to know whut the Japs are goin' to do, an' whut's the Russians' next move, and the like o' that. Morrison's the uncrooned king o' China; and if he'll talk to ye, ye'll know more about China than these mushionaries and poleetical agents can tell ye in a year.'

September 17th 1901. I found Morrison at a watering-place outside Chefoo. I knew his record fairly well; for, as a young man, he had explored New Guinea and northern Australia in the days when the blacks were bad. The blacks put a spear into him. He got his black boy to cut off the shaft of the spear, but never had the head of the spear taken out till he got to Melbourne. A man like that takes some stopping.

In person, he was a tall ungainly man with a dour Scotch face and a curious droop at the corner of his mouth – a characteristic I had noticed in various other freaks, including Olive Schreiner, the gifted authoress of the *Story of an African Farm*. Morrison had with him a China-coast doctor named Molyneux who acted as a sort of Dr Watson to Morrison's Sherlock Holmes. At first Morrison talked mainly about women, and if there was any unbalance in his mentality it was probably in that direction. I plied Molyneux with questions and thus got Morrison talking. Any answers that Molyneux gave me were annotated and corrected by Morrison, and by the time we had lunch I had got the uncrowned king of China talking freely.

It was an education to listen to him, for he spoke with the self-confidence of genius. With Morrison it was not a case of 'I think'; it was a case of 'I know'. Of the three great men of affairs that I had met up to that time – Morrison, Cecil Rhodes, and Winston

The Foreign Legion

Churchill – Morrison had perhaps the best record. Cecil Rhodes, with enormous capital at his back had battled with Boers and Basutos; Churchill, with his father's prestige and his mother's money to help him, had sailed on life's voyage with the wind strongly behind him; but Morrison had gone into China on a small salary for the *Times* and had outclassed the smartest political agents of the world – men with untold money at the back of them.

A triangular conversation between Morrison, Molyneux and myself ran on the following lines:

PATERSON: 'What started this Boxer trouble anyhow?'

MOLYNEUX: 'Well, you see, the Boxers –'

MORRISON: 'No, it wasn't the Boxers. You've got Boxers on the brain. The Boxers were just a rabble, washermen, and rickshaw coolies. Old Napoleon with his whiff of grapeshot would have settled the Boxers before lunch. The trouble was that the Chinese Government couldn't handle their job and the whole world was waiting for England to declare a protectorate over the Yangtze valley and stand for fair play and open the door for everybody. All the nations trusted England to give them fair play.'

PATERSON: 'What was the fighting like?'

MORRISON: 'Ask Molyneux. He knows all about war. Give him a rifle and a tin of bully-beef and he'd drive the Chinese out of China. The first man shot in Peking was the Chinese tailor, and I've always suspected Molyneux. He owed that tailor a lot of money.'

— Excerpt from *Happy Dispatches*, a collection of Paterson's essays on famous men he had met, published in 1934.

5 | Good sports, bad sports

A chip off the young block

There were 144,319,628 men, women and children in Bangladesh on 18 June 2005 and every one of them over the age of five almost died of joy. Playing in a one-day cricket match, the Bangladesh XI soundly trounced the Australians on that historic day. It was – the experts were as one on this – the most unexpected and astonishing win in the long history of cricket.

Well, no. It wasn't. That distinction belongs to an Australian XI – the very first eleven players selected to play for their country. And they beat England on 15 March 1877. The joy in Bangladesh 128 years later was unconfined. But the thrill that had rushed through the colonies with the news that the English had been beaten was almost palpable. Keith Dunstan, the journalist and author, has described it as cricket's Gallipoli: 38 years before the landing at Anzac Cove, the win at the Melbourne Cricket Ground welded the colonies into one nation.

The loss, on the other hand, was a traumatic shock to the Mother Country's psyche. It badly damaged England's image of itself as the imperious ruler of the world, superior to all others in all ways. The very large chip which had rested on the shoulders of the young nation had been put on that of their masters. In the 310 Test matches played between the two countries since then it has remained on their shoulders.

Until 15 March 1877 it was universally acknowledged that the English could not be beaten at cricket. The game belonged to them. They invented it and they played it at a level the Australians (and the Canadians and Americans, until they came up with its cousin, baseball) simply couldn't

Like a big-game hunter and his 'bag', John Quinlan, a renowned sharpshooter, poses with the corpse of Mad Dan Morgan. Quinlan shot Morgan in cold blood and from behind – as Morgan had done to others – with the huge Colt revolver placed in his lifeless hand. Even in death the police description of Morgan, '6 Feet, black hair very long and curly… expression of face ferocious' was, plainly, not understated. Morgan's head was later decapitated, 'Dr Dobbyn, the Coroner of the District being under the impression that it was usual to take a cast of the head of any great criminal'.

State Library of Victoria

The four principles in the Monty Python Murder farce. CLOCKWISE from top left: Henry Louis Bertrand, the Wynard Square dentist who was married to Jane, sweet and put-upon, but who lusted for Ellen, the promiscuous wife of Henry Kinder, the unfortunate around whom the knockabout comedy revolved. After Bertrand tried to blow from Kinder's head what few brains he had he popped a pipe back in his victim's mouth and went out to make love to Kinder's wife.

Errol Flynn's love life is legendary but the Hollywood grapevine had it that he was a man of ordinary sexuality, haunted and mocked by the legend. The most remarkable thing about Flynn was his tempestuous life out of the bedroom. He was a thief, a con-man, a slave trader, a man who fought off cannibal head-hunters, beat a murder charge, wrote two passable novels, went to the Spanish Civil War, lived in a cave in Sydney's Domain and was three times charged with the rape of under-age girls. And he was a likeable bloke. He's seen here with Olivia De Havilland, one of his innumerable conquests.

In June 1955 the young Queen Elizabeth knighted Sir Eugene Goossens. Nine months later his career was in ruins, undone by 1,700 pornographic photographs, films, books and three rubber masks. The two women in his life failed him. His wife, seen here with Goossens, hid from reporters in a convent in France, and the woman who had introduced him to 'sex magic', Rosaleen Norton, probably gave him up to the Vice Squad. The renowned conductor and composer had been pressing for Sydney to have an opera house at Bennelong Point and though he died dishonoured that is his great legacy.

National Library of Australia, Canberra

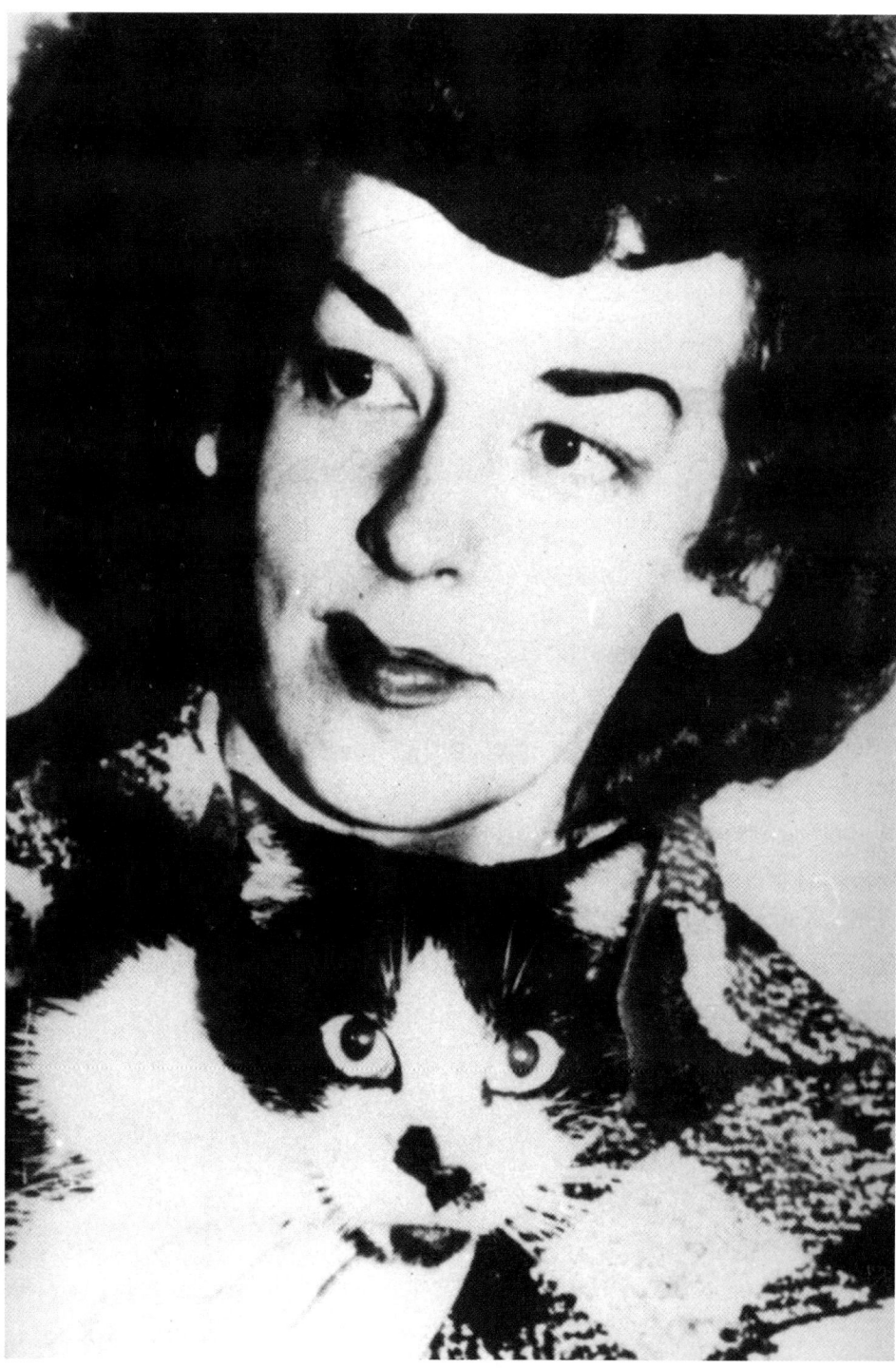

The Witch of Kings Cross and her 'familiar.' Rosaleen Norton and her malevolent-looking moggie were not gifted with supernatural powers but they acted the part and Norton was certainly interested in exploring its possibilities. An ardent exponent of 'sex magic' she destroyed two men, the poet Gavin Greenlees, who was eventually committed to a mental institution by the Lunacy Court, and Sir Eugene Goossens, the eminent international musician. She ruined his health, his career and his reputation. Norton lived on, surrounded by her paintings of the occult and the erotic, and the newspaper cuttings that recorded her lurid life. *NewsPix*

RIGHT: It was a story that moved Australia, and the press and the people desperately wanted young Eva Carmichael and Tom Pearce to become sweethearts. The only survivors of the wreck of the *Loch Ard*, Tom had risked his life to pull Eva from raging seas and then climbed a steep cliff face to go for help. She waited, 'Cold and terrified… I heard a strange noise. I imagined it to have been the war-cry of the Aborigines,' she later wrote. The strange noise was Tom returning and rescuers 'Cooeeing'. When they reached Eva's hiding place she was gone.

BELOW: The only survivor of the wreck of the *Dunbar* at Sydney Heads, 'Lucky Jim' Johnson clung for his life on a tiny ledge high on a cliff. There were 10,000 people – a fifth of the population of Sydney – watching helplessly and in horror at South Head as mountainous waves dashed the mangled and mutilated remains of 121 men, women and children on the rocks and tossed them 20 metres high. Suddenly there was a cry: 'A live man on the rocks! There he is!' Johnson became a lighthouse keeper and rescued the sole survivor of a wreck with 60 on board.

'I have been unavoidably detained, old boy, for reasons beyond my control,' Francis James said soon after he was released from a Chinese prison. More than three years of interrogation and solitary confinement had given him plenty of time to work on and polish that quote. Almost everything James had to say about his incarceration was amusing, and he fascinated the international media. His black hat with its enormous rim, his scarlet-lined cloak, his studied urbanity and his flirtation with the truth all said, 'Look at me, everyone!' On 15 January 1973, as he stumbled to freedom, almost everyone did.

Fairfaxphotos

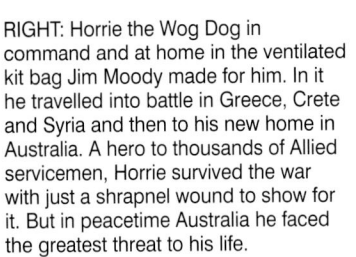

RIGHT: Horrie the Wog Dog in command and at home in the ventilated kit bag Jim Moody made for him. In it he travelled into battle in Greece, Crete and Syria and then to his new home in Australia. A hero to thousands of Allied servicemen, Horrie survived the war with just a shrapnel wound to show for it. But in peacetime Australia he faced the greatest threat to his life.

BELOW: On guard at the AIF camp in the Western Desert, Egypt. Horrie is wearing the khaki army coat cut down to make his uniform. Eventually he won his corporal ensigns.
Australian War Memorial, Canberra

match. The only way to give the English a run for their money was to set the odds in your favour: play twice as many men as they put on the field. And even then, even with 22 players to their 11, they'd still beat you.

The Englishmen, not surprisingly, suffered from a marked superiority complex, tinged with more than a touch of condescension. Asked what he thought of colonial cricketers, Roger Iddison, a Yorkshire all-rounder, said: 'Well, I don't think much of their play, but they're a wonderful lot of drinking men.' This characteristic was to distinguish Australian sides for the next century and more.

But pride comes before a fall and perhaps the first premonition that the English might one day come a cropper came when an all-England XI, under Mr H. H. Stephenson, started its 1861 tour of the colonies on an unheard-of note: a team of 15 New South Wales players beat the English by two wickets. Stephenson took his team to Victoria. The Melbourne Cricket Ground astonished him: England had no oval so well prepared and so suited for cricket, and the grandstand, 700 feet long, was the finest in the world. The Victorian team of 15 promptly repeated its rival colony's victory, and then New South Wales won again – this time by 13 wickets.

Stephenson came home humiliated. But despite the embarrassing losses the tour had been a financial bonanza and it was followed by a series of tours, each showing that the gap between the two countries was closing.

On 15 March 1877 at the Melbourne Cricket Ground that had so impressed Stephenson 16 years before, it closed emphatically. For the first time the intensely competitive colonies, New South Wales and Victoria, put aside their jealousies and agreed to play a combined intercolonial team that would be called the Australian team. In recompense for holding the game in Melbourne and not Sydney, six New South Wales players were selected, one more than Victoria. Of those selected, Frederick Spofforth, 'The Demon Bowler' refused to take his place because he would not bowl to the Victorian wicketkeeper, the brilliant J. M. Blackham, and the Victorian Frank Allen, the 'Bowler of the Century' was not inclined to play, preferring to attend the Warrnambool Fair. The wrath of the newspapers in Melbourne and Sydney was considerable.

More than 1000 spectators were there when the match began on Thursday and by the end of the day their numbers had trebled. By lunch the Australians had lost three wickets for 41 runs and the captain, Dave Gregory, had made history by being the first man run out in test cricket. Charlie Bannerman, however, was holding things together, driving superbly while watching wickets fall. By close of play Australia was 166 for 6, and on Friday, the following day, Bannerman might have gone on to become the first man to carry his bat through a Test had he not been injured by a sharply rising ball and retired on 166, a huge total for those days. England replied with 196, leaving them 49 runs behind. Australia's second innings was a disaster: Bannerman, his hand heavily bandaged, made just four, and the top score, from Horan, was 20.

England began its second innings needing just 154. They fell 45 runs short. Kendall, who played only one more international game (he was a wonderful drinking man) took seven for 55 in 33 overs.

One hundred years later, at the Melbourne Cricket Ground, the two teams played the famous Centenary Test. And once again Australia won by 45 runs. The chip was safe.

Black day at Rushcutters Bay

Big Jack Johnson, Tommy Burns was well aware, liked to start cautiously. He'd stay on the defensive for maybe four, five rounds, and then he'd build up, become aggressive. The trick was to score the points in that early round, Tommy Burns thought, and then get on the velocipede. He had the speed and the ring craft, all he had to do was stay out of reach of those long black arms. He'd done it before with men almost as big as Johnson and he could do it again. Hell, he was heavyweight champion of the world.

The Aussie referee, McIntosh, the man who was paying Burns a fortune to be in the ring with Johnson, dapper in his cap and his white turtleneck and trousers, called them in and they touched gloves. 'Well boys, you've both been dying to fight each other. It's all in except kicking and biting, so far as I'm concerned. On your way!'

McIntosh's unorthodox departure from the referee's standard, 'Now I want a fair fight,' was not a good omen. Burns looked up into Johnson's grinning face. Johnson, he knew, was taller and heavier – five inches taller and two stone heavier – but up close, with those gold teeth – God, he was gigantic!

Still, he reminded himself again, he was Tommy Burns, heavyweight champion of the world. He was fast. He had ringcraft. All he had to do was stay out of trouble. Stay on his bicycle. Johnson was a slow starter. Box him; build up the points in the early rounds.

They came together centre ring and Burns hit Johnson with a right. Johnson took it on his biceps. He ripped a left hook, into Johnson's stomach. It had no visible effect other than to get the big man chatting.

'Ahl right, Tahmmy,' Johnson said conversationally as they clinched, as if Burns had asked him to pass a slice of sponge cake, and then he caught Johnson's uppercut and went flying through the air. It had hit him right under the chin.

The roar from the 20,000 was shattering. At once savage, shocked. This arrogant black giant had put the white heavyweight champion of the world on the canvas. And round one had barely begun.

Though he was short, Tommy Burns, a French-Canadian, was fast, ring-wise and had an abnormally long reach. Holding his hands low he would dart inside bigger, slower men to score with a punishing left hook. It was a technique that had worked well enough for him to beef up and advance successfully through the weight divisions until, in 1905, he met and, in 20 rounds, defeated the world heavyweight champion Marvin Hart.

That didn't mean that Tommy Burns was the best heavyweight in the world. Far from it, as Johnson was about to prove, and there were other black fighters, such as Australia's adopted West Indian, Peter Jackson, who would probably have beaten him with ease. But in the US an unwritten colour bar forbade 'mixed fights': white men and black men meeting in the ring.

Burns had held the heavyweight title for three years and the record for the most consecutive defences by knockout when, in 1908, the Sydney entrepreneur Hugh D. McIntosh brought him to Australia to defend his title against the local hero, Bill Squires. Burns, who acted as his own manager, had made a lot of money, and McIntosh who had made his fortune by the time he was 21, had plans to make a lot more for both of them.

To stage the title defence McIntosh built a huge open air stadium in Rushcutters Bay. The stadium and the event were a sensational success. Seventeen thousand paid to see Burns knock out Squires in the thirteenth round; the first official world championship fight staged in Australia.

Burns fought again, in South Melbourne, at a smaller replica of McIntosh's Rushcutters Bay stadium, this time against Bill Lang and 7,000 saw him knock Bill out in six. Now McIntosh was ready for his big pay day.

A 'preview' of the Burns-Johnson fight, reproduced on the cover of Lone Hand *magazine. Syd Miller's caricature of the entrepreneur who staged it, Hugh D. McIntosh, also depicts 'Bash' and 'Ballet' the two passions in McIntosh's life. An international figure in the world of entertainment, McIntosh was an immensely wealthy man who mixed with the high and the mighty*

- Courtesy of Frank Van Straten, author of Huge Deal: The Fortunes and Follies of Hugh D. McIntosh

That year, 1908, *The Bulletin* changed its masthead slogan from *Australia for Australians* to *Australia for the White Man,* and McIntosh, scenting big money in a fight between the reigning champion and the unofficial black champion of the world, went after Jack Johnson. He wasn't hard to find. Wherever Burns fought Johnson was likely to turn up, sneering that the champ was avoiding him.

Arthur 'Jack' Johnson, from Galveston, Texas, was a superb fighter, a man with a record of 52 fights and only three losses. Out of the ring he was said to be amiable enough except when Tommy Burns' name came up. Then he turned bitter. Because of the colour bar he could not fight Burns in the US. He had followed Burns around the world taunting him, telling Burns he could whip him if only Burns would agree to get in the ring with him outside the US.

Burns countered these taunts with the unfeasible and extremely unwise accusation that Johnson was yellow.

McIntosh had asked Burns what it would take for him to fight Johnson in Australia, and had opened negotiations by suggesting Burns take £4,000 or half the gate. 'If I had agreed to half of it, my share would have been £13,000,' Burns later recalled. 'But I didn't. I stipulated £6,000 win, lose or draw. I'll admit it. I didn't want to meet Johnson. I thought he was too big for me. I never thought for a moment that Mr McIntosh – or anybody else, for that matter – would put up the £6,000. I was the most surprised person in the world.

'But having said that I would appear for that sum, I felt that as a man I was bound to do so.'

There was no problem getting Johnson into the ring: and not a lot of money was needed. McIntosh offered £1,000 and expenses and Johnson was glad to get it.

Now McIntosh had his dream bout: one that would be watched by the world. 'The first time in history,' as his advertisements had it, 'that champion representatives of the black and white races have met for racial and individual supremacy.'

It was hot and humid when, at 11 a.m., Johnson entered the ring to polite applause and some boos. Burns ducked under the ropes to a primeval roar from 20,000. They cheered their hero for five ecstatic minutes. They had paid from 10 shillings for seats in the 'bleachers' to £10 for ringside and all of them had come to see the white man give the black giant a hiding.

At ringside were the usual mix of dilettante high society and well-heeled lowlife. 'One-Eye' Connelly, an American who made it a point to gatecrash major sporting events (he'd got through the guards at the gate carrying two big, empty, boxes labelled: Boxing Gloves) was there, and, among the reporters, two of America's finest writers, H.L. Mencken and Jack London, the famous short story writer and novelist.

Johnson came into the ring wearing a dressing gown over his boxing trunks. Burns entered in street clothes and, while the crowd goggled, proceeded to strip until, to everyone's relief, he stopped at a pair of tight cotton boxing briefs.

His elbows were bandaged. When Johnson saw this he refused to fight until they were taken off. The 'Godfather' of Australian boxing, Larry Foley, one of the last great bare-knuckle fighters, was at ringside and was called in to adjudicate. The bandages were against the rules, he said, but what was Johnson concerned about? They couldn't hurt him or give Burns an unfair advantage. Still Johnson refused to go any further until they were taken off.

McIntosh warned him: 'In one minute from now the timekeeper will strike the gong and start the fight, and if you don't fight I will declare Burns the winner.'

Johnson scowled. 'You can do as you damn well like!' and turned his back on McIntosh. The timekeeper was just about to raise his hand and strike the gong when Burns jumped up and called out, 'I'll take the bandages off!'

He was a brave man, Burns, and he was soon to regret it.

When Jack Johnson sent Tommy Burns crashing to the canvas in the first minute of the fight he had begun a slow torture of the champion that would continue for 14 cruel rounds.

Burns bounced to his feet after the round one knockdown and flung himself at Johnson. The big man swatted him back, hitting him with left leads and right crosses as he pleased. Sometimes he'd pull him in and tie him up as he conversed: 'Aal right, Tahmmy... poor little Tahmmy ... don't know how to fight Tahmmy?' And he'd give that wide, golden-toothed smile as he pounded Burns's ribs. Other times he'd stand back and say, 'Say, little Tahmmy, you're not fighting. You can't? I'll show you how,' and he'd rip uppercuts and left and right crosses into Burns's burgeoning and bloodied face.

It was, said the *Bulletin's* man at ringside, 'the most beastly exhibition of rubbing it in by a man determined to impress on this crowd of white trash whose champion he was beating.'

The crowd, so delirious before the fight, sat stunned and silent as Burns, more and more battered, staggered back to his corner at the end of each round. 'Jewel [Burns's wife] won't know you when you go home, will she?' Johnson told him.

By round fourteen even Johnson had tired of this, and went for the kill after Burns, down for a count of eight, had gamely struggled to his feet for more. As Johnson swarmed over Burns a police superintendent with a riding crop jumped into the ring and shouted, 'Stop, Johnson!' and it was all over.

McIntosh declared Johnson the winner on points.

The news swept the world. Whites were outraged. African Americans were delirious with joy. In the Deep South the news led to lynching. Texas legislated to ban the film of the fight to avert more lynching, and in Harlem there were race riots. At once the hunt began for the 'Great White Hope', the man who could return the heavyweight title to its rightful owners: the whites of the world.

'There was no fight!' Jack London wailed in print. 'No American massacre could compare to the hopeless slaughter that took place in the

Sydney Stadium. The fight, if fight it must be called, was like that between a pigmy and a colossus ... of a grown man cuffing a naughty child...

'So far as damage was concerned, Burns never landed a blow ... I was with Burns all the way. He was a white man and so am I. Naturally I want to see the white man win... But one thing remains. Jeffries [James J. Jeffries, the former heavyweight champion] must emerge from his alfalfa farm and wipe the smile from Johnson's face. Jeff, it's up to you.'

Jeffries, who had won the title from Bob Fitzsimmons, duly came out of retirement to fight Johnson in Reno, Nevada, the following year. Hugh D. McIntosh had bid for the rights to stage the fight in Australia – a colossal $100,000 and a quarter of the film rights – but he was topped, just, by the famous American entrepreneur, Tex Rickard. McIntosh still made a pile from the fight. 'I bet all I could on Johnson,' he said, 'I was convinced he could not lose.' McIntosh won $15,000.

Jack Johnson finally lost his title to a white man, the towering Jess Willard, in 1915. It was a dubious decision and there is a strong likelihood that Johnson threw the fight. The bout was held in Cuba because Johnson had fled the US, to avoid a charge of violating the Mann Act – transporting white women across state lines for the purpose of prostitution. He returned to the US in 1920 and was sentenced to a year's imprisonment. He died in a car crash in North Carolina in 1946.

Tommy Burns took a year off, came back to win the British Empire heavyweight title and fought five more times before retiring to become an evangelist. He died of a heart attack in 1955.

Hugh D. McIntosh made an immense amount of money from entertainment, boxing and theatre but in 1942 when he died in London, aged 65, his friends had to pass the hat to cover his funeral expenses.

The only lasting winner from the great Boxing Day Burns-Johnson fight was the dawning of the realisation among African Americans that they could hold their heads high, that one day they would fight for and win their rightful place in the US.

The Godfather, Larry Foley

Larry Foley once walked 15 miles in rain and through swamps to get to a bare-knuckle fight and famously knocked out his opponent after 30 minutes – a short and sweet affair by the standards of the day. His most famous fight, though, was at Echuca, in 1879. Foley put 'em up to an American bruiser, Abe Hickin, come to fight for the Australian championship. Hickin told the press he wanted nothing to do with the new Marquess of Queensberry Rules, boxing with gloves.

'I want a fight, not a pillow fight,' he said, and Foley obliged, brutally re-shaping Abe's features. When he'd finished, the *Riverina Herald* reported, Hickin, 'presented a horrible sight. Both eyes were nearly closed, his lips were cut and blistered, his nose knocked out of shape, and his whole face pounded almost to jelly.'

As Foley stepped from the ring after the fight, he was congratulated, he said, by a tall dark man who introduced himself as the champion boxer of north-east Victoria, Ned Kelly.

Kelly had indeed won that unofficial title at Beechworth. Five years before, in a long and bruising 20-round bare-knuckle bout he had stopped the aptly named 'Wild' Wright. A photograph taken to commemorate the bout shows a young and determined Kelly, bearded and businesslike, both fists cocked, and wearing silk shorts over 'Long John' underpants.

Five weeks before the Foley–Hickin match Ned and the Kelly Gang had held up the bank of New South Wales across the river at Jerilderie, and got away with £2,000. Foley's ecstatic admirers took up a testimonial and presented him with half this amount when he beat Hickin. It was enough for him to build his White Horse Hotel and the Australian Academy of Boxing.

Hugh D. McIntosh went to Foley's boxing school as a young

man, and later told the London *People* magazine: 'Under his tuition such world famous boxers as Peter Jackson, Frank Slavin Jim Hall, Young Griffo, Bob Fitzsimmons, Mick Dunn, Abe Willis and Mick Dooley spread the reputation of Australia as a home of champions.

'It was Larry Foley who taught them to become stars. It was he who schooled and disciplined them into world beaters. His gymnasium was the Mecca to all aspirants to fistic honours. All the famous boxers congregated there; and at Larry's Saturday night shows, where the purses ranged from £1 to £5, you saw the sorts of fights that get spectators jumping out of their seats with excitement.'

The look that lost the race of the century

Don't tell anyone, but the first person to run under four minutes in a mile race was not Roger Bannister but John Landy. Landy would deny this. But then he would, wouldn't he?

John Landy was the second man to run a mile in under four minutes, but the first to do so in a race. Roger Bannister did not run his sub-four minute mile in a race. He was paced by runners who were on the track solely to push Bannister under the magic four-minute mark.

John Landy beat Bannister's time a few weeks later. He held his record for a goodly time, then he was beaten in 'The Mile of the Century'. Then he finished third at the 1954 Olympics.

That sums up his international career.

Yet there's a statue of him at the Melbourne Cricket Ground, one of a dozen honouring sporting heroes and heroines who had some of their finest moments at the ground. Landy's statue stands alone, apart from the rest. His is a monument to what is finest in life.

Landy was a mile runner; in his day, the best. For decades men had tried to run a mile in under four minutes. It couldn't be done. They could get close, but it was simply physically impossible. There was a school of thought that believed you could die trying. That was the theory.

But in the early 1950s three men determined to break the barrier even if it meant dying in the attempt. In the US, a brash young man, naturally gifted, Wes Santee, the son of a rancher, declared he would be the first to do it. Roger Bannister in England, a medical student, and Santee's almost exact opposite, was quietly obsessed with making history; doing it for Britain. And in Australia, John Landy, a quietly modest but intense young man, the pride of the nation, was running the fastest miles ever, week in week out.

As all three came closer and closer to the magic mark the world began to watch. Their attempts were front-page news. Which of them would go under four minutes first? Or would they all fall short, as every aspirant had? Then, one of the three did it. On 6 May 1954, Roger Bannister crossed the line in 3:59.4. He was the first man to run a mile under four minutes. But he didn't do it in a race.

Bannister ran with pacemakers – hares who set a pace that suited him, and who he followed until they dropped away, leaving him to run for the record with his famous finishing 'kick'. The other runners were there simply to make it look like a race.

Chris Chataway a world-ranked three miler and Chris Brasher, who would win a gold medal in Melbourne in the steeplechase, were Bannister's pacemakers, and the plan was devised in a London teahouse, by their coach, the Austrian Franz Stampfl.

Only weeks before, Bannister had made an attempt with pacemakers – one of them the Australian Don Macmillan – and had failed by two seconds. Around the world knowledgeable people reacted with scorn.

'Maybe I could run a four-minute mile behind one of my father's ranch horses,' said Wes Santee.

'Let's keep it kosher,' said the New York *Herald Tribune*, and the London *Daily Mail*, like much of the British press, declared the race 'not bona fide'. British athletic officials, opposed to pacemaking for the purpose of setting records, debated whether the record should be ratified.

But they all sang a different song after 5.50 p.m., on Thursday 6 May, when Bannister, Brasher and Chataway lined up at Oxford for Event Number Nine, the One Mile.

'The gun banged, and Brasher shot forward as arranged,' Neal

Bascomb wrote in *The Perfect Mile.* Norris McWhirter [the public address announcer], as arranged, read off the time every half-lap. 'He had hired an electrician to wire two speakers to the microphone, one pointing down the home straight and the other on the back straight. Bannister however, didn't hear him correctly and felt so fired with energy in that early part of the race that he thought Brasher was setting too slow a pace ...

'In the back straight Bannister yelled, "Faster, Chris! Faster!" ... As they approached the two-and-a-half lap mark, Brasher was struggling. Bannister sensed that his friend was about to stall and called for [Chris] Chataway to take over. "Chris!" Bannister yelled. Chataway was tired, but on hearing Bannister he found the strength to spring forward and Bannister passed him in the straight to win, looking like Christ crucified, in just under four minutes – 3:59.4.'

When it was over, Chris Brasher, who had a talent for getting straight to the point, told the *Daily Mail*'s Terry O'Connor what many were thinking. 'Well, we did it,' he said. 'That means Landy and Wes Santee can never break the four-minute mile first.'

All of England rejoiced. 'This magnificent man,' sang the *Daily Mail*, which only weeks before had demanded a bona fide attempt on the record. 'The Empire is saved,' one editorial, quite erroneously, shrieked, and, evidently forgetting Trafalgar, Waterloo, the Relief of Lucknow and the Battle of Britain only a dozen years before, went on to bellow: 'Roar! Roar! Roar! There's been nothing to compare with this since the destruction of the Spanish Armada.' In the previous year a British-led climbing team had conquered Everest (all right, technically it was conquered by a New Zealander – almost the same thing – and a Nepalese, necessary to have chaps like that along on a mountain like that.) And now a British runner had done the impossible. British joy was unconfined. 'Only a British man could have done it, son,' one English journalist recalled his father assuring him. It was a record, many felt, that would never be broken, unless it was by another superman. British, of course.

Forty-six days later in Finland John Landy ran a blistering 3:58 – almost two seconds faster than Bannister's time. He did it in a race. There were no pacemakers. There was no-one helping him over the line.

The Finnish promoter of the race had invited Chris Chataway to compete. Chataway accepted and told Landy he would act as pacemaker, just as he had for Bannister. Landy was underwhelmed and unconvinced. 'He came over to try to beat me – which is what he should have been trying to do.' But in any case Landy had made it clear that if he had the slightest suspicion that anyone was playing the hare, with or without his approval, he would immediately step off the track.

In Australia, by necessity, Landy had always run out in front and he had told friends that he needed someone on his elbow to break the mile barrier. He had finally found that someone. 'Chataway clung very close to me and, particularly when we began the last lap I was aware he was there and all I was trying to do was beat him,' Landy said later. Chataway pulled up second, knowing that he had played a crucial role in breaking Bannister and Britain's still warm mile record. Damn!

Immediately the focus shifted to the coming Empire Games. Newspapers internationally recognised that the world was about to see a race without precedent. Two men, the only two, ever to do the 'impossible,' racing against each other in what was quickly, and for once quite correctly, dubbed, 'The Mile of the Century'.

The media went into a feeding frenzy. This was a sports story the like of which athletics had never known. 'It was like a world title fight,' Landy recalled. 'It went on for weeks.' The Mile of the Century was also a milestone in sporting and television history: the first time any sporting event had been televised in the US from coast to coast. A hundred million watched it in North America, a huge audience 50 years ago when only a minority of people had a television set, and millions more heard it over 560 radio stations. *Time Life* held its first issue of *Sports Illustrated* until a plane on standby rushed the photograph of the finish to the printers. In England and Australia 50 million sent up prayers.

Both men stepped up to the starting line with strategies based on their knowledge of each other. Landy's was simple. He was going to try to run Bannister off his feet. 'Essentially he [Bannister] ran a waiting race and usually made a long sprint with about 300 metres to go. I, on the other hand, had won my races by running fairly evenly, but nearly always taking the lead,' Landy said.

Bannister, too, was going to run his usual race. He'd let Landy make the running. Don Macmillan, who had raced against Bannister many times, had begged Landy, his roommate at the Games, not to run from the front. 'Roger's going to sit you ... and then jump you,' he'd said. 'That's all he'll do. He'll sit, sit, sit. John, you'll be a sitting duck!' Landy thanked him and stuck to his strategy.

Landy's plan worked better than he had anticipated up until the halfway mark. He had opened a huge gap, around 15 yards. But then Bannister began to reel him in.

'When they rang the bell for the last lap I could see him on my shoulder,' Landy said. 'I knew the worst had happened and that I then had to apply another tactic. I thought he would go at 300 so even though I was running out of strength I made an effort at 300 and began to move away.

'Coming down the back straight I was aware where Bannister was because the sun was in the right position to show our two shadows, and I could see myself moving away from him a little. I guess I wasn't thinking clearly at that stage about the position of the sun and the fact that you wouldn't always see the shadows.

'When I came round the corner at the 1500 metre point, say with 120 yards to go, I was aware that Bannister's shadow had disappeared. My first reaction was one of hope that I had got away from him – and that's when I couldn't resist looking back.'

Landy looked the 'wrong' way – over his left shoulder. Bannister at that moment was about to come in line with his right shoulder. Why didn't he look right?

'I looked to the left because that was the position I would be able to see where he was (as I thought he might have been) about 15 yards behind me. I looked, and he wasn't there. I looked a bit further – all in a split second of course. When I looked up the other way he was going past my right-hand side and of course the race was all over.'

Both men had run sub-four-minute miles, but Bannister had won the Mile of the Century.

In Australia the public – every bit as parochial as the British – felt let down. Landy was faster than Bannister over a mile. Why hadn't he run a better tactical race? Why did he look over the 'wrong' shoulder?

Could he have won if he'd looked right, first? 'That's nonsense,' Landy said. 'It was a matter of who slowed down first – and it was me rather than Bannister who did that ... The truth of the matter is if you're not good enough you don't win, and that's precisely what happened.'

Well, he would say that, wouldn't he?

What he didn't say was that he had cut the side of the instep of his right foot two days before the race. Jogging barefoot, he had stepped on a photographer's flashbulb and opened a five centimetre long gash. It needed four stitches, a doctor told Landy. He could forget about running the next day. Landy told him to tape the gash and tell no-one.

A Canadian sportswriter, Andy O'Brien, had discovered Landy's secret when he burst in on him in his room and saw the floor smeared with blood. In return for an interview he, too, had agreed to keep the story a secret. Now that the race was over he told the world, via CBS, what had happened. John Fitzgerald of the Melbourne *Herald* dashed to find Landy. 'Did you step on a flashbulb?' Landy replied, 'How do I know if I stepped on a flashbulb? All I'm saying is I went into that race 100 per cent fit.' He walked away. He was favouring his right leg.

He went back to Australia. He had lost interest in running. The headmaster of his old school, Geelong Grammar, persuaded him to take up a position as a biology teacher at Timbertop, the school's secluded bush campus. There, away from the fierce focus of the press, he gradually got back his love of running.

In January 1956, he returned to Olympic Park, Melbourne and ran the second fastest mile in history, second only to his own record. A few weeks later he was set to try to smash that record in the Australian championships

There were 20,000 at Olympic Park when, in the third lap, the 19-year-old unknown Ron Clarke, caught in the hurly burly as the field bustled to go into the last 440 yards, clipped another's heels and sprawled to the ground. Landy, running behind for one of the few times in his career and trying to hurdle him, caught his spikes on Clarke's arm.

Landy stopped dead. He turned his back on the fast disappearing field, bent down to see if Clarke was injured. Clarke said he was fine, jumped to his feet and rushed past the stock-still Landy to re-join the race. Landy, sprinting hard, took after him. He had given the lead runner, Merv Lincoln, his greatest Australian rival, a lead of around seven seconds and 40 yards, but by the time they reached the turn he was just 15 yards adrift and into the back straight he was within five yards. He surged past Lincoln on the final turn and won by 12 yards. His time was 4:04.2

The race, and the moment when Landy stopped and bent over the fallen Ron Clarke, is commemorated in the statue at the Melbourne Cricket Ground.

The Melbourne *Sun News-Pictorial's* Harry Gordon wrote an open letter that said it for all Australians.

Dear John,

The fellows in the Press box don't have many heroes. Often they help to make them – but usually they know too much about them to believe in them. Up in the Press seats they don't usually clap ... Mostly they've mastered the art of observing without becoming excited. On Saturday at 4.35 p.m., though, they forgot the rules.

They had a hero – every one of them. And you were it. In the record books it will look a very ordinary run for these days. But, for my money, the fantastic gesture and the valiant recovery makes it overshadow your magnificent miles in Turku and Vancouver. It was your greatest triumph.

He had one last grasp at glory. In the 1500 metres at the 1956 Olympics in Melbourne, Landy, the world record-holder for the mile, was the home-town favourite. This time, we all just knew, he'd do it. This time he'd show them! At the bell for the last lap he was in a tightly bunched field with 10 metres separating first from last. From the bunch a long-shot 'unknown' emerged, the Irishman Rob Delaney. He had never before run a race like it and he never again would, but it was good enough to win gold. Landy came around the final bend with plenty in reserve and belatedly sprinted into third place, his anguish and exasperation undisguised.

Later, however, Landy took it with his usual frankness and dignity. He spoke in a way that sports stars today might find incomprehensible: 'I was disappointed, but there was no excuse. I trained wrongly and I didn't run a very good race. But I believe that on the day, no matter how I had run, Delaney would have won.'

Well, he would say that, wouldn't he?

6 Mad, bad and dangerous to know

The gold pirates of Port Melbourne

'Things are coming to a pretty pass indeed!' The *Argus* leader writer was working himself up to a fine state of apoplexy. 'Day by day we are wading deeper into crime, lawlessness and insecurity. The topic of today is the piratical robbery of twenty-five thousand pounds worth of gold dust: that of yesterday, a murder in Little Bourke Street; the day before, we talked of another murder at Geelong. Will tomorrow's furnish murder in Collins Street, a ransacking of the banks, or the town on fire?'

The leader writer was in grand form and with reason: things in Melbourne Town in 1852 were indeed in a pretty pass and things were about to get worse before they got better. Half the police force were trying their luck at the goldfields where in just 30 months time there would be the armed uprising at Ballarat's Eureka Stockade (and, simultaneously, the birth of Ned Kelly). Those police who remained in the service had to deal with a burgeoning criminal underworld fed by the yellow metal that was literally the talk of the town.

In the week that had the *Argus* so agitated, the big gold story, as the editorial said, was piracy: the skillfully planned and executed robbery of a ship's cargo of 8133 ounces of gold.

Worth the immense amount of £25,000, the gold was in sealed, marked boxes in the hold of the *Nelson*, a barque anchored off the lighthouse at Williamstown, and that could be seen from the roof of the *Argus*. On 2 April 1852 the *Nelson* was being readied for her voyage to London carrying the cargo that was causing a social upheaval without precedent. The discovery of gold at Ballarat eight months before had emptied the town. Rich and poor, saints and sinners, sailors and servants, clerks, public servants, merchants, farmers and farriers, they were all to be found either on their way to Ballarat, prospecting on the goldfields, or back in Melbourne Town exuberantly spending, in many cases, like the proverbial drunken sailor.

At around one a.m. on the morning of 2 April, it's fair to say, most of the sailors from the *Nelson* were busy getting drunk. Melbourne, a century and a half ago, was notorious for its dedication to excess. Scores of taverns, thousands of prostitutes, footpads in the alleys and highwaymen on the St Kilda road just a mile from the Town Hall: and with all this, very few policemen to stem the tide of sin.

On board the *Nelson* seven seamen were below in their cabins. No-one was on watch as two longboats, their oars muffled, slid silently alongside and as many as 22 men, most black-masked and armed, swarmed up the side of the barque.

Henry Draper, the first mate, was in his cabin when he was woken by Carr Dudley, the ship's second mate, with the news that pirates had taken over the ship and all the crew on her were locked up. Two masked men verified this when they burst in and put pistols at his head, one shouting, 'We've come for the damned gold, and the gold we'll have or blow your brains out!'

Henry Draper was a brave man with an inordinate sense of propriety and responsibility: he asked the pirates to allow him and Dudley to put on their trousers, and he was concerned that the pirates might do damage to his ship. 'As I was coming into the cabin I saw someone throw some muskets overboard, and seeing them prepare to enter the captain's cabin, I was fearful that they would injure the chronometer or do some other damage. I wished to remonstrate with them, and therefore asked who was their captain, when they said, "We have none, and we are all captains." At this moment one of them fired a pistol at me, and the ball inflicted a slight flesh wound in my thigh.'

This may have concentrated Draper's mind, focusing it on the priority of keeping his brains in his skull. He took the pirates to where the 23 gold boxes were stored and they lowered them, one by one, into the longboats. They might have lowered 22 but for Henry Draper's foolishness. One of the pirates cavalierly – why it's impossible to guess – offered Draper the last box of gold. And Draper, that good man, said stoutly through the pain of his wounded leg: 'I have lived honestly till now and shall take none of it.' This was all very well, and nobly said, but the owners of the gold no doubt would have urged him to reconsider the kind offer.

'Well,' said the pirate, 'if you won't have it we will.'

And they did.

The newspapers broke the sensational story the next day after a lone sailor in hiding on the *Nelson* had freed the crew and sent for the police. The *Argus* leader writer was called in, too, and settled into his task with relish. 'Without attempting to get up a "sensation", or to frighten the ladies,' he wrote with precisely that in mind, 'we may ask if it is unlikely that the next step in this progress of villainy in Melbourne will be seizure of a vessel in the bay by a band of marauders, and the establishment of a system of actual buccaneering along our coast?' From the banks being ransacked and the town on fire he was upping the ante now.

And the next day another *Argus* sensation: this time Mr Masters, a compositor in the paper's typesetting room, was ambling along the beach not far from Williamstown when he discovered boxes in the tea-trees. He 'immediately despatched some boys who were at hand to give information to the police who speedily arrived and brought the boxes to town. They are now lying in the watch-house, together with the stock of a gun which has been broken in two by the force used in breaking them open. A fancy pipe was found nearby, as well as a blue shirt which perhaps may afford some clue to the perpetrators of this daring deed.

'In the hurried division of the spoil, some of the gold had been spilt about the place, and several people were employed yesterday afternoon in carrying away the sand for the purpose of washing it. One man was seen to slip away with a nugget of considerable size, and others obtained a quantity of the [gold] dust.' Mr Masters, who probably set the type for the story, was one of them.

The clues left lying near the boxes, the fancy pipe and the blue shirt, yielded nothing. But as so often happens in 'capers' of this kind, the clue that undid the perpetrators of this daring deed was supplied by two of their own, informants, rumour, hunches and a considerable amount of bad luck. John George James was the first to be arrested. He was about to sail for Sydney when the Water Police caught him. Henry Draper identified him as the ringleader of the pirates and said James had pricked him with a sword. In his possession they found 20 gold sovereigns and, in his carpet bag, 'every description of dress fitting for one who wished frequently to change his outward appearance'.

Within the week a man having an ale in the Union Inn at Geelong was approached by three strangers who came in wanting to sell gold. They emptied a pouch of nuggets onto the bar and the merchant immediately recognised them as among those he had packed for shipment not long before. Someone slipped out the back door and shortly after, the police arrived. The men were armed, they violently resisted arrest and each had a draft on the Union Bank for £500.

The gold trail led soon after to another watering hole, the Ocean Child Inn at Cowie Creek, where four men were taken after a fight, and later that day, a fifth. The evidence against all the men was largely circumstantial but they came up against the inflexible and ruthless Justice Redmond Barry, a man in whom the quality of mercy was strained. All were sentenced to 15 years hard labour.

Barry's sardonic attitude to the strong possibility that the men were innocent – he was always inclined to believe the worst – emerges in his advice to the accused that 'if however, any of you can show the Executive that you are innocent of the crime impugned to you, you are at perfect liberty to do so, and then, and not until then, may you hope for a remission of sentence'.

This consolation aside, Redmond Barry gave the pirates a backhanded compliment – and the *Argus* editorial writer a few pointers on how to keep outrage on the boil. 'The idea of capturing a merchant vessel quietly reposing within our harbour within almost a gunshot of the shore, and abstracting from its stronghold the whole of the golden treasure with which it was freighted, was, in itself, sufficiently atrocious,' he said, 'but when we consider the manner of its execution, the number of the marauders engaged in it and the determination with which it was carried into effect, the character of the outrage assumes a complexion altogether new to me in the annals of modern crime.

'It is clear that an organisation of brigands is being carried on in such a manner, and on such a scale, as to deceive even the vigilant eyes of the police, or a greater number of perpetrators of the offence of which you have been found guilty would, by this time, have been discovered.'

The vigilant eyes of the police were not deceived, however, and a greater number of perpetrators were soon discovered. Three months later three more men were arrested and tried for piracy. One was given 15 years on the roads, the other, an escaped convict, was found not guilty but returned to prison and the third was found not guilty and released.

Every one of the men had a considerable bank draft: all up police recovered more than £10,000. The remaining £15,000 was never recovered. And the remaining dozen or so pirates were never caught.

The Monty Python *murder*

> OPEN: on a dental surgery in 1865, sun streaming in through the upstairs windows of a large terrace house. A small man in his mid-twenties, a mass of dark curly hair, moustache and nervous energy, and dressed in his wife's clothes, has a brace of pistols before him beside the surgical instruments on a small table.
>
> He picks one up, aims, and fires.
>
> CUT TO: a sheep's head mounted across the room. Bones shatter and fly as the bullet crashes home.
>
> SFX: Pistol crack, bones exploding. Then another pistol crack.
>
> CUT TO: our hero, now lowering the second pistol, blowing the smoke from its barrel, as he does so.
>
> HERO: 'And now my dear Kinder, I think it's time to call on you and your very naughty, utterly adorable wife.'

Murder can be comical. In the hands of the cinema's master of the macabre, Alfred Hitchcock, we can laugh at what would be terrifying in real life. But the circumstances of the real life murder of Henry Kinder, you suspect, would be beyond the powers of even the Master. A movie on the killing of Kinder could be directed, and performed, only by the team from *Monty Python*.

Louis Bertrand, 25 years old, was an extrovert who liked to roar like a lion as he walked the streets of Sydney. When he wasn't roaring or being overly charming, he was morose. (Today we'd know he suffered from bipolar disorder.)

Jane Bertrand, his wife, a shy, timid young woman four years younger than Louis, seemed, acquaintances gossiped, to be mesmerised by her extraordinary husband. She was asleep much of the time. (Today we'd know she suffered from narcolepsy.)

Louis Bertrand was passionately in love with the wife of his friend, Henry Kinder, an amiable New Zealander who drank too much and consequently seemed unaware that his sultry wife, Ellen, was having affairs with his friends, Louis Bertrand and an old flame of Ellen's, Frank Jackson, and, probably, others.

Finally, there was Louis Bertrand's dental assistant, Alfred Burne, 20, an uncomplicated young man of not much intelligence. Between these five characters – and they could be played by any number of permutations from the cast of *Monty Python* – you have a peerless murder farce.

Louis Bertrand's dental practice in fashionable Wynyard Square, Sydney, was prospering when, in January 1865, he met Ellen Kinder. They fell in love almost at once. Her husband Henry, recently arrived in Sydney, was a teller with the City Bank on the corner of King and George Streets. The Bertrands and the Kinders each had two young children and the families soon became close friends – Louis and Ellen as close as it's possible to be.

Six months later an old flame of Ellen's, Frank Jackson, arrived from Auckland and for a time there was tension until Ellen, with both men waiting on her word, opted for Louis, and Frank, who was not in love with her, accepted her decision. Bertrand thought to soften the blow by offering Frank lodging at his Wynyard Square house with the added inducement of having an affair with his downtrodden wife, Jane. Jackson declined.

'It's a pity,' Bertrand said, 'that my wife is so virtuous. It makes it so hard to get rid of her.'

Bertrand wanted to divorce or kill Jane so that he could marry Ellen. And, of course, he told Jackson, he'd also have to kill Kinder. He'd already tried a couple of times. With young Alf Burne he'd rowed across the Sydney Harbour at night to the Mosman home of the Kinders. On the way over, a tomahawk under his coat, he'd told Burne that it was likely that Kinder would be discovered dead the next morning, and that the coroner would find he had killed himself.

Bertrand took his boots off and climbed through the window of the Kinders' house, Burbank Cottage. He was gone for some time and Burne was asleep when he reappeared. He was in a state of irritation, as he often was. Kinder had refused to drink a drugged bottle of beer he'd bought him. They'd have to try again another night.

A week later Bertrand blacked his face, put on a red shirt and a slouch hat and a mask over his eyes and, looking like Al Jolson, Superhero, had Burne row him once again to the Kinders'. This time he told Burne he would require his assistance. Alf Burne was not very bright but he drew the line at this and Bertrand, foiled again, took a long draught of whisky and told Burne to turn the boat around; they were going home.

Louis Bertrand now decided to do the job in daylight and without assistance. Over the next weeks the dimwitted Alf Burne watched bemused as the dentist shaved his beard, dressed in women's clothing and went shopping at a gunsmith's. Under his master's – or mistresses's – guidance Alf bought a brace of second-hand pistols and handed them to Bertrand, who tucked them under his dress and bade the gunsmith g'day. With them and a sheep's head for a target, he practised his marksmanship in his surgery. When his visiting mother-in-law heard shots in the surgery and rushed in Louis blithely told her he was conducting an anatomical experiment; he wanted to discover the thinnest part of a sheep's skull.

On 2 October, with Jane, Louis went visiting Burbank Cottage. While Jane and Ellen chatted, Louis and Henry strolled to the pub at Milson's Point for a refreshing ale.

Henry was still wearing a hangover from the previous night. Louis was wearing a top hat, and gloves that he did not take off for the remainder of the night. When they returned the men sat down to a game of cards over a glass of sherry. Their wives, with their backs to the card table, were on a window seat looking out over the harbour when there was a sudden loud retort.

Jane and Ellen spun around. Henry Kinder had fallen back in his chair unconscious, his ear partly blown away and his jaw shattered. Jane saw a smoking pistol at Louis's feet as he coolly picked up Kinder's pipe and jammed it back in his broken jaw. Ellen shrieked and ran from the room. Louis went after her, dragged her back and pointing at her bloodied husband rasped melodramatically and enigmatically, 'Look at him well. I wish you to see him always before you!'

Then, while Jane tried to staunch the blood, Bertrand and Mrs Kinder went outside to the darkness of the verandah where they kissed passionately. When they returned and began pacing restlessly up and down, Jane handed her husband the bullet that had wounded Kinder. The three manhandled Kinder into bed and some hours later called a doctor.

At 11 p.m., when Doctor Eichler arrived Henry Kinder was semi-conscious but able to talk. Bertrand told the doctor that Kinder had shot himself, and Kinder told the doctor his wife had shot him from behind and then ran from the room. Doctor Eichler ignored this. Had the doctor the benefit of seeing endless episodes of *CSI* he would have noticed that the wound behind Kinder's ear indicated the bullet was travelling upwards, meaning that unless Kinder was an India rubber man he could not have shot himself. But television was yet to be invented and the doctor was not observant and not inclined to believe Ellen Kinder would shoot her husband. He recommended to Kinder that he prepare to meet his maker.

Two days passed before the shooting was reported to the police. Senior Constable Emmerton of the North Shore police arrived at Burbank Cottage to find Henry Kinder in bed, his head heavily bandaged, and enjoying a pipe.

'What lies are these people saying about my shooting myself?' he asked Emmerton, while Bertrand, who was present, rolled his eyes heavenward. Senior Constable Emmerton ignored this. Outside Bertrand explained that Kinder had tried to kill himself after he and his wife had argued over another man. The policeman went away satisfied.

Two days later, however, Kinder was still alive, and even recovering. This was unconscionable! Bertrand was outraged. 'He must not live! Bring the milk and mix the poison!' he screamed at his wife and fell flat on his face in a fit. When he recovered he mixed either aconite or belladonna in a glass of milk and ordered Jane to give it to Kinder. Kinder died the next morning. The coroner found he had killed himself while emotionally insane.

Three months later Louis Bertrand was charged with murder. That it had taken so long was astonishing. Bertrand, of course, could not keep quiet about his cleverness. He told his sister for instance, 'I had to kill him, I had no use for him,' and increasingly he complained Kinder was haunting him. Detective Elliot of the new investigation branch of the NSW police force began talking to people like Alf Burne, Bertrand's dental assistant, and Frank Jackson, who Bertrand had caused to be jailed for 12 months for trying to blackmail him.

Bertrand alone was charged with Kinder's murder. Jane Bertrand, his frightened, wretched wife, it emerged, was often beaten by him and feared for her life, and was allowed to go free. And there was no evidence that Ellen Kinder had conspired to have her husband killed.

The jury could not reach a verdict on the first trial. Bertrand told them that the shooting of Kinder was a practical joke that had ... misfired. He and Kinder had got drunk and Kinder had agreed to pretend to shoot himself 'to amuse the ladies'. This was why no bullet was found, and

Bertrand explained that the gun had been loaded only with powder and wad, and some doctors testified that a wad could have been the cause of Kinder's wounds.

Bertrand at Darlinghurst Court in February 1865.

Bertrand's behaviour in court was bizarre. He paced to and fro in the dock, roared with laughter at times and had to be reminded by the judge, 'You ought to realise you are being tried for a most serious crime.'

The case went before a jury again. This time Bertrand admitted telling his sister he had to kill Kinder but, he explained, once again it was only in jest. If he had really killed Kinder he would hardly tell a woman. 'A certain amount of intelligence and ability is imputed to me and yet it is assumed I would entrust such a terrible secret to women, who are not known to be in the habit of keeping secrets.'

He was found guilty notwithstanding this well-known fact, and in passing the death sentence on him the judge, Sir Alfred Stephens, said,

'You cannot but be regarded as a fiend ... It is distressing and sad that a father of any family should die on the scaffold for a crime that makes human nature shudder.'

Louis Bertrand did not die on the scaffold. His sentence was commuted to life imprisonment, whereupon he immediately confessed his guilt and happily told the whole story. He served 28 years in jail before being released and immediately sailing to obscurity in England – the future home of *Monty Python*.

The husband who murdered her wife

*I*t's a beloved cliché of the horror movie genre. The rain coming down, a thunderous black night lit by lightning flashes revealing a maniac muttering gibberish as he digs a grave.

In the cinema, with our popcorn in one hand and our partner on the other, and though we have seen this kind of thing many times, we still feel a frisson of unease.

But when it's happening in real life and you're looking on at arm's length, drenched to the skin, shivering with fright and the cold as the thunder rumbles on and the lightning flashes across the Sydney sky, and the grave the madman is digging is just big enough for you – a 14 year-old boy – well you'd think it was strange, to say the least.

But the whole story of Eugenia Falleni, the man–woman, is strange, not least the fact that she was married for three years to Anne Burkett, an attractive young woman, before the bride noticed that there was something very basic missing in their marriage. When she did correct this oversight, when she discovered one shocking day in September 1917 that the man she had wed was not a man, she lived to regret it. But not for very long. Stranger still, after murdering Annie Birkett, Eugenia Falleni married again, and again her bride had no doubts that her husband was not, as they said in those days, 'the full two bob'. What on earth was happening in marital beds in 1917?

Eugenia Falleni was born in Florence, Tuscany, in 1876 and went to New Zealand with her parents at an early age. At 16 she ran away to sea, told people her name was Eugene and, dressed as a man, worked as a cabin boy on a Norwegian barque. Why did she do it? Generally it's believed she dressed as a man simply so that she could go to sea, and for the next half dozen years she carried off this deception on a variety of ships plying the South Pacific.

One man knew her secret. Martello, a fellow Italian sailor, got Eugenia pregnant in 1899 and disappeared from her life, dropping her off in Newcastle. There she gave birth to a daughter, Josephine, and resumed her life as a man. By now she was accustomed to passing herself off as a man, and as a man she was able to get work that paid considerably more than she would get as a woman. Of course Eugenia may have been a lesbian, but there is no indication of this in what we know of her private life, and the fact that her first wife, Annie Birkett, was shocked to discover her deception suggests otherwise.

Calling herself Harry Crawford, she told a childless couple called de Anglis that the infant's mother had died and asked them to raise the girl as their grand-daughter. Sporadically, and usually drunk, 'Harry' visited Josephine in the de Anglis home in Double Bay, Sydney. Sometimes 'he' left money for her keep.

Harry Crawford was unstable and quarrelsome and drinking exacerbated his dark nature. He was in and out of menial jobs until in 1912, a Dr Clarke of Wahroonga, employed him as a general hand and coachman. Dr Clarke's housekeeper was a pretty widow, Annie Birkett, 30, who had a young son, also called Harry. For two years Crawford courted Annie Birkett, until, in 1914, she left Dr Clarke's, opened a corner store in Darling Street, Balmain and married him.

Soon after, Josephine moved into the Balmain home. Her guardians had fallen out over her: she was a difficult, moody girl and they couldn't handle her. Mr de Anglis gave up, left his wife and went back to Italy and when Mrs de Anglis died Josephine moved in with her 'father'. By this time Josephine knew Harry's real identity but told no-one. How did it affect her? We will never know. The trauma of discovering that your father is your mother is one that few have experienced.

Inevitably Annie Birkett and Josephine fell out – not surprisingly Josephine was an unhappy, wilful teenager who defied her stepmother and her 'father', stayed out late at night and caused much anguish. In addition, Annie and Harry fought constantly. Annie gave up on the marriage, left home with her son and moved in with her sister in Kogarah. When Josephine found a job and lodgings, however, Harry persuaded his wife to come back and they took a house in Drummoyne.

In September, 1917, Annie breathlessly told a relative, 'I've found out something amazing about him [Harry].' What that was she didn't say, but held the discovery secret until 28 September when she and Harry went for a picnic in Lane Cove, off Mowbray Road.

There, in a secluded spot, she was battered to death and her body thrown on to a bonfire where, three days later, a boy stumbled onto her charred remains.

The discovery of an unknown body at Lane Cove was reported and quickly forgotten. In France that week the Australians were stranded waist-deep in mud in Flanders, coming under heavy poison gas bombardment and losing 5000 in the advance on Passchendaele. In five months between Messines and the taking of Passchendaele, on 6 November, 38,000 Australians were killed or wounded in France, so one unidentified body in Lane Cove had little impact.

Harry Crawford went home and told his stepson that Annie was visiting friends and took him to Watson's Bay. The two climbed up to The Gap and Harry, slipping though the safety fence, went to the edge of the cliff and invited the boy to join him. Young Harry declined. For some reason he felt nervous.

Now Harry Crawford was telling the neighbours his wife had run off with a plumber. He sold their furniture and moved out with young Harry to a boarding house in Cathedral Street, Woolloomooloo, where one night in the same month, October, he told young Harry they were going out.

The two walked out of the boarding house into a thunderstorm and trudged uphill through the rain. The man carrying a spade and, in his pocket, a bottle of brandy, the boy, drenched, lagging behind. Young Harry was nervous at first, when they got on a tram at Kings Cross. His stepfather sat silent, brooding, clutching the brand new spade. When they got off at Double Bay and walked into the scrub the boy was frightened. And when they came to a secluded clearing and the man started to dig he was terrified.

Despair and pain are etched in the countenance of Eugenia Falleni, also known as Harry Crawford. She duped three wives, and began to go insane when she murdered the second.

By now Harry Crawford too, was near hysterical. Taking deep swigs from the brandy bottle he handed young Harry the spade and told him to keep digging. The two kept at it, taking it in turns, while the thunder rolled and lightning lit up the lonely grave until the grave – it had to be a grave, the boy realised – got big enough for ... him. Shivering, wet to the skin, he waited and Harry Crawford suddenly threw the spade into the trees and told the boy they were going home.

By now Harry Crawford was going insane, drinking heavily and having hysterics, telling his landlady, Mrs Schieblich, 'Madam! Madam! I am haunted. I think the room is haunted!'

Shrewd Mrs Scheiblich replied, 'I think it is your wife haunting you. I think you killed her.' Harry slumped to the kitchen table and began sobbing. He virtually admitted killing Annie, telling his landlady he had argued with his wife and given her 'a crack over the head'.

Mrs Schieblich was no fool. She did not go to the police. She was German and it was wise for Germans to keep a low profile at a time when her countrymen were killing Australians by the thousands. But she wanted Harry out of her house. His stepson, by now, was living safely with Annie Birkett's sister, and Mrs Schieblich sent Harry packing when she told him detectives had called looking for him. He left the house at once.

Amazingly, in 1919, he married again, and again duped his wife who praised her 'dear loving husband'. But Harry Birkett, now 16, and his aunt, never having heard from Annie or the plumber she was said to have eloped with, finally decided to go to the police. Dates were checked, dental remains were shown to Annie's dentist and on 5 October 1920, three years after the fatal picnic, Harry Crawford was charged with the murder of his wife and taken to Long Bay Goal. There he was told to strip, have a bath and put on prison clothes. Harry agreed, but said he would have to do it in the women's section.

At first the prison authorities refused to believe her. A doctor was called. 'I knew within a matter of seconds that she was a woman,' he announced. 'There was not the shadow of a doubt of it.'

The trial of the 'man–woman,' Eugenia Falleni was a sensation. She appeared in court in women's clothing, the first time in 30 years she had worn them. Found guilty of murder and sentenced to death, the sentence later commuted to life imprisonment, she was released in 1931 and lived the remainder of her life, in women's clothing, as Mrs Jean Ford.

Mrs Ford bought a house in Glenmore Road, Paddington, where she lived quietly, always maintaining her innocence to those few who knew her real identity. On 9 June 1938, she stepped off the kerb in Oxford Street and was hit by a car.

No-one could trace Mrs Jean Ford's relatives, or discover her background. They took fingerprints. The dead woman had been Eugenia Falleni.

The Desperate Housewife of Frogs Hollow

She was known, in her day, as the Borgia of Botany Bay, but this does a disservice to the Borgias – Lucretia, her brother Cesare Borgia and her father Pope Alexander VI – Rome and the Renaissance's leading family of poisoners. Louisa Collins was from Frogs Hollow, Botany, Sydney, and she was an independent operator. Less a Borgia, more a very downmarket Desperate Housewife, she was the last woman hanged in New South Wales.

Louisa was born in 1849 to a couple employed at Belltrees, an imposing country property in the Upper Hunter Valley near Scone, where she grew up an eye-catching teenager. Twenty years on, in the dock and charged with murder, she was described as 'pleasantly plump, with bold good looks and a flighty disposition'.

In Scone, she must have been a cracker. Charlie Andrews, the local butcher, thought so, and although Charlie was exceedingly dull and 20 years older, Louisa followed her mother's urgings and married him at Merriwa Church of England in 1865. Charlie did his best – they had seven children – but the problem was that Charlie was a plodder and Frogs Hollow, an isolated patch surrounded by swamp and reached only by a small bridge, its population mostly wool washers, was not the place to be married to a plodder. And the problem was exacerbated by the fact that Charlie was not the only one who thought Louisa was a cracker. Those admirers tended to be located at the bar at Amos's Pier Hotel overlooking Botany Bay, where in time Louisa became celebrated for her kindness to strangers. Soon she was installing them at the boarding house she ran while Charlie worked at the butcher shop. Frogs Hollow society was scandalised. But when Louisa took in a new boarder, Michael Collins, a 22-year-old very casual labourer from Victoria, tongues wagged so vigorously that even Charlie Andrews noticed. Louisa and Michael openly conducted their affair, canoodling on the tram and cuddling in the bushes, and just before Christmas Charlie finally seemed to notice what was going on. He wanted Collins out, and when Louisa tried to debate the matter he took Collins by the scruff of the neck and threw him out of the house. Beside herself with rage and grief at her loss, Louisa rushed off to the police station where she was told to go home and have a nice lie down.

If only she had.

Not long after Charlie found his food was disagreeing with him. He couldn't keep anything down. The truth, of course, was that his wife was disagreeing with him. Michael Collins was calling at the Andrews home while Charlie was at work. On Monday 29 January, however, Michael Collins didn't come around: Charlie was home, ill in bed. He couldn't go to work and the next day Louise went to see the man from the insurance. She wanted to know, in the event of the untimely demise of Charlie, how soon she could collect the money. 'Poor Charlie is very close to death,' she said.

Charlie died four days later. Doctor Marshall identified the cause of death as acute gastritis and within the hour Louise was on the tram on her way to town to claim the £200 insurance money from the Australian Widows Fund. 'I didn't want to dwell on things over the weekend,' she later explained in court. Somehow she found the strength to come back to the house and cook for the family and boarders and later that night called a neighbour and asked her to help her lay out the body. 'I want you to help me with my husband,' she began, and the neighbour interrupted, 'How is he?' 'Oh he died this morning, I want you to get him ready for the funeral,' said Louise.

Three days later Louisa held a rowdy wake at the home and when the last guest had finally left Michael Collins remained. They married almost immediately, on 9 April, and had a son seven months later, but they didn't live happily ever after. Michael was lazy and shiftless and he was a gambler. Within 12 months he had spent all her money. She had given him her last £20 and he had gone into the city to gamble. When he came home, she said, 'He struck a match and lit a candle and said: "Louisa, I have lost all the money." He began to cry and I cried too.'

Their baby died suddenly, and Louisa began drinking again, telling patrons at the pub that Mick was a useless layabout. Then Mick passed away. He had complained about Louise's drinking and she went out shopping for rat poison. In June 1888 he was in bed in agony when Dr Marshall visited. He saw Louise tenderly holding Mick's head in bed and trickling milk down his throat. For some inexplicable reason Michael Collins was wearing his best trousers under the sheets. He refused to take them off – if he'd done so right from the beginning he and Charlie Andrews might have enjoyed life for a considerably longer period.

Dr Marshall could find nothing specifically wrong with Collins and fell back on his gastritis diagnosis, but an hour after he left Collins was dead and even Dr Marshall thought he should reconsider things. He went to the police.

Two days later, while Louise was on a drinking binge they looked around the house and found the unwashed glass Dr Marshall had seen Louise use to give Mick his milk. It was found to contain traces of arsenic, and when the bodies of Charles Andrews and the Collins' baby were exhumed they too were found to contain traces of the poison.

Louise Collins stood trial four times for one or other of the murders with which she was charged. She claimed that Collins had killed himself – a slow suicide by poison. Such a suicide would have been a world first. But though her claim was ludicrous Louise swayed juries with her looks. 'She is tastefully attired, cool and collected, and intelligently alert, while modest in demeanour. She can best be described as a fine looking woman,' one reporter wrote.

Finally, on 8 December 1888, she was found guilty and sentenced to death. She went to the gallows calmly and with great courage. Her hanging was more ghastly than usual. Gruesomely bungled, it led to the New South Wales decision to never again hang a woman.

The witch who danced with the devil

Rosaleen Norton, the Witch of Kings Cross, did her damnedest to be the Wicked Witch of Oz.

She was frequently photographed with her 'Familiar' cat pressed to her angular face, or kneeling half-naked before an altar to Pan, the pagan god with the horns, hindquarters and sex drive of a goat. Her paintings won her singular notoriety: she is the only Australian painter ever to have her work burned by order of the censor. She conducted 'sex magic' covens and ruined the lives of at least two sensitive and highly creative men who were undeniably under her spell, and she is unquestionably the most famous witch Australia has known.

But Rosaleen Norton was a woman known to her friends as Roie, and you can't be a witch called Roie. Contracting names to give them an 'ie' ending was the vogue when Rosaleen was one of the 'characters' of Kings Cross and were she living in Sydney today her friends at the Cross would undoubtedly call her Norto. Roie or Norto – either way it just isn't a proper name for a witch.

The former *Daily Mirror* crime reporter, 'Bondi' Bill Jenkings may disagree. 'I'd encountered her on many occasions and I reckon she was on the lowest rung of humanity,' he said. 'She was the epitome of depravity, but she must have had some sort of diabolical charm, because she had a circle of devoted worshippers around her ...

'She exuded evil – I used to feel like sprinkling myself with Holy Water whenever I was in her presence.'

Rosaleen was lax about personal hygiene, too, and 'Bondi' might have been better advised to carry a can of disinfectant. A more charitable view, from this distance, might be that Rosaleen was born before her time: she experimented with drugs, she had strong feminist inclinations and she was sexually voracious and uninhibited.

But her real appetite was for notoriety. Her gift was a very modern understanding of the cravings of the media and the sexual bent of a certain type of man and woman. She'd be a third-rate ad agency's art director today, spicing up the shoe campaign. Or perhaps a much photographed dominatrix, seen stalking the Birdcage at the Melbourne Cup and looking sultry for the cameras at *Star Wars* premieres. She'd make a wonderful surprise guest on *Big Brother*.

Rosaleen claimed to have been born during a violent thunderstorm on 2 October 1917 with two blue spots on her left knee – the indelible mark of a witch – and a sinewy, sinister, strip of flesh running from her armpit to her waist. As an adult Roie certainly looked the part. Long jet-black hair framed plucked, arched eyebrows, high cheekbones, and a mocking, faintly malicious smirk. Her ears were pointed and her eyes were cold and dark. But she had a perfectly normal childhood with perfectly normal Protestant parents in that least satanic of towns: Dunedin, New Zealand.

That may have been Rosaleen's problem.

The Nortons came to Sydney when Roie was seven and although she liked to say she was expelled from school for her disturbing drawings, the few known drawings of her childhood show she was a girl who liked drawing fluffy bunny rabbits in a style firmly fixed in the School of Beatrix Potter.

She was a bright student with an aptitude for drawing and won a place at the art school of East Sydney Technical College where she developed a fascination for the macabre, fed by her readings of pulp fiction such as the American paperbacks, *Amazing Stories* and *Weird Tales*, and the classics by Edgar Allan Poe, Mary Shelley and R.L. Stevenson.

At 15 she wrote three short stories good enough to be published in *Smith's Weekly*, then famous for publishing many of Australia's best writers and artists. The editor, impressed, offered her a job as a writer. Roie accepted, but then insisted that her illustrations be published rather than her stories. She lasted eight months, was fired, and when her mother died she left home. In 1935 she met 17-year-old Beresford Conroy and hitchhiked with him around Australia, supporting herself waitressing and as a pavement artist.

When the teenagers returned to Sydney they married and lived in a bohemian corner of the Rocks called, perhaps ambiguously, Buggery Barn. Kings Cross, inevitably was the next stop. She eventually made her home in a tiny, dark, basement bed-sit in Brougham Street, where she was to live for the rest of her life.

By now her conventional teenage interest in the macabre – Dracula and Frankenstein horror films were top of her pops – had led Roie to immerse herself in the study of the occult and ritual magic, the Kabbalah, pre-Christian and primitive beliefs, Satanism and Jungian psychology and such texts as Fraser's *The Golden Bough*, and the perverted philosophy of Aleister Crowley (called with good reason The Beast).

She became a proponent and practitioner of 'sex magic' and her art increasingly mirrored her interests: a meticulous, competently drawn and painted phantasmagoria of leering satanic beings and menacing creatures, witches, and covens, naked hermaphrodites, phallic snakes and proud-breasted naked nuns who appeared to be in the wrong business. (The artist whose work in part inspired her, Norman Lindsay, is said to have called Rosaleen 'a grubby little girl with great skill who will not discipline herself'.)

At the same time as she was beginning to explore this nether world on paper and canvas, Roie found work as an artists' model, posing nude to cover the rent and starring at artists' balls and parties where she rapidly became one of the 'characters' of the Cross – a woman whispered to be promiscuous, to take drugs and worship the devil.

Norton divorced Beresford – he'd gone to the War – in 1945 and took up with a young poet, Gavin Greenlees. Greenlees came from one of the best-known families in Australian journalism and was considered to be a pleasant fellow with promise. She had the first showing of her art in 1943, but it wasn't until 1949 that she made an impact. At Melbourne University's staid Rowden-White Library she showed the finest 47 pastels and sketches of her last decade. The exhibition had considerable press attention before its opening: the subject matter was a long way removed from the landscapes of Hans Heysen and Albert Namatjira then in vogue. Hardly had it opened than the Vice Squad visited and carried away four of Norton's works: *Witches' Sabbat, Lucifer, Triumph* and *Individuation*, and charged her with having exhibited obscene articles.

Norton won the case and got wide publicity but the show was a failure. The university restricted public access to her show and she failed to sell almost all her work. She was exasperated by press stories that she was some kind of witch and that the four paintings that had been seized had been done while she was in some kind of trance.

'Trance nothing!' she said, irritated. 'Certainly I told a few arty busybodies that, because they wanted to know oh-so-much. I said I did those works after coming out of trances. Most of my stuff is drawn around witches, I've read a lot about witches and old folklore. But the witch stuff is tied up with those trances. It suited me and my work, and even now there are people in Melbourne and Sydney who reckon I'm a witch who can go into a trance when I feel like it.' (Later, Roie was to recant: recycling her story of paintings-in-a-self-induced-trance to the mutual gratification of the Sydney press and herself.)

In 1951 she and Gavin settled into the tiny Brougham Street flat and the following year they jointly produced a book, *The Art of Rosaleen Norton*, with poems by Greenlees and illustrations by Norton.

It proved catastrophic for all concerned. The publisher, Walter Glover, had printed 500 leatherbound copies of the work but almost as soon as it was released it was declared obscene and was banned. Glover went bankrupt. Greenlees had a breakdown – he attacked Norton with a knife – and Norton, who was perpetually penniless, made nothing from the venture but priceless publicity.

The Witch of Kings Cross, as she was now dubbed, was at the height, of her Sydney celebrity status when she got a phone call from the most eminent cultural figure in Australia, Sir Eugene Goossens (see *The obscene end of Eugene Goossens*, page 246). His interest in her had been sparked by the furore over the banned book and artworks and his subsequent association with her – Goossens took part in her sex magic ceremonies – led to him being found guilty of importing pornography and forced to slip out of the country under a pseudonym, his dazzling career spectacularly shattered and his personal life an empty husk.

In August 1955 she exhibited at the Kashmir Cafe and the Vice Squad once again removed some paintings. Norton was again charged with breaching the *Obscene and Indecent Publications Act*.

A long drawn-out series of court cases followed until Norton was eventually found guilty of executing three paintings deemed to be obscene and they were ordered to be destroyed. At the same time she and Greenlees were fined £25 for assisting an unknown photographer in the making of obscene photographs, but they escaped a conviction for committing an 'unnatural offence' – sodomy. It was this charge, and Sir Eugene Goossens' failure to use his influence on her behalf, that some say prompted Norton to contrive Goossens' destruction.

As the court case against her began, a New Zealand teenager, Anna Hoffman, picked up by police in the Cross and charged with vagrancy, told them that Rosaleen had inducted her into a coven and that she had participated in a black mass. Hoffman later said she had invented the story but Norton's reputation as the Witch of Kings Cross was now irrevocably established.

'I yearned to be a witch and made an absolute neophyte of myself hanging around her basement flat in Brougham Street,' Hoffman wrote years later.

'I was hoping she would divulge to me her occult secrets. She was very generous and lent me books from her vast collection ... Other times she acted mysteriously and wouldn't even let me in the door when I called. I once smelt a secret perfume wafting from the smoke-filled room behind her. I knew she smoked hashish to open doors to her subconscious for painting, and to prepare for magical rites while in a self-induced hypnotic trance.' (The unkind might say that Roie was in a self-induced stoned state.)

A few weeks after the Hoffman scandal *Australasian Post*, a national weekly devoted to pinups of girls in the newly invented Bikini swimsuits, landscape photographs of the Outback and politically incorrect cartoons much loved by men, ran a feature grimly headed: 'Warning to Australia. Devil worship here!' Accompanying the story was a photograph of Norton in her flat, kneeling in adoration before a larger than afterlife painting of Pan. In a lengthy interview the man from *Post* probed: 'Have you ever seen the devil?'

Norton replied haughtily, 'If you mean the being whom I know as the god Pan, I frequently have that privilege.'

Asked if she yearned for a more normal, ordinary, life she was, for once, shocked: 'Oh, God, no! I couldn't stand it! I'd go mad or sane, I don't know which!'

Throughout the sixties – now without Greenlees who, in 1957, had been committed by the bluntly named Lunacy Court to a hospital for the mentally ill – Norton managed to maintain her position in Kings Cross society by dint of reports such as that in *Post* and this, from a 1965 paperback, *Kings Cross Black Magic*, purporting to describe a night at Rosaleen Norton's coven:

'There were about eight or nine cult members present. They all wore hideous masks so were quite willing to be photographed, although they pointed out that there were certain rites which could not be performed before outsiders or cameras.'

Rosaleen, in a cat mask, was nude except for a black apron and a black shawl. She was smoking from a long cigarette holder. Then she took off the shawl: 'Miss Norton had modelled in her time, and she was as unselfconscious with the shawl off as with it on,' the writer reported, not giving much away.

'What did people get out of the coven?' the writer asked Rosaleen, and was told, 'I get a life that holds infinite possibilities and is entirely satisfactory to me on all planes of consciousness.'

But by the seventies Rosaleen Norton was largely forgotten and friendless, a pensioner in failing health. Richard Moir, who published a memoir of her, saw her in her last days before she died of colon cancer on 5 December 1979 at the Sacred Heart Hospice for the Dying.

'I was ushered into the visitors lounge room, strange, I thought, as Roie couldn't walk,' he wrote.

'I waited in the lounge room for some time patiently, suddenly Rosaleen Norton appeared physically standing on both legs, welcoming me, escorted by two sisters. The vision I beheld was breathtaking.

'Rosaleen Norton (not Roie) standing there in full garb, her hair flaming back, carefully arranged in her look. Her make-up had been carefully applied, the face powder, the Rosaleen Norton full eyebrow makeup and eyebrows, the red lipstick. It was the Rosaleen Norton as I had always remembered her, but even more so.

'She stood for only one minute ... The last words Rosaleen Norton ever said to me were, "Darling: I can't stay too long, I just came to say hello. Ah! I must go, Darling." And with her head in a proud position Rosaleen Norton was escorted away out of my sight forever.'

But where exactly was Rosaleen going?

Surrounded by Catholic nuns in a hospital honouring the Sacred Heart of Jesus, she was heading in completely the opposite direction if she intended visiting the great god Pan.

7 Beating the cruel sea

The soul survivors

The first time Eva and Tom met she was in her nightdress, in his arms. Around her were the dead and the doomed, and Tom, she knew, was her only hope.

They were teenagers. She was 18, he was 19. Theirs is one of the sea's most romantic, dramatic and noble stories; a true story that picks up where the *Titanic* movie theme music swells up over the concluding credits scroll. Unlike the *Titanic*, this story had a happy ending, though not the one their adoring public demanded.

The story of Eva and Tom and the wreck of the *Loch Ard* began in the last days of sail. The *Loch Ard*, 90 yards, 1500 tons, one of the last and fastest of the clippers that raced between England and Australia, was beautiful to behold and it could cut through the oceans at 14 knots – 16 miles an hour. But like all sailing ships she lacked the manoeuvrability of the steam-powered rivals who were destined to make them obsolete. That inability to quickly change direction – that and a lot of bad luck – was the undoing of the *Loch Ard*.

The *Loch Ard*, in May 1878, was at the end of an 80-day voyage that had taken her 18 passengers, a crew of 36 and a fortune in cargo – £53,000 – from the English port of Gravesend to within a few hours of landing in Melbourne. Among the passengers were the Carmichael family from Ireland, Dr Emery Carmichael, a GP, his wife, and six of their seven children. The seventh, William, had quarrelled with his parents and like so many disaffected or disappointed young men in those days, went to Australia to seek a new life. He had decided, however, to reconcile with them and took ship to return home as they were coming out: ships that pass in the night.

The Carmichaels, like all the passengers, planned a new life in Australia, and looked forward to it with optimism and excitement, tinged with a little trepidation. Eva Carmichael, for instance, feared falling into the hands of the Aborigines: like thousands of others in Britain and Ireland, she had heard and been terrified by melodramatic accounts of the awful fate that befell Mrs Eliza Fraser, the white woman shipwrecked and held captive by savage Aborigines half a century before.

On the afternoon of Friday 31 May, the *Loch Ard* was preparing for her arrival in Melbourne. The weather was fine, there was a good breeze filling the sails and all on board were celebrating the end of a successful voyage. Captain George Gibb started to reduce sail and set his course for Cape Otway. He anticipated that the *Loch Ard* would arrive there at around 3 a.m., on Saturday morning. And from Cape Otway he needed to 'thread the needle' – sail the narrow passage into Bass Strait between the Shipwreck Coast and the west coast of King Island, the treacherous stretch where the *Cataraqui* had sunk with the loss of more than 400 lives in 1845. After that tragedy they had built a lighthouse at Cape Otway and it was this light that Captain Gibb expected to see within 12 hours.

When that time came, however, the flashing light was not to be seen in the darkness and Captain Gibb began to be concerned. He calculated that he was miles from land. But how many miles? He couldn't see. The weather had turned and a bank of fog lay ahead. But, strangely, above him he could clearly see the stars. At four o'clock the fog bank north of the *Loch Ard* cleared and Captain Gibb understood. The fog bank was coming off land and the land – towering cliffs that rose steeply from the sea – was less than a kilometre away. They were about to sail headlong into those cliffs.

The *Loch Ard* had a slim hope.

Gibb knew that if he could turn the ship south and sail it back into the wind. He needed all sails hoisted at once.

Tom Pearce, apprenticed to the *Loch Ard*, told the Steam Navigation Board inquiry some weeks later, 'Our watch was going below – some had gone – when I heard the order to hoist up the staysails, and at the same time the captain ran forward ordering all hands on deck. We got sail on her as quickly as possible by hoisting the main and mizzen topsail, set the spanker, and hoisted the upper mizzen topsail.'

The three-masted clipper was now sailing fast towards the cliffs – Captain Gibb wanted her to have all the momentum she could gather before turning into the eye of the wind. At the last possible moment Gibb gave the order: 'All hands ready about!'

The *Loch Ard* turned away from the cliffs and began coming back into wind. She couldn't do it. 'The ship just came up head to wind,' Pearce said, 'and then commenced to fall off again, as there was not enough sail on her to bring her around.

'As soon as the captain saw she was beginning to fall off again, he ordered both anchors to let go ... we were among the broken water ... we could soon see the anchors were not holding for every time the ship lifted with the sea she brought the anchors home. We gave her a little more cable, but could not give her much as we were afraid of a rock astern to which we'd gone very close.'

Captain Gibb now tried to tack out to sea but though the *Loch Ard* was gathering speed she was being taken inexorably towards the cliffs, and then, said Tom Pearce, '... she struck. Her starboard quarter appeared to strike a ledge that was just awash. It was not far from the land and at every roll of the sea her yards would strike against the cliffs ... I believe the rock made a great hole in her bottom, for she was bumping very heavily.'

They were about to sink in the icy waters. From both sides waves were crashing over the decks and Eva Carmichael heard the Captain tell someone, 'If you should be spared to see my dear wife, tell her that I stuck to the ship to the last, and went down with her like a sailor.'

He was true to his word. Tom Pearce said, 'I saw the captain on the poop. The ship seemed to be gradually sinking by the stern. I saw several of the seamen clinging to a portion of the upper main-topsail yard which had been broken by striking against the cliffs. The spars were falling in every direction, so much that some of the sailors got into the cabin with the passengers in order to save themselves. I believe some ladies had put on cork jackets and were going on deck, when they at once washed away.'

Pearce and the lifeboat were also swept into the sea. 'When the order was given to clear away the boats, I and five others went to the lifeboats ... There were six of us in the boat. I cut the after-gripe, and just then a sea came onboard and washed us all away ... When the sea struck the lifeboat and knocked it overboard it capsized and I was underneath it. I never saw any of the others who were with me. I was under the boat for some time ... The boat floated very high and there was plenty of air under her.'

Eva Carmichael, meanwhile, had found the most unlikely lifesaving device: an empty hencoop – a wooden cage for hens. She was one of the ladies who put on cork jackets – there were only six – and had come on deck in her nightdress, only to be immediately washed overboard. She almost drowned then, as she narrated in an account of the disaster written by Richard Bennett in 1878: 'One of the strings of my lifebelt broke and the belt shifting up and down forced my head under the water several times, which almost cost me my life. Seeing a hencoop I swam towards it. God taught me to swim in my blessed plight, for I never swam before. I succeeded in getting hold of the hencoop and so did Arthur Mitchell. This hencoop had been an object of ridicule among the passengers on board; but I felt thankful for it in the water.

'By this time *Loch Ard* had disappeared under the waves. Seeing a spar, I let go of the hencoop and made for it. In a few minutes Mitchell and Jones were clinging to the spar also. Mitchell began to shiver frightfully, and to despair of ever reaching the shore. He had a lifebelt:

but poor Jones kindly took off the life-buoy that was around himself and put it around Mitchell.

'Poor Jones and Mitchell soon let go the spar, and after swimming some little distance they disappeared, and I saw them no more. I was now left alone, and could see nothing but the waves rolling and a rock at a little distance. I let go the spar and made for it. The waves dashed me against the rock, and then sent me spinning round its point. I went down under the waves three or four times and began to despair of life. In a few minutes after turning the point of rock I saw Tom Pearce standing on the beach.'

Tom Pearce picks up the story. 'I suppose I was under the boat for about three quarters of an hour, but it seemed much more. The backwash, together with the ebb tide, must have taken the boat out to sea. When I came from under the boat I could see nothing of the ship, nothing but a lot of floating wreckage. I could not see anybody else floating. I went under the boat again, and the flood tide must then have drifted me in shore again, as the first thing I was aware of was the boat striking against a rock at the entrance of an inlet. This righted the boat but as she was floating in I still kept to her; but when about halfway up the inlet she struck against the sides of the cliff and threw me out. I then struck out for the beach, which I reached and found it covered with wreckage.'

Tom found a cave and threw himself on to its floor, exhausted. After resting, he went looking for something to eat – there seemed no hope of getting off the beach in the dark and under the sheer cliffs. 'I then heard someone calling out and at first thought it was somebody on the cliffs above me, but I could not see anybody. I heard a second cry, and then looked out to sea and saw a lady clinging to a spar.'

It took Tom an hour, Eva believed, before he could get her safely in to the beach. He half carried her to his cave, found a case of brandy, 'broke the neck of one of the bottles and made me swallow almost all of its contents, after which he swallowed a drop himself. Cold and exhausted – for we must have been in the water for about five hours – we lay down on the ground. I soon fell into a state of insensibility and must have been unconscious for hours.'

Tom Pearce had enjoyed two strokes of luck that saved them both. He had accidentally found the shelter of the upturned lifeboat, and the lifeboat had drifted into the only possible landing spot for many kilometres – the gorge now known as the Loch Ard Gorge. While Eva lay unconscious he set out to get help. He started to climb the cliff face, finding a point where it was at its lowest and least dangerous. After several attempts, when he almost fell, he finally made it to the top. There he had a third, crucial piece of good luck. All around was a wilderness of scrub. He chose, for no reason, to go west and quickly stumbled on a rough track that brought him, an hour or so later, to the sound of two young station hands out mustering sheep.

While the two rode furiously back to the Glenample Station to rouse their boss, Hugh Gibson, Tom staggered back to the cliff. Halfway down he was stranded, and then Gibson arrived and helped him. Gibson, alerting Eva that rescue was at hand, gave the Australian bush call – 'Cooeeee!' Eva, now awake and wondering where Tom was, 'heard a strange noise. I imagined it to have been the war-cry of the Aborigines.' She crept from the cave and hid in the scrub. Then she heard someone say, 'Yes' and she cried out, 'I'm dying.'

The survival of the two, and the story of their heroics, thrilled Melbourne. They were seen to hug, Eva called Tom 'my saviour' and the newspapers were almost demanding a marriage. It wasn't to be. The two remained friends in the weeks Eva took to recuperate, and Tom was there to see her off when she sailed back to Ireland. She didn't want to stay in Australia. She wanted to be with her brother and her granny, all that was left of her family.

She went on the *Tanjore*, a steamship. Eva married, had three sons and lived in England, where she died in 1934. Tom married the sister of one of his mates – an apprentice, like him, on the *Loch Ard*. Both his sons – like Tom's father – lost their lives at sea. Tom Junior was on the *Loch Vennacher* when it disappeared off Kangaroo Island in 1905, and his other son, Robert, was commanding a ship in a convoy bound for Malta when it was sunk in World War Two. Tom himself died of illness in 1908.

The curse of the Lochs

Eighteen of the 24 ships operated by the Loch Line went to the bottom of the ocean. The *Loch Ard* tragedy was just one of an extraordinary series involving ships with the name beginning 'Loch.' Eighteen years before the *Loch Ard*'s last voyage the *Loch Maree* vanished in the same notorious seas, in Bass Strait. Three years later, in the Atlantic, the *Loch Earn* took 226 passengers and crew with her when she went down in the Atlantic. In 1883 *Loch Fyne* was never again seen after sailing from New Zealand for England. *Loch Long* was only three hours out of Melbourne when she too disappeared in 1903. Tom Pearce Junior's *Loch Vennacher* disappeared two years later and three years later, in 1908, *Loch Lomond*, en route from New Zealand to New South Wales, disappeared. During World War One *Loch Carron* sank in the Atlantic and *Loch Awe*, *Loch Torridon* and *Loch Groom* were sunk by German submarines.

Small wonder that many sailors, superstitious at the best of times, regarded sailing with the Loch Line as signing their death warrant.

'A man on the rocks! There he is!'

He must have had the nightmare many times: that he was in a wild, drenching squall on a pitch black night, the wind shrieking as it tried to tear him from the tiny ledge halfway up the sheer cliff face and hurl him down into the sea below where broken bodies swirled and crashed among the rocks. In his dream he'd been there for many hours – days it seemed – and he could hold on no longer. He was going to fall like the others!

He was falling!

Then he'd wake and realise again that he'd lived his nightmare and survived.

James Johnson, an Irish sailor, spent 36 hours on the cliff face near the Gap, the awesome entrance to Sydney's harbour. He had been left on the cliff with three others. Weakened, one by one, his companions fell from the cliff during that first black night. He was the sole survivor of the wreck of the *Dunbar*, one of 122 men, women and children who had sailed on her from England to Australia. After that he was known as 'Lucky Jim'. It was an uninspired, absolutely accurate, nickname.

Lucky Jim's survival and his subsequent account of what happened on the night of 20 August 1857, ensured that what might have been a mystery – how the clipper *Dunbar* came to be dashed and shattered on the cliffs at the base of the Gap – was seen to be an understandable, if tragic, error on the part of her captain.

The *Dunbar*'s captain, James Green, an experienced master well known and well liked in Sydney, had sailed her from Plymouth on 31

May. She was carrying 63 passengers, many of them families, a crew of 59 and 1,980 tons of cargo valued at £22,000. She enjoyed a swift passage and after just 82 days – almost two months faster than the average time for the trip – *Dunbar* was approaching Botany Bay at around 7 p.m. James Johnson was about to come on watch.

Captain Green took it slowly. The weather was worsening. A gale was blowing from the east-south-east; the ship was wallowing in rough seas; squalls and rainstorms and the encroaching darkness of the night made it difficult to see. But through the breaks in the weather Captain Green and his officers could see land. They were from six to eight miles out, they estimated. But then the darkness closed in and all that could be seen, now and then, was the revolving beam from South Head lighthouse.

'When night came on we kept on course and shortly afterwards we saw the Sydney Light,' Johnson later told the *Dunbar* inquest. The lighthouse was on the cliff tops close to South Head and the inexperienced – Captain Green was not – might think it was directly on South Head: the entrance into Sydney Harbour, however, was a significant distance further north.

Slowly Green took the *Dunbar* towards the light. Aboard the clipper few thought he intended to take her into the harbour. They would have to wait until morning; surely, the seas would be calm then. The captain of a passing steamer saw the *Dunbar* and hardly gave it a second thought. 'I considered the ship perfectly safe,' he told the inquest, though, 'It was blowing heavy squalls, the weather stormy, with torrents of rain; there was a very heavy sea on ... I am sure the captain of this ship could not have seen the Heads.' And James Johnson, on watch, corroborated: 'We could not see a hand before our face ... we could not see the land but only the Light occasionally ... nobody ever thought that the Captain would have tried to get in that night.'

But the Captain did try. He had calculated that his ship was about six miles from land, but in fact it was much closer – just two miles. And she was making so much leeway, he reckoned, that unless he could run her into the shelter of the harbour and anchor her the *Dunbar* would be driven ashore.

Only one survived the wreck of the clipper Dunbar. *'Dead bodies by dozens were every minute being dashed upon the rocks...hurled in the air some 60 or 70 feet by the violence of the waves.'*

Johnson finished his watch at midnight and as he prepared to go below noticed that the sails were set. The ship, he believed, was keeping a good distance from land, squaring away. '... there was no opening that I could see that would lead anyone to believe [we] were going into port.' Then he heard 'a faint cry from the second mate on the fo'c'sle head, "Breakers ahead!" Captain Green called to the steerman to put the helm hard aport.'

It was too late. Green had mistaken the inlet of the Gap for the entrance to the harbour. The clipper was heading straight for towering sandstone cliffs. Next, Johnson heard a frightful grinding sound: 'She struck the rocks below first, and then bumped heavily over them' to smash against the base of the cliffs, 'shiver' and break up.

'And then the screaming began,' Johnson recalled, 'The passengers running about deck screaming for mercy. The captain was on the poop; he was cool and collected; there was great confusion and uproar on the deck with the shrieks of the passengers ... I made for the cabin, but the sea was coming down there enough to smother one ... saw some of the young ladies, when going into the cabin, running about in their chemises, screaming, screeching and crying... I was washed away with planks and broken timber upon a shelf of rock but immediately on the sea receding I got up a bit higher out of the reach of the back current.'

Johnson had been incredibly lucky. Below deck most of the passengers and crew were quickly drowned when the seas swamped in. Those on deck were washed helplessly into the swirling waters and pounded against the rocks. The *Dunbar* itself was shattered and scattered. But Johnson and three other men were swept onto the cliff face. By morning, precarious on a small ledge about 50 metres up, he was looking down on the disaster, the only survivor.

In the darkness the calamity went unnoticed by those few who lived around the Gap. The lighthouse keeper, however, had had a bad night. He had been kept awake by his agitated dog. It cried constantly, and, later, he saw it had worn a fresh path going to and from the cliff edge. In the morning, tired and irritable, he listened as his wife told him she had a nightmare about a man drowning. The man, she later told the inquest, was the image of James Johnson.

Dawn revealed a macabre scene. Bodies – scores of them – were swilling in the sea, washing in the foam around the rocks. 'By three o'clock,' said Bradshaw's *Narrative of the Wreck of the Dunbar*, 'some hundreds of cabs from Sydney, as well as several omnibuses, loaded to excess, had brought people to view the heart-rending scene of destruction going on at the Gap. Dead bodies by dozens were every minute being dashed upon the rocks by each wave, mountainous in themselves. Presently bodies without hands, legs, arms, bale goods, bedding, beams and every imaginable article was being hurled in the air some 60 or 70 feet by the violence of the waves.' Bradshaw reported that cargo littered the beach. Beer casks branded Tooths, bits of bodies, flooring timber, the corpse of 'a little boy, quite naked, and apparently about four years of age, with black hair, was picked up; also a cow, red with white spots, and short horns, was floating near this spot, surrounded by sharks, who were devouring the animal.'

There were hundreds of people – ghouls – now at the wreck. Looking down from the cliff tops, showered with spray, the *Sydney Morning Herald*'s man wrote, 'We found the residents of that locality watching with great horror the dead and mutilated bodies as they were thrown upon the rocks, the succeeding waves washing off again the naked remains ... the bodies were thrown up on the ledges of the rocks and again taken off by the violence of the surf.'

All but one. Clinging to the cliff high above the seething mass of bodies and wreckage, calling for help and waving a handkerchief as vigorously as he dared without risking a fall, was 'Lucky Jim.' And still no-one noticed him.

On Saturday morning a fifth of the population of Sydney – 10,000 people – were at South Head. 'I, like most of the spectators, mingled in the general excitement then prevalent,' said the *Herald*'s reporter, 'when, behold, the joy of everybody was expressed by a shout of "A man on the rocks! A live man on the rocks. There he is! There he is!"'

For days after, bodies, mangled beyond identification, were washed ashore on the beaches of Middle and North Harbour along with the wreckage of the ship. Thousands lined the route as the bodies were taken to Campbelltown and buried in a common grave.

Jim Johnson's evidence at the inquest on August 24 helped clear Captain Green's name and a joint statement from the masters of 35 ships then in port supported the jury's finding: 'There may have been an error in judgment in the vessel being so close to the shore at night in such bad weather, but they do not attach any blame to Captain Green or his officers for the loss of the ship.' It seems a kind finding.

Jim Johnson stayed on in Australia, and was working on the Newcastle lighthouse, when on 12 July 1866, the steamship *Cawarra*, with 60 people aboard, was wrecked trying to enter the port during a gale. There was only one survivor, Frederick Hedges. He was saved by 'Lucky' Jim Johnson.

8 Deep secrets

HMAS Sydney *and the riddle that remains*

She starts signalling with helio lamps. We do not answer but maintain our speed and course 250 degrees. Steadily nearer comes our doom and we distinctly recognise the vessel as an Australian cruiser of the Sydney class.

That's Sub Lieutenant Wilhelm Bunjies talking, one of 314 seamen who survived the naval battle between the *Kormoran* and the Australian light cruiser HMAS *Sydney* in November 1941. Many of the survivors gave similar accounts of the battle to their rescuers. But all the accounts give only one side of the story. The other side of the story – the story from the Australians' side – will never be given. There were no survivors on that side. Captain and crew of HMAS *Sydney* – all 645 – went down with the ship.

When, where and exactly how *Sydney* was lost may never be fully known. But there are many who believe HMAS *Sydney* may have been sunk after she surprised the *Kormoran* rendezvousing with a Japanese submarine, a nation that was not then at war, but, just 19 days later would enter the conflict with its attack on Pearl Harbor.

Suddenly, Australia, the nation that had never known war on its shores, was faced with the realisation that its naval defence was not impregnable and now there was the frightening prospect of an invasion by the Japanese.

The loss of 645 men from virtually every major town and city in the nation affected almost all Australians. And the sinking of *Sydney* was all the more traumatic because it came eight months after a victory parade through the streets of Sydney that celebrated her triumphs in recent sea battles. In July 1940, after sinking an enemy destroyer and weathering heavy air attacks the month before, *Sydney* heroically appeared on the horizon just as three British destroyers were about to be overwhelmed by two of Italy's fastest cruisers. *Sydney* opened fire from 20 kilometres and scored direct hits on the fastest cruiser afloat, *Bartolomeo Colleori*, crippling it. Then she badly damaged the *Colleori*'s sister ship, *Giovanne delle Bande Nere*, sending it scuttling for safety. Under the command of 40-year-old Captain John Collins, the idol of his crew, it had come out of these engagements virtually unscathed. Australians dubbed the cruiser 'Lucky *Sydney*'. She was popularly believed to be invincible.

Now she was coming home after escort duty along the coast of Western Australia, where the *Zealandia* was taking 1,000 troops of the Australian 8th Division to Singapore. In the Sunda Straight HMS *Durban* took over and *Sydney* turned for friendly Fremantle.

HMAS *Sydney* was under a new commander, Captain Joseph Burnett. A friend of Collins, he'd joined the Australian navy as a 14-year-old, the year before him, in 1913. Joe Burnett was at Jervis Bay Naval College where the contrasting personalities of the two were summed up in the college magazine's analysis of their cricketing styles: Collins 'the white hope of the team. Goes in to hit and keeps on hitting ... Burnett, a very sound bat ... and has the sense to wait for the ones to hit.' Burnett had seen service in two wars. He had been in the North Sea during World War One, and he was Executive Officer on the battleship HMS *Royal Oak* during the Spanish Civil War. He'd been Deputy Chief of Naval Staff when given command of HMAS *Sydney*, and few were better qualified.

Late afternoon on Wednesday 19 November, less than a day from port, someone on the bridge spotted a plume of smoke on the horizon. There was another ship in the neighbourhood and *Sydney* would have to check it out. She turned and headed that way. Almost certainly the ship would turn out to be a rusty old freighter, but there was a slim chance, too, that she could be one of the small fleet of German raiders, the *Kormoran* notably, which had caused real trouble at the beginning of the war. Heavily armed, almost the Australian cruiser's equal in firepower, she was larger than *Sydney* and could cruise at 18 knots. In the previous 11 months, in the Atlantic and Indian Oceans, and under various guises, the *Kormoran* had sunk 11 Allied ships. Now, however, the raiders' ploy of sailing as cargo ships had lost its surprise element, and increased vigilance and aggression had made them less encountered.

The first sign that things were not quite what they seemed that Wednesday afternoon was the smoke plume. It increased, almost as if the ship wanted to disappear behind it and into the glare of the sun setting on the horizon. And the ship had altered course. That was odd.

Captain Burnett knew well the procedure to follow in instances like the one he was sailing into. Stay ahead to thwart submarines that might be hiding in the wake of the ship being inspected. Keep your distance. And position yourself so that you can't be the target of torpedoes. They were basics. Then you asked the ship to give its four international signal letters. You then gave it the two inner letters of the Admiralty's secret call sign and asked it to supply the outer two letters. If the ship didn't, you fired a shot across its bows. After that the ship had better respond to your liking.

It was an uncomplicated system but it was not foolproof. As the *Sydney* had found, freighters challenged in this way often made a mess of it, not knowing the call sign or even how to show it. The crew of *Sydney* took up action stations as she closed in on the unknown vessel, guns for and aft trained, her amphibious aircraft fuelled and ready for take off.

'What ship?' *Sydney* signalled and the reply came – after a while – '*Straat Malakka*'. Burnett checked the code book for an outline of the Dutch freighter *Straat Malakka*. The ship he saw, as she came within range of his guns, resembled the outline reasonably closely. The ship's signalled destination, Batavia[Djkarta], made sense too, although she had turned when *Sydney* saw her and was now steaming in completely the opposite direction to Batavia.

Burnett gave the order to signal 'IK', the middle letters of the *Straat Malakka*'s secret code. But IK was also the international code for 'Have you suffered damage from cyclone, typhoon or tempest?' That could be confusing to the skipper of the cargo ship. Burnett waited for the response and while he waited he broke the rules. He allowed *Sydney* to come alongside the cargo ship. It meant that he could bring his ship's arsenal directly to bear on the *Straat Malakka*: eight 15-centimetre guns, four torpedo tubes. He had the cargo ship covered but Burnett would have been aghast at what happened next.

It was 5.30 and Burnett saw the Dutch flag the ship was flying hauled down and the German swastika run up in its place. At the same time camouflage screens fell to reveal six 13-centimetre guns, machine-guns and six torpedo tubes that now opened fire on him. The first salvo and the first torpedo from the *Kormoran* mortally wounded *Sydney*. Shells hit her bridge and gunnery control tower and put her two forward gun turrets out of action.

The aircraft on deck exploded in a mountain of flame and only her after-turrets, each with 15-centimetre guns, could return the fire continuing to come from the *Kormoran*. Convulsed by explosions *Sydney* turned and tried to ram the German ship before passing under the *Kormoran*'s stern and drifting, still firing but blazing from end to end, to the south.

She was last seen, a glow on the horizon, the Germans said, around 10 p.m.

Dying though she might be, HMAS *Sydney* managed to take the *Kormoran* with her. She hit the enemy's bridge and then the engine room. Dead in the water, aflame, the *Kormoran*, under Captain Theobold Detmers, continued firing as the *Sydney* limped away until, at 6.25, he gave the order: 'Cease firing! Abandon ship!'

Five hours later with most of her crew in lifeboats and on rafts the raider blew up.

That was the end of the battle, and the start of one of the great naval mysteries. What made Captain Burnett put his ship in such peril? Burnett, 'a very sound bat ... and has the sense to wait for the ones to hit ... '? Why hadn't he used her spotter aircraft to have a good look at a freighter acting a little oddly? *Sydney*'s gunners were renowned for their expertise. Yet somehow the 'freighter' had lowered its Dutch flag, dropped its camouflage screens to reveal its guns, hoisted the swastika and opened up a torrent of gunfire – all before *Sydney*'s gunners could react.

Wilhelm Bunjies, one of the German survivors from the *Kormoran*, told interrogators how his ship deceived the *Sydney*:

'The cruiser keeps asking us for our name. She is so close that it is impossible to overlook her helio signals. We answer *Straat Malakka* and hoist the Dutch ensign astern. All disappear from deck, but behind the camouflage flag shutters everyone stands in feverish excitement and holds his breath. We can distinguish every single man on board; the bridge is full of officers. She is now travelling parallel to us ... '

He didn't say, however, that, as many still believe, the deception went beyond flying a Dutch flag and tricking up the raider to resemble a freighter.

He didn't say, as some theorised, that Captain Detmers flew a white flag of surrender and lured *Sydney* close to allow a boarding party to launch its boat before running up the swastika and giving the cruiser a tremendous broadside. Captain Detmers was wary with his account of what happened. Had he lured Captain Burnett into the belief that the mystery ship was surrendering he could have been charged as a war criminal.

Other Australians believed that there was a German submarine. That the cruiser was torpedoed and the survivors machine-gunned.

Or – on the eve of Japan's surprise entry into the war with her attack on Pearl Harbor – was a Japanese submarine involved? And did she sink the cruiser and kill all the Australian witnesses to its war crime? Just 19 days later, on 7 December, an Australian, Colin 'Ike' Treloar of Adelaide, attached to 205 Squadron, RAF, at Singapore, had been one of a crew of eight aboard a Catalina flying boat that came across a Japanese task force of 44 ships north-east of Malaya. Before its crew could report the sighting it was sent down in flames by Japanese fighter planes. A few hours later the Japanese attacked Malaya and Hawaii and over the next two days Thailand, The Philippines, Guam Island, Hong Kong and Wake Island. The war in the Pacific had begun and 'Ike' Treloar was the first official Australian casualty.

Or was he the 646th?

In 1997 a parliamentary inquiry into the disappearance of HMAS *Sydney* investigated these theories and others. It found no substance in them. Cynics were not surprised.

The 645 men from HMAS *Sydney* have been dead now for more than six decades. But the suspicions will never die.

The bathtub revelation of Claude Sawyer

Claude Sawyer saw something in his bath that made him think his nightmare could come true. He'd had this bad dream that the ship he was on, the *Waratah*, the pride of the Blue Anchor Line fleet, had foundered and sunk in heavy seas.

Now he was watching the behaviour of his bath water with keen interest. When the ship rolled, he later told the court of inquiry, the bathwater slid to a steep 45 degree angle and stayed that way for an unnerving time before sliding back to horizontal. He didn't like the way the *Waratah* pitched in high seas, either, sometimes ploughing through waves instead of riding over them. Sawyer had strong misgivings. He thought it was time to get off.

Claude Sawyer was the only one of the *Waratah*'s 212 passengers and crew who had a premonition that the ship was doomed. All but he were lost when the ship disappeared at sea. Nothing was ever found of them, or the *Waratah*. Not a single piece of wreckage or flotsam was ever found. And not a single cause was ever satisfactorily advanced as to why she vanished.

She was the pride of the Blue Anchor Liner, a passenger–cargo liner built by a renowned firm of shipwrights and launched at the famous Clyde shipyards in 1909. The *Waratah* could cruise more than 300 knots a day, she had seven watertight compartments and 16 lifeboats. Her appointments were luxurious, the most expensive and lavish ever built for Blue Anchor.

Her maiden voyage from London to Sydney and back was a triumph. On her second voyage she left Adelaide with 10,000 tons of cargo, a crew of 119, and 93 passengers, almost all of them Australians from Sydney, Melbourne and Adelaide.

Crossing the Indian Ocean, the *Waratah* ran into strong winds and the way she handled them caused Claude Sawyer to have his premonitory dream. On 25 July, when she reached South Africa, he disembarked at Durban and sent Mrs Sawyer a telegram: LANDED AT DURBAN, THOUGHT WARATAH TOP HEAVY.

The next day the *Waratah* headed for Cape Town, 790 nautical miles south. The following day, in heavy head seas, she passed a tramp steamer, the *Clan McIntyre* and they exchanged signals, identifying themselves. In the afternoon she made signal contact with the Union Castle steamer, *Guelph*, and that was the last that was ever seen of the *Waratah*.

Twelve days later, when she failed to arrive at Cape Town, there was no concern; heavy seas, in a day or two she'd be in. After a day or two they thought that perhaps her two sets of coal-burning engines had broken down and three warships went in search. They came back reporting no sign of her.

In Australia the families of the passengers were praying when the news came through from South Africa. The Blue Anchor vessel sighted a considerable distance out slowly making for Durban could be the *Waratah*. The news thrilled the nation.

In Melbourne, the seat of Federal Parliament, the Speaker was handed the cable, stopped the debate and read it as Members of the House sprang to their feet cheering. In theatres performances were stopped while the joyous news was announced.

The sighting was wrong. The ship was not the *Waratah*.

In the next three years numerous reports of sightings of the *Waratah*, its remains, or the bodies of its passengers, were investigated and found false. Search vessels were charted, criss-crossing the ocean for any trace of the liner. All fruitless. In December 1909 a court of inquiry began a 14-month investigation that looked into the possibilities that she had been powerless and had drifted to her doom in the Antarctic; that she had been wrecked on reefs; that she had been hit by a gigantic wave that swallowed her and sucked her down into the darkness of the ocean floor. No conclusion could be reached.

But the truth could surely be found in Claude Sawyer's bathwater.

The canine clue to the Bogle–Chandler mystery

Can the clue to the Bogle–Chandler killings, one of the great murder mysteries of the 20th century, a puzzle that has baffled the best international forensic experts, be traced to the roly-poly stomach of a puppy dog?

A brilliant scientist and an attractive young woman found dead near a Sydney suburban Lovers' Lane, their nakedness inexplicably covered – presumably – by their killer, Dr Gilbert Bogle's and Mrs Margaret Chandler's deaths remain the source of never ending speculation.

They died on that morning on New Year's Day, 1963, it was mooted by some journalists, because of a devious security conspiracy involving atomic espionage: British Intelligence – or perhaps the CIA – wanted Gilbert Bogle out of the way. Others, among them the young newspaper proprietor Rupert Murdoch, believed the two were poisoned by a brittle, spurned lover of Bogle. Some wondered, was it an aphrodisiac overdose? A double suicide? A murder–suicide? Was it weedkiller? Did Russia's master spy Kim Philby order Bogle killed to hamper America's development of anti-missile devices? There was speculation about a mysterious death ray. Dry ice, perhaps. Was it LSD, the new and little known hallucinogen that was covertly manufactured, people whispered, at the CSIRO laboratories where Bogle was a star scientist? What about snake bites, or spiders, trapdoor, redback or funnel web? Nerve gas pellets concealed in Bogle's car? Did a jealous man or woman inject them with a new, untraceable poison, or spray them with a toxic substance from a tropical shellfish?

None of these theories held up. Tests revealed nothing. Police, forensic experts and scientists around the world were fascinated by the challenge but all, eventually, confessed they were at a loss.

'It wasn't just a medical thing that went wrong,' Dr John Laing the director of forensic medicine at the Public Health Department of NSW once said.

'Specialists from all walks of life – detectives, civilians, university professors and me – we all delved into it. Nothing proved rewarding; everybody came to a dead end. There were magnificent theories but there was something wrong with each one. They didn't fit the facts. Sherlock Holmes once said something to the effect that if it ever gets to that stage, then maybe the facts are wrong.'

So could it have been, perhaps, an accident?

It was around 7.45 a.m., and the first morning of the new year was already hotting up when the two teenage boys foraging for golf balls near the Chatswood golf course came across the body of a man, blue in the face, blood tricking from his nose, in the bush on a bank of the Lane Cove River in suburban Sydney.

It took police three hours to arrive. (Like the boys, they may have presumed the dead man was a derelict.) When they did get to the scene they were met with a gullet-heaving stench of excreta, vomit and death. The dead man – his wallet identified him as a Dr Gilbert Bogle of Turramurra – lay on his stomach, his arms spreadeagled, his legs extended and his shoes mudcaked.

Rigor mortis had set in. He was half naked, clad only in shirt, tie, socks and shoes. His trousers were neatly folded to cover his legs and under them was a grimy piece of carpet covering his nudity. His jacket covered his back, the sleeves following the spread of his arms. Semen was later detected on it but this fact (like others), was suppressed by the circumspect coroner. Clearly this wasn't a suicide, or death by natural causes.

Then, a shout from a motorcycle policeman around 15 metres away, closer to the river.

'Hey! Sarge! There's another one down here!'

Around 11.30, when the first report of the discovery of the body came in, Bill 'Bondi' Jenkings had been drinking at a city pub with some Criminal Investigation Branch detectives, as you do early in the morning on New Year's Day when you're the *Daily Mirror*'s chief crime reporter. He raced to the scene just in time to be there when the second body was found. 'In my haste to get over there I lost my footing and almost tumbled into the corpse,' he says in his book, *As Crime Goes By: The Life and Times of 'Bondi' Bill Jenkings.* 'I can still see her pretty face looking up at me.'

Margaret Chandler, her body still warm, was lying on her back in a slight hollow, a leg protruding from three sheets of a flattened-out beer carton put together to cover her nakedness. She might have been asleep, one hand languidly across her stomach under her right breast, but she too was nude from the waist down and a man's underpants lay between her ankles. Her rose floral dress was rolled up to her waist and her strapless bra was pulled down to expose her breasts. Abrasions on her torso indicated she had crawled or stumbled around – or been dragged by someone. Her white panties and brown shoes and Dr Gilbert Bogle's belt were down by the dry riverbed, just above water level.

And again the sickening sight and stench of vomit and diarrhoea, the smell and signs of violent physical purging in the weeds, reeds and tangled grass where both bodies lay.

Almost at once the blunders that would frustrate the forensic scientists began. The police were careless in the way they replaced the clothes and the beer carton parts after examining the bodies. They should have been more rigorous protecting the crime scene: 'Before long the whole area was swarming with coppers and journos,' 'Bondi' Bill recalled. And, crucially, it was a public holiday and the coroner couldn't be found. The bodies were left baking in the hot summer's sun until the middle of the afternoon when the stench was almost overpowering. Taken away, the corpses were refrigerated overnight and the autopsy performed the next day – more than 24 hours after the discovery and too late to trace possible poisons.

Poison, it was generally agreed, was the cause of death. The autopsy showed both victims had almost identical symptoms. And, it was also generally agreed, a third party had been at the death site. It was possible – just – to concede that Margaret Chandler, a nurse before she was married, might have covered Bogle's body to keep him warm before he died. But Bogle died at least an hour before her so it was inconceivable that she covered it herself; that she found three convenient pieces of beer carton exactly the size to cover her, and then lay beneath them, her bra below her breasts, her skirt still furled around her waist and her arm resting across her stomach, waiting for death.

But if they were poisoned who did it, and what was their motive? The Bogle–Chandler mystery still intrigues armchair detectives. But today, perhaps, an equally fascinating aspect of the case is the glimpse it gives us into an Australia that came to an abrupt end around the time of the double killing.

On New Year's Eve, 1962, Australia was the land of the Sunday Roast. Millions of people – certainly all practising Catholics – sat down after church on Sunday to an unvarying and eagerly awaited lunch. Very well done roast lamb and mint sauce, pumpkin, potatoes, and peas. There was no wine on the table or in the cellar. There was no cellar, and as for wine most Australians would have identified Riesling as the premier of South Korea – or was it Singapore? Marijuana was beginning to be heard of, but few knew much about it. The Australian Football legend, Jack 'Captain Blood' Dyer believed marijuana to be a sauce they put on spaghetti. Homosexuals were known, but it was also known that they were easy to spot – they had hair that needed a good cut, limp wrists, spoke in an effeminate way and wore suede shoes – and there were very few of them. Unmarried young men and women didn't live together. They had sex, of a sort, in the back seats of cars at the drive-in movies or at the front gate where the goodnight kiss sometimes led to 'heavy petting'. When it got past that stage it was time to think of getting married. Most married in their early twenties. And they stayed together even when the marriage was a failure.

All that was about to change, rapidly. The Bogle–Chandler deaths came just a year after Australia was introduced to the Pill – and swallowed it with hardly a second thought. The following year, 1964, an astonishing fashion craze swept Sydney: the topless look. Women boarded buses wearing hats (practically compulsory for all women over 25) frocks, stockings and high heels – but with their breasts exposed.

Two years later, the censor's office, until then vying with the Vatican in its zeal to stop people from reading and seeing what the censor knew they shouldn't read or see, collapsed almost overnight, thanks to the *Lady Chatterley's Lover* 1966 landmark court case.

These dramatic social changes meant that by the end of the sixties unmarried teenage girls were 'on the Pill' and sleeping with – and increasingly, living with – whoever took their fancy. Porn newspapers and magazines were on sale at some corner milk bars alongside the *Truth* (More Shock Photos Inside!), *Australasian Post* and *Pix* and just below the counter with the Black Magic chocolate boxes, the Cherry Ripes and the jelly babies.

Today the main figures in the Bogle–Chandler case would, characteristically, be divorced or still single. Margaret Chandler, 29, and her husband Geoffrey, 32, would most likely be single, meeting partners in nightclubs, living together for a year or two perhaps, and agreeing to part when, as happened, they sought other lovers.

On the first day of the New Year of 1963, however, unaware that the revolution had begun, Australians woke up to news that would have them agog. Here was a Rhodes scholar – the secular equivalent of a saint – a brilliant scientist at the famous research laboratories, the CSIRO, a man who apparently could speak a number of languages and could play the clarinet – he could probably make a decent fist of Artie Shaw's 'Frenesi' – a married man with four kiddies, here was this estimable and remarkable man, found dead with his trousers off and reputation in tatters.

And Margaret Chandler. She was the mother of two little kiddies – and she had been a nurse! More saintly connotations. Here was Mrs Chandler, also half naked, and found (but the public were not told this) with a man's underpants between her ankles. Worse, far worse, it quickly emerged, her husband, also a CSIRO man, apparently didn't give a hoot if his wife was having an affair with Dr Bogle – in fact he encouraged it! And he too was having a bit on the side.

On the surface Geoffrey Chandler and his wife Margaret seemed to be a happily married couple living in Croydon, a middle-class Sydney suburb. They had two small children, Gareth, two, and baby Sean, and common interests in dachshund dogs and veteran cars. He was a scientific photographer employed by the CSIRO, and she had been a nurse.

On the surface, Dr Gilbert Bogle, 39, a colleague of Chandler's, was a seemingly happily married father of four, whose wife Vivien was the daughter of an Anglican bishop. A New Zealand Rhodes scholar at Oxford who got his doctorate of philosophy in physics, he had come to the CSIRO in 1960. There he was working – blazing a dazzling trail – on solid-state physics, specialising in masers, the precursors of lasers. His work was not classified top secret but its ramifications for military use were extremely significant.

Within a few weeks of the New Year Dr Bogle was to take a position with the Bell laboratories in America, the world centre for new engineering programs. The laser was developed at Bell and Dr Bogle's expertise would have been called on in the further development of laser, and, probably, in advancing Bell's anti-ballistic missile systems.

But 10 days before New Year's Eve he met Margaret Chandler.

The Chandlers and 'Gib' Bogle were at a CSIRO Christmas barbecue at Murraybank and Bogle, Geoffrey Chandler later said, was in excellent form. He was clearly smitten by Margaret and there was instant rapport. 'They struck a spark, one off the other. In a way I was flattered. At least two women had told me that Gib was a fascinating man and it is always gratifying to have one's choice in one's wife borne out by another man's attentions to her.'

These three sentences from *So You Think I Did it?*, the book Geoffrey Chandler wrote in 1969, sums up the man's breathtakingly cavalier attitude that he professed to have about other men and his wife. Chandler didn't know Bogle well, but he must have known, from CSIRO scuttlebutt, that Bogle made a practice of seducing the wives of friends and colleagues. Bogle, he later learned from one of Gib's former conquests, was a man who was apparently not particularly ardent, but who liked to 'renew himself' with other women.

Geoffrey Chandler, too, liked to renew himself. He was a member of the Sydney Push, described by Barry Humphries as 'a fraternity of middle class desperates, journalists, drop out academics, gamblers and poets manqué and their doxies'.

Chandler was a little more circumspect, describing the Push as anti-authoritarian, republican, and humanist, but then warming to the 'doxies': 'Casual love-making was part of the Push life ... One of the attractions of the Push undoubtedly was that there were always a number of good-looking young girls around.'

Bob Ellis gushed that the 'members of the Push loomed as Homeric giants, whose life was one long adventure, night after night, party after party, race meeting after poker session and tragic love after tragic love, following only the minute's need or desire – arguing and drinking far into the night, taking round the hat for incidental abortions, offering no rebuff to anyone who showed up at midnight and wanted to sleep on the floor, and having their parties, parties, parties – all the parties I missed'.

At the time they met 'Gib' Bogle was having an on-and-off affair with a woman, Margaret Fowler. Geoffrey Chandler was 'constantly seeing' an attractive member of the Push, Pam Logan. And Margaret Chandler had come out of an affair with another single man who told police that Geoffrey Chandler had suggested that he visit Margaret when he was not at home.

Margaret Fowler was also at the barbecue and her husband, an academic, later told police that his wife had gone on at great length about how Gib and Margaret had gone off into the bush together and how her husband Geoffrey had not seemed to mind. She had discussed the party 'ad nauseam', he said, and said, 'I pity ... Bogle if he's going to get mixed up with the Chandlers.'

Driving home from the barbecue Geoffrey Chandler could see his wife was excited. The following day, he said, as they lay in bed talking about Gib, Margaret wondered what he would be like as a lover. Geoffrey told her, 'If you want to have Gib as a lover, if it would make you happy, you do it.'

That was Chandler's style. 'Margaret and I learned about love together,' he wrote. 'We realised in our relationship everything that love could mean. It may have been that when I made love to other women, as I occasionally did, I was testing myself against other standards.'

On New Year's Eve, after the Chandlers had left their children with Margaret's parents at Granville, the three met again at the Waratah Street, Chatswood home of Ken and Ruth Nash on Sydney's North Shore. Ken Nash, a dapper man, was Chandler's superior in the photographic branch at the CSIRO. The Chandlers, it transpired, had been invited at late notice – and only at the prompting of Gib Bogle, the star guest among the 22 who came – suitably dressed – to the party. Only Geoffrey Chandler declined to come in the stipulated jacket and tie for men. He wore what Ken Nash testily told the inquest was 'sandals, casual slacks and some form of long shirt-like object that hung outside his trousers with an open-neck collar, although I had explained at great length that dress for the party was to be a frock-type dress for the women and jackets and tie for the men'. And he didn't bring an original 'work of art' as guests were instructed. Gib Bogle brought his clarinet and a sketch parodying Picasso's drawings, the 'message' behind which was later to be the subject of endless conjecture.

Inside the thirties suburban home Geoffrey Chandler looked around and didn't much like what he saw: about 20 people talking quietly and not doing a lot of drinking. He slipped out around 11 a.m. and went to a Push party in Balmain. There he met Pam Logan and went to her bed-sitter in Darlington for about half an hour before returning to Chatswood to the Nash's party at between 2 a.m. and 3 a.m. in time for supper.

No-one seemed to have missed him and Mrs Nash told him cheerfully that Gib was going to drive Margaret home.

After supper Chandler, Margaret and Gib sat 'in what I think Ken Nash called his den ... it was at this time I should have said to Margaret, "Come on, we're going home." But I didn't. So it was really I who forced the issue. I could tell that Margaret was somewhat disenchanted, and that what had started as a half joke, a possible experiment, had gone stale. She had been saying she was interested in Gib but really all she wanted was to get in the car and go home with me. And I think Gib felt the same way. But he was a man and he had said he would take her home, and he certainly wasn't going to revert on this.'

Chandler asked Bogle if he still wanted to drive Margaret home. Bogle, he said, looked at him intently for a moment and then said 'Right.' It was taken for granted that Chandler would go to Granville to pick up the children, leaving the Croydon home empty.

Chandler mooched out of the house, not bothering to say goodbye to anyone, sat outside for a while smoking – waiting to see if Margaret might change her mind – and had a last cigarette in his car before starting the engine and driving his silver vintage Vauxhall to Pam Logan's. He woke her up and she went with him to pick up the boys.

The distinctive car was seen on the Parramatta Road between 4.45 and 5 a.m. by two witnesses. One of them recognised Chandler and said to his wife that the woman in the car wasn't Margaret Chandler. At Granville, while Pam waited at a discreet distance from the house, Chandler picked up his children and they all returned to the Logan flat at Darlington. It was 6.30 a.m. There Chandler stayed until 10 a.m., when he returned to his Croydon home, tumbled into the empty double bed and slept.

At 1 a.m., there was a knock on the door. It was the police.

When Geoffrey Chandler slipped away from the party at the Nash's around 11 his absence went unremarked. Ken Nash gave evidence at the inquest that he had become aware that Chandler was not in the house an hour later, some time around midnight (when Chandler was arriving at the Push party). Around that Auld Lang Syne time, Nash told the coroner, he had seen Margaret Chandler and Gib Bogle standing together a few metres from the back door. They were on the lawn, about a metre apart, just looking at each other.

'Partly in jest, from a point of view of puckish humour, I switched off the light which spilt on to the lawn. They returned to the house immediately.'

The party went on with a few diehards staying until, at around seven in the morning, the Nash's phone rang. It was Mrs Bogle. Did Ruth Nash know where Gib was? Mrs Nash lied. Gib had left a little while before, she told Mrs Bogle. Ten minutes later the last guest left – and perhaps 20 minutes after that Bogle's body was discovered about five kilometres away. Ken and Ruth Nash went to bed not knowing that the party was well and truly over.

Fifteen minutes after Geoffrey Chandler had returned to the party and finally driven off, disconsolate, to wake up Pam Logan and go with her to pick up his children, Gib Bogle said goodnight to Ruth Nash, asked to take his Picasso home to show his children and beeped farewell in his Ford Prefect.

Margaret Chandler waited a few minutes and then also left. She got into Bogle's car and they drove off and were next seen driving into Lane Cove River Park, five kilometres from the Nash's around 4.30. Bogle drove across Fuller's Bridge, turned to the right, off the road and on to a narrow dirt track, on the eastern bank of the Lane Cove River, a well-known Lovers' Lane.

Why?

What were they doing on this squalid riverbank, littered with broken bricks, beer bottles, condoms and rusted cans? If they wanted to make love why not go to the Chandler's Croydon home? Geoffrey Chandler had made it quite clear he would not be there. If they hadn't wanted to do that, if they couldn't wait, Bogle could have driven his car a minute or so further along the track where there was an open stretch of riverbank with little rubbish and a lot more privacy. (It appeared it was Rush Hour at the Lane Cove Lovers' Lane by the time Gib and Margaret arrived.)

A witness told the inquest that he had seen Bogle seated in the car looking quite pale. Another saw the car a few minutes later, but it was empty. Ken Challis said he saw a couple in the Ford Prefect who were not there when he returned half an hour later. But he did see a muscular man in a dark T-shirt and long blond hair, who, Challis said, shot in front of his car and slithered down the bank and out of sight.

Another man, Eric McGrath, drove by the deserted car at around 5.10. A few hundred metres further on he came across a boy, aged around five. He asked the boy if he was lost and, as Challis appeared from the trees, the boy – who seemed stunned and kept repeating, 'No. No. No. I want to go home!' – ran away.

A courting couple saw the Bogle car but were frightened when they spotted a man in the bushes. They drove off.

Three hours later Gib Bogle's body was found.

The other, other woman

Margaret Fowler, a prime suspect. Fairfaxphotos

One Sunday morning in 1959, in his little 1948 green Ford Prefect sedan, Gib Bogle pulled up outside the squash courts at Turramurra, not far from his home where he had left his wife and four children. On the courts a woman who had caught his eye, Margaret Fowler, was playing. She was 35, a librarian and fellow employee at the CSIRO. She too was an academic with a degree in physics and maths, and married to a professor of chemical engineering. She was about to begin an affair that would continue, on and off, until Bogle's death.

Gib drove Margaret to a local park where 'he kissed me a great deal. He did not undress me,' she told police who interviewed her several times. 'I said to him, "I'm frightened. This is very serious for me and it's only fun and games for you." (She was an intelligent but foolish woman with a masochistic itch

Gib would quickly scratch.)

'It's too unequal,' she said as Gib came back with a callous and glib answer: 'Yes, but it would be fun all the same.'

They were petting in the Prefect for an hour and in that time Margaret Fowler fell in love with this man whose idea of fun was seducing desperate wives. A few days after their pash in the park she caught his train and already the pattern of their affair was clear. He admonished her:

'You are a very possessive woman.'

She wasn't, she insisted without conviction, but he brushed her denial aside. In any case, he told her, he was 'interested in someone else now'.

This sort of brutal treatment was apparently not enough to dampen her ardour. For the next three years, and though he was often impotent and unsatisfying sexually, she was obsessed with him, took his cruel and cursory treatment and always came back for more.

Once, after lovemaking in his office, she told him: 'You can't treat me like this!' He rapped: 'I only like you when you don't talk. Once you start reproaching me I don't like you any more and it's coming over me now and I'm going home. Get up!'

She slapped his face and that should have been the end of the affair, but whenever Bogle tried to end it, as he often did, she would threaten him. 'I'll die if you do!' When she learned that the Bogle family was planning to move to the US early in 1963 she told a friend that she would take a fatal dose of the poison, phenobarb, but by November 1962, she told police, they made arrangements to live together in London. Bogle had told her they would share a flat together. (Presumably he would pop over from the US and meet her, as he had popped over to the Turramurra squash club.)

Margaret Fowler was interviewed by the police six days after

> the deaths but had an alibi. She was at another party, in Turramurra, several suburbs away.
>
> She and her husband had left the party at 3.45 a.m. (about the time Margaret Chandler and Gilbert Bogle had left the Nash's) and gone straight home. The police interviewed her four more times and she wrote a long statement about her involvement with Bogle.
>
> Margaret Fowler left Australia for England immediately after the inquest. Her husband divorced her four years later claiming he had come home to find her and another man naked in bed. She died in 1977.

'Two bodies in an almost normal anatomical presentation, but the people were dead and the authorities wanted to fill in that vacant little square at the bottom of the report,' Doctor John Laing, the director of forensic medicine at the Public Health Department said years later. 'So surely – and this is not an uncommon experience in a pathologist's life – if anatomy won't give you the answer it is obvious that the New Year's Eve party must.

'They overindulged, they were full of alcohol, they got themselves into a posture where they asphyxiated, that or they took sleeping pills and goodness-knows-what and went for a row without meaning to. So all we had to do was put the specimens in the bottles, send them to the government analysts and Bob's your uncle.

'Oh boy, how wrong can you be! It was not until the analyst sent back his magnificent document in which he said no poisons and, so help me, a New Year's Eve party – no alcohol – that we realised we were up the original gum tree.'

One thing the post-mortem did reveal was that whatever killed Dr Bogle at around 5 a.m., that New Year's Day, almost certainly killed Margaret Chandler a few hours later. And poison, it was agreed, was almost certainly the cause of death. But what poison it was impossible to tell.

When the City Coroner, Mr Jack Loomes, opened the inquest into the deaths, in March, Sydneysiders queued for seats each day, bringing with them flasks of tea and packed lunches and over its 15 days the media held the front pages for the sensational evidence that was surely to come as witness after witness – 50 in all – took the stand.

It didn't happen. Chief among the witnesses was the government analyst Mr Ernest Stanley Ogg, who told Mr Loomes that he had examined the pair's brains, hearts, livers, spleens, kidneys and blood. He had tested hair for arsenic poisoning, durata seeds (a poison used by Asian criminals) cocaine, henbane and Queensland conefish venom among many tests for known poisons. But, he said, there were thousands more available. 'There are about 40,000 new chemical substances every year. The majority of them are toxic in varying degrees.

'No-one can say these substances can be detected. No-one can say of any of these substances, that if they had been used to poison someone, they could be detected.'

Finally, to the immense disappointment of the public, Mr Loomes released his findings. The facts were, concluded the coroner, that 'each of the unfortunate persons died an unnatural death' and that they died because they stopped breathing after their hearts stopped beating; or because their hearts stopped beating after they stopped breathing.

Well, yes.

He also said that 'every person who I felt could give any information as to the deaths of these unfortunate persons has been summonsed to appear ... One would like to think feel that no stone has been left unturned to have all available evidence that could assist in any way placed before this inquest.'

Well, no.

In truth, he left unturned the stone of the spurned lover of Dr Bogle – Margaret Fowler – a woman many police considered the prime suspect.

On 27 May, it was Margaret Fowler's turn to give evidence. She had no sooner sworn to tell the truth than her counsel and the counsels for both the Bogle family and Geoffrey Chandler objected to the truth being told. The coroner agreed with the three learned men, saying, 'I feel her evidence could not now help in any way in the charge that has been placed upon me,' at which many an eyebrow was hoist among Sydney detectives.

(On the same grounds the coroner also discharged Margaret Chandler's self-described former lover, Bill Berry).

Nonetheless, the complexities of the love life that the deaths had revealed were laid bare at the inquest, and at one poignant moment, Geoffrey Chandler an urbane man, calm and collected, lost his composure. In answer to a question he said, 'One tried to find a solution for these things ... '

Mr Looms didn't ask about the worm tablets for dogs.

Bill Jenkings, the veteran *Mirror* crime reporter reckons he knows how Margaret Chandler and Gib Bogle died. It was not murder, he says.

In *As Crime Goes By: The Life and Times of 'Bondi' Bill Jenkings*, he writes: 'I have no doubt it was a stupid practical joke that badly misfired. This I base on my own investigations and the many frank discussions with that shrewdest of detectives, Jack Bateman ... I believe that one of the guests at the party slipped tablets[the worm tablets] into cups of coffee Dr Bogle and Mrs Chandler drank just before they left the party.'

Bateman, Bill Jenkings, says, knew who did it but said the evidence was circumstantial: it could not be proved in court.

Bateman was convinced that the person, knowing the couple were about to have a liaison, thought that while the pair were lovemaking the worm tablets would act, causing diarrhoea and vomiting. But the chemical in the tablets, arecoline hydrobromide, proved deadly.

The 'joke' that backfired theory is supported by Brian Hansen, a highly regarded writer, first as a specialist crime reporter and then as a sports reporter and author of 20 books. In *The Awful Truth. The Inside Story of Crime and Sport*, Hansen tells of a meeting arranged by John Bryan Kerr, the star radio announcer 'celebrity killer' who once dominated the Melbourne headlines. He and Hansen continued to stay in touch after Kerr served his time for murder and when *Truth* sent Hansen to Sydney to cover the Bogle–Chandler case he got a call.

It was Kerr and he claimed to have a contact who would reveal how the couple died.

Hansen says he was told to take a ferry to Manly where he went to a house and was met by a well-dressed middle-aged man.

The man gave him details of the case that Hansen knew to be true but had not been made public. He told him he was one of the dinner guests at the Nash New Year's Eve party. He wanted it made clear that the party was perfectly normal.

'There has been so much written about this ritual and that ritual and that we were a collection of ratbags doing all sorts of obscene things. It was just rubbish. We were simply a group of intellectuals having intellectual discussions over a few drinks and some good food.'

Then he told Hansen his theory, which he said, was shared by other dinner party guests but, he believed, had not been passed on to the police.

'Gib fancied himself as a ladies' man and was known to us as a bit of a smoothie. We knew he was having an affair with Margaret although she was much younger and less mature than Gib. They did slip away from the function late in proceedings. We all noticed including Chandler, nobody was surprised.'

He said a little later another member of the party also wandered off and he had no doubt the guest was following the couple. 'He told me in strict confidence the identity of that shadowing guest ...

'The guest said that he and others, particularly the women, knew that Bogle kept a small hip flask in the glove box of his car. The flask was invariably filled with spirits for a social sip with his companion as they parked in convenient tail-light locations.

'The flask wasn't there when the police examined his car, because there was no mention of it being found or even that they knew of its existence. It is obvious to me somebody slipped something into the flask and it is pretty clear that this had to happen while they were at the party.

'They couldn't have been contaminated until after they left the party because the stuff had a stupendous effect on them. They certainly hadn't consumed anything that toxic at the Nash's or they would have died there. It is highly probable that somebody who knew about the flask loaded it up while they were still at the party.

'... somebody anticipating they would be slipping off for a bit of slap and tickle decided to play a silly practical joke on them and poured some form of aphrodisiac into the flask. I think it quite possible the joker followed them in his car just to watch what transpired. What he saw was it all go horribly wrong. He couldn't help because they were beyond help. He made the bodies decent and took away the flask for obvious reasons.'

In 1976 Ken Nash, the New Year's Eve party host with a mischievous sense of humour, wedged a .22 calibre semi-automatic rifle between his legs, stooped his head over the barrel and squeezed the trigger.

The dapper man who was affronted by the casual wear of Geoffrey Chandler left a note for the neighbours apologising for the mess and the inconvenience to whoever found his body. One of the neighbours said Nash, widowed in 1974, had become a recluse for the last two years of his life. Once, however, Nash had invited him in for a drink and the two men had talked through the night about little else but the Bogle-Chandler mystery. Nash, the neighbour said, was obsessed by the case.

Nash killed himself on the thirteenth anniversary of the death of Gilbert Bogle and Margaret Chandler.

Who dunnit – and how? The theories

A former senior detective involved with the case believed a jealous Margaret Fowler murdered the pair, says Marian Wilkinson in *The Book of Leaks*. 'I'm satisfied in my own mind she did it. It never went out of my mind,' she says he told her.

'He pointed to her affair with Bogle, and that he had "wiped her" and to a report early in the case that said she was seen outside the Nash's house party on the morning of January 1. He said he had not wanted the Fowlers to leave the country but there was nothing to hold her on, no evidence against her.'

* * *

Keith Paull, who was at the Lane Cove death site on New Year's Day and who later became the chief superintendent of the NSW police was interviewed after his retirement and said: I'm inclined to think that LSD might well have been a cause. But whether it was self-administered by force or trickery, it's hard to say. At this stage I suppose we'll never know for sure. There may still be someone out there who knows what happened – but it's unlikely they'll come forward now.'

* * *

Two years after the deaths, the Hong Kong police force's Director of Forensic Medicine reported two deaths which exhibited precisely the symptoms found in the Bogle-Chandler case. The two Asians died, he found, after taking 'Japanese Chocolate' – the Asian aphrodisiac, Yohinbine.

* * *

Margaret Fowler and Geoffrey Chandler gave credence to an extraordinary theory by the widow of Dr Cliff Dalton, a friend of Dr Gilbert Bogle's. Catherine Dalton's husband, like Bogle, was an eminent New Zealand physicist, and had helped invent the first fast breeder reactor. He was a member of the Australian Atomic

Energy Commission in Sydney and died two years before Bogle in mysterious circumstances.

Catherine Dalton wrote a book linking the two men's deaths. She believed Bogle was assassinated because he was poised to disclose Australian Atomic Energy Commission security leaks and CIA illegal activities in Australia.

Later, following revelations by the British intelligence officer Peter Wright, Geoffrey Chandler speculated that Bogle had been 'eliminated' as a Soviet agent.

* * *

The respected journalist Marion Wilkinson, in *The Book of Leaks*, an investigative book jointly written with Brian Toohey, agrees with the conspiracy theory. She believes that the FBI, which J. Edgar Hoover ordered keep files on the case, can shed light on the deaths, but refuses to release the files.

'When Mr A.F.A Harper, head of Gib's section at the CSIRO was called in at the last stages of the inquest he said in answer to questions ... that Gib was not engaged in any research into what might be called a "death ray". Nor was he involved in anything that might have international repercussions on the grounds of security ...

'But although the work in solid state physics was not classified [secret] it had classifiable possibilities. In any case it is the bulk of knowledge that can be vitally important, especially unclassified information, obtained when people are working in free fields where some sharp-eyed scientist can immediately see new values ... it is possible that he had stumbled on to something during his research that someone or other did not want brought into effect or circulated among scientists.

'This is speculation – but it is in my opinion a more valid theory than any other that has been advanced.'

9 Ratbags and rogues

The comet who crashed

When Crown Prince Frederik, heir to the throne of Denmark, wedded his Tasmanian wife Mary in 2004, he said he followed in the footsteps of an earlier Dane, Jorgen Jorgenson, with just as much hope and just as much confidence.

But Frederik will need a lot more than hope and confidence if he is to come near to matching the extraordinary adventurer who was 'one of the most interesting human comets recorded in history', as the novelist Marcus Clarke said.

A CV of the life of Jorgen Jorgenson might read like this: 'Anglophile, spy, sailor, author, revolutionist, artist, privateer, vagabond, preacher, explorer, policeman, editor, exile, dramatist, naval officer, debater, convict, whaler, drunk, devoted husband'.

Oh. And King of Iceland.

Jorgenson was a fraud or a genius, according to circumstances. Eminent men like Sir Joseph Banks held him in the highest regard. Others thought him little more than a blowhard. In a tavern he could be a thundering bore or an exhilarating conversationalist, depending on how much you each had to drink. At the casino he could be a bad loser. In the wild he was indefatigable. And in times of danger he was a good man to have at your side.

A compulsive man, Jorgenson constantly sought action and excitement in Britain, on the Continent, in South Africa, New Zealand, Tahiti, and the colonies of New South Wales and Van Diemen's Land, where finally he lies in an unmarked grave, but not forgotten. It would be very hard to forget Jorgen Jorgenson.

He was born in Copenhagen in 1780. He came out bawling and already bellicose, the son of Denmark's royal clock-maker whose genes surely suggested that the boy would grow up meticulous, methodical and ... quiet.

Quite the opposite. Jorgenson was more the son of the Viking he would have been had he been born 1,000 years earlier. As a child he had been appalled by the horrors of the French Revolution and became an Anglophile, with a determination to visit the British colonies on the other side of the world that were then in their infancy. Inspired by Captain James Cook who was killed in Tahiti the year before his birth, he signed on – as Cook had done – with a British coal ship, the collier *Jane*, and for the next four years sailed between the Baltic ports and Newcastle-on-Tyne. Then, on a jaunt to London, he was press-ganged into the Royal Navy.

In 1801, then 21 and with an exceptional command of English, spoken and written, he arrived in Sydney and joined Matthew Flinders' survey expedition on its east coast leg of the circumnavigation of Australia. Jorgenson was second mate on the *Lady Nelson* and remained in that post until 1804, witnessing the abandonment of plans to establish a settlement in Port Phillip and the transference of the settlers to Risdon Cove on the Derwent River, where they established a colony in Van Diemen's Land.

Jorgenson went into the bush exploring, armed with a Bible in one pocket and Dr Johnson's novel *Rasselas* in the other. He climbed Mount Wellington and harpooned a whale in the Derwent (the first European to do so in both cases).

When he sailed from Hobart Town he might reasonably have felt that he would never again see the Derwent or Mount Wellington.

In 1805 after leaving the *Lady Nelson* and whaling and sealing throughout the South Seas he returned to England and then went home to Copenhagen. In 1807 he found himself embroiled in a war between England and Denmark. The English, to prevent the French seizing the Danish fleet, attacked Copenhagen and for three nights bombarded the terrified citizens with rocket-propelled incendiaries. Denmark sided with Napoleon, and Jorgenson, who had commanded a ship in the South Seas, was given a privateer, the *Admiral Juhl*, and took three prizes until he found his ship outgunned and dismasted by the British warship *Sappho*.

Now a prisoner at large and back in England, Jorgenson mixed with Cabinet members and such illustrious and influential men as the Prime Minister, Lord Castlereagh, and Sir Joseph Banks. In 1808 he and an English merchant came up with a plan to ship goods into Iceland, breaking a Danish embargo on trade with England. He went to Reykjavik, the capital, and quickly convinced himself that the Icelanders needed deliverance from Denmark's oppressive terms of trade. The country, he thought, ought to be brought under the protection of Britain. He led a bloodless and farcical revolution. Count Trampe, the Governor of Iceland, was surrounded and arrested, and Jorgenson became benign dictator under a new flag, three white cod on a blue background. Jorgenson proclaimed himself the country's Protector and declared Iceland a republic.

'I was fully determined to seize the first opportunity to strike some blow to be spoken of. It was not love of liberty which influenced me on this occasion ... I have in the course of my life been under the malignant influence of other passions besides pity,' he wrote later. The fiasco might have been avoided if Jorgenson had been more determined to resist the random impulses that played such a key role in his life.

The 'Dog Days Revolution' as it was called, ended ignominiously when the British, not sure they needed another protectorate, ordered the Royal Navy to Copenhagen, and Jorgenson, shipped back to England as a prisoner, was committed to a Thames River prison hulk. Held among fellow Danish officers, he produced his analysis of the revolution in Iceland, an autobiographical novel and two plays.

After being released, he lived in London on and off for the next 10 years, a period marked by dissolution and much time spent in ale houses rowdily 'debating' and carousing with lowlife, or at the card tables. 'I am always wise everywhere else, and mad in London,' he said, talking of his reckless gambling. He spent time in sponging-houses (privately run debtors' prisons). He spied in, and wrote a travel book about, France and Germany. And, inevitably, he ended in Newgate prison for stealing his landlady's bed linen.

He was sentenced to seven years' transportation. He suggested directly to Castlereagh that he be allowed to transport himself to a foreign place, and Castlereagh agreed to allow him to do so. He stayed on in England, however, and when recaptured he was sentenced to transportation for life. In 1826, 22 years after he had left, he was taken back to Van Diemen's Land,

'Strange fortunes and great activity,' he said, marked his life in Van Diemen's Land, and for once Jorgenson was understating the fact. He earned his ticket-of-leave within a year but even while a prisoner Jorgenson was an explorer in wilderness that still defies the most experienced bushwalkers. For the Van Diemen's Land Company he became an official pathfinder, setting out to find a route from the Shannon River to Circular Head, the company's base. Plunging into the tangle of forest and mountain scrub around Ironstone Mountain and discovering Lake St Clair, he retreated only when his rations and his torn and ragged clothes were both on the point of giving out.

Two years after he won his ticket-of-leave Jorgenson signed on as a field constable in the Midlands town of Oatland, a hunter-down of Irish and English bushrangers, earning himself the enmity of his former fellow convicts and winning the love of one of them.

Norah Corbett was a dark-eyed laughing Irish lass half his age, transported for petty theft and working as a laundress. Like him she loved to talk and to drink. They were made for each other. They married in 1831 and for the remainder of Jorgenson's life they quarrelled violently and were fixedly devoted to each other. Drink fuelled both emotions.

Something of the eccentric genius of Jorgenson can be seen in his self-portrait, painted in 1807. The following year he fought against England, the country which transported him to Van Diemen's Land.

In 1830 Lieutenant-Governor Arthur attempted to save the few hundred surviving Aboriginals from destruction – there were, says Manning Clark, from 3,000 to 7,000 on the island when the white man came in 1804. Twenty-six years later, Arthur organised the infamous man-hunt, 'the Black Line,' a human cordon of 3,000 men who went into the bush to herd the natives into the Tasman Peninsula and were able to capture just one man and one boy. Jorgenson, as a field constable took part in the cordon and led his armed men into the wild back-country. A friend to the Aborigines, nevertheless, Jorgenson, typically, had compiled a written vocabulary of their language.

In 1835 he and Norah were pardoned and the pair spent the next five alcohol soaked years scandalising the people of Ross, where Jorgenson was now a constable. They died within months of each other. He was just 60 when he was buried in an unmarked grave in 1841.

The comet had burned out.

The obscene end of Eugene Goossens

*H*e must have felt it when he approached the men at the Mascot airport Customs counter. Heart pounding, stomach churning, the sweat beginning to break out on his scalp and prickle among the thinning, swept back hair: he must have felt the fear.

Ahead of him, behind the counter, he could see four or five men stolidly studying him. Oh, Christ! They didn't look like a welcoming committee.

Could he dump it here ... just a few paces from them?

He should have dumped it! Was that a crime? Or should he just march through, show them a European blend of mild irritability and a lot of urbanity? He was, he reminded himself, respected and admired around the world, a Knight of the Realm: the memory was still fresh and wonderful. The young Queen, Elizabeth II had dubbed him so; he'd knelt before her as she rested the sword on his shoulder at Buckingham Palace just months ago.

Straight ahead, stand tall, be polite but aloof, patrician: let them know that it was Sir Eugene Goossens they were talking to.

In his heart Sir Eugene Goossens had a gift for music that had made him one of the world's most renowned classical musicians. In his mind Sir Eugene Goossens held visions of a world-class Sydney symphony orchestra playing in an opera house that would be the envy of the world. And in the bag he was carrying, his briefcase, was ...

But now, heart thumping so loudly that they could surely hear it he was at the counter ...

'Anything to declare, sir? Other than this?' The man nodding at the declaration form he had passed across the desk.

'No. No, nothing.'

'What's in that?' The man now pointing to his briefcase.

'Oh, that's only my musical scores.'

'Well, let's have a look at it.'

Goossens was the most powerful figure in Australian music: conductor of the Sydney Symphony Orchestra and head of the Conservatorium. As such he was earning more than Robert Menzies, the Prime Minister, and he was well worth it.

Eugene Goossens was a man of great artistic talent wedded to ruthless drive and a grand plan to drag Australia out of its cultural desert: he envisaged a splendid opera house for Sydney, built, he suggested, on the site of the ugly tram sheds at Bennelong Point.

He believed, too, he could take the mediocre Sydney Symphony Orchestra to the front ranks of the world's finest. He wanted the ordinary men and women of Sydney to enjoy classical music and he gave outdoor concerts that were attended by crowds of 20,000 and more. And he saw that the nation had a latent talent of immense potential: a Sydney stenographer named Joan Sutherland who he cast in the lead role – her operatic debut – in his own opera, *Judith*.

Above all, Sir Eugene Goossens was a cultivated and intelligent man with the aloofness that comes with being the conductor of great orchestras. Before he was recruited to Sydney in 1947 he had distinguished himself in concert halls throughout the UK, Europe and America. Noel Coward said, 'My heart loosens when I listen to Goossens.'

Goossens himself once said, 'The living of a musician is a very dignified one. I'm very grateful.'

But intelligence, urbanity and dignity don't always come with wisdom, as Sir Eugene no doubt frequently reflected for the six years of his life that remained after 9 March 1956 when he arrived at Sydney's Mascot airport from London and Customs stopped him.

They were expecting to find what they did: pornographic photographs, films and books in his luggage, although the quantity – around 1,200 items, and the three phallic rubber masks – may have had them tut-tutting with pleasurable surprise. They would have smiled too, at the medal they found among the items: the medal given to him by the Queen on his recent investiture as a knight.

The scandal rocked Sydney and the international arts world. Nevertheless, Sir Eugene might – just – have survived (today it would not be a scandal: an amused par or two in the gossip columns, perhaps) had it not been for Rosaleen Norton.

Sir Eugene, his biographer Carole Rosen says, was searching for 'the mystical truth that was the fount of artistic inspiration and enlightenment', but if he was looking for it in the arms of Rosaleen Norton he was looking in a very rum place.

Like Sir Eugene, Rosaleen Norton (see *The witch who danced with the devil*, page 188) was a conductor, of sorts. Flickering film footage shows her conducting a 'black magic' ceremony. The Witch of Kings Cross, as the press called her, is seen waving a knife around and intoning banalities borrowed in part from the *Rubaiyat of Omar Khayyam*: 'In the name of the horned god ... above and below ... within and without, around and about, here and there ...'

Norton was a third-rate artist, but a first-rate self-publicist. In 1952 her book, *The Art of Rosaleen Norton*, a collection of grotesque, erotic paintings illustrating poems by her young lover Gavin Greenlees, had attracted the interest of the Postmaster General, who judged the book obscene, but not before Eugene Goossens had bought a copy: he had a secret interest in the occult and the book fired it. He wrote to Rosaleen Norton and she invited him around for tea.

Tea with Rosaleen Norton at her seedy Kings Cross flat was a long way removed from the Twinings and cucumber sandwiches that Goossens was accustomed to serving at his elegant North Shore home.

Goossens, however, did not take tea with his wife. Marjorie his third wife, a wealthy and glamorous American, no longer loved him and lived a cosmopolitan and luxurious life in Europe. Goossens, loveless, found Sydney provincial and strait-laced and boring and Norton's cramped, dingy Kings Cross flat must have excited him; the makeshift altar before which her coven worshipped stirred something deep and dark and prurient inside him.

Goossens, like Gavin Greenlees, fell under Norton's spell. He, too, became Norton's lover and for the next two years took part in the humpo-bumpo-mumbo-jumbo of the coven's 'sex magic'. (Later he also began a more refined relationship with an 18-year-old admirer, an Adelaide pianist, Pamela Main.)

Goossens' biographer explains his involvement with Norton as a search for his Muse. 'For the majority of participants,' she wrote, 'the ritual worship of Pan had provided sexual excitement that was both erotic and illicit. But for Eugene it was something much more, a search for the mystical truth that was the fount of artistic inspiration and enlightenment.' This explanation would have cut no ice with Bert Travenar.

Travenar, a NSW Vice Squad detective at the time, picked up the story in the ABC program, *Rewind*, aired in September 2004.

'Well, two young fellows were hawking some photographs around the newspapers. [Bondage pornography, the photos showed Gavin Greenlees in ceremonial costume and Norton in nothing but liberal make-up, earrings and ropes.] Eventually they went to the *Sun* and the fellow from the *Sun* got in touch with the chief of the Vice Squad and he detailed me to ... continue with the enquiry.' (The Vice Squad already had suspicions that Goossens was among a small and elite group of Sydneysiders who were members of a circulating library of pornography.)

Travenar already had in his file letters written by Goossens to Norton: signed letters that confirmed their intense sexual relationship. They had been stolen and given to the police by a *Sun* crime reporter, Joe

Morris, who had infiltrated the coven to get a story on the Witch of Kings Cross but who now discovered that there was a far bigger story waiting to be splashed.

'Rowiewitch,' one of Goossens' letters to Rosaleen began, 'You came to me early this morning, about 1.45. I realised, by a delicious orificial tingling that you were about to make your presence felt.'

And another, 'We have many rituals and indulgences to undertake. Even now, my bat-wings envelop and lift you.'

And – fatefully – 'Anonymity is still best. Destroy this.'

She didn't of course. She kept his letters stuffed behind her sofa where Joe Morris found them and handed them over to the Vice Squad. The police were ready to pounce, said Travenar, 'but unfortunately, before I was able to effect an arrest on that occasion, he'd left the country and gone on a concert out of Britain and the Continent.'

For Goossens the highlight of that tour was his knighthood. But the lowlight, as it proved, was the time and money he spent in Soho sex shops – visits that were recorded by private investigators, hired by the *Sun,* who followed him in London.

'Joe [Morris] rang me,' said Travenar, 'and said, "That friend of ours that's overseas is coming back on the Qantas flight so-and-so from London." Then he said he was carrying a briefcase and his information was that the briefcase probably had indecent photographs that he had, in fact, bought.'

Detective Travenar, along with Ron Walton, head of the Vice Squad, and a photographer from the *Sun,* were waiting with the customs officer when Sir Eugene arrived at Customs. Bag by bag, customs searched his luggage and then Goossens and Travenar went to an upstairs room at police headquarters in the city.

'I said, "Do you know a woman named Rosaleen Norton?" he said, "Yes. I've known her and Gavin for some time."

'I said, "There was repeated mention of 'SM' rites between you and Norton and Greenlees made in your letters. What is that?"

'He said, "That is sex magic. It is a symbolic ceremony involving sex stimulation."

'I said, "How is that rite conducted?"

'He said, "We undressed and sat on the floor in a circle. Miss Norton conducted the verbal part of the rite and then I performed the sexual stimulation on her."' (This stimulation might best be understood in Rosaleen's own chant: 'In and out, above about, below, here and there.')

Sir Eugene Goossens, a harmless, naïve and foolish gentleman, talking to the Vice Squad without a lawyer, now faced his fall.

Sir Eugene stood down from his positions and the following day was charged with bringing prohibited goods into the country. A much more serious charge of scandalous conduct – something that though done in private outraged public decency – a charge that could have meant him going to jail, was yet to be laid.

On the Customs charge he was fined £100 ($200), but, to Bert Travenar's chagrin, evident even 40 years later, the Attorney-General decided not to go ahead with the scandalous conduct charge, with all its likelihood of the naming of well-known figures in the pornographic library circle and sensational 'revelations' from the publicity-hungry Rosaleen Norton. Implicit in the failure to press the charge was the understanding that Sir Eugene would leave Australia forever.

The newspapers had been salivating on the disclosures that were yet to come. Two days after Goossens was stopped at Customs the Sunday Telegraph reported: 'Big Names in Devil Rite Probe. Police have disclosed that "black masses"' and other devil worship ceremonies have taken place in luxurious homes on the North Shore.

'A banker, a lawyer and one or two radio artists are said to be among those involved. Police disclosures followed an intensive Sydney-wide check on practising satanic rites. The extent of devil worship in Sydney amazed police. They are expected to make shock disclosures soon.'

The papers were to be denied more shock disclosures and one or two 'radio artists' must have breathed huge sighs of relief when the further charge against Goossens was not proceeded with. Bert Travenar was devastated. 'I'd been dudded,' said Travenar 40 years on, still bitterly regretting that Sir Eugene hadn't been humiliated and disgraced in court.

One autumn morning six weeks after his return to Sydney Sir Eugene slipped out of the city and under the name of Mr E. Gray took a KLM flight to Rome. At the last minute he had sent his friends – few of whom stood by him publicly – a form letter claiming that he had been forced to bring the pornography into Australia 'as a result of persistent menaces involving others'. That was the tack Goossens' barrister took at his trial.

No-one has ever given this explanation the slightest credence. But was there a sinister link between Rosaleen Norton and the set-up that undid Goossens? Was she the menace Goossens referred to? Did Norton betray Goossens to the Vice Squad because of his failure to help her when she and Gavin Greenlees (her other lover) were on charges of committing 'unnatural offences'? Did she plant the incriminating photographs in her bed-sit so that they could be found by the reporter Joe Morris?

The veteran Sydney crime reporter, Bill Jenkings in his memoirs, *As Crime Goes By*, says Rosaleen Norton played a key, behind-the-scenes role in Goossens' fall. 'Her role in the scandal was never made public but Rowie the Witch was involved up to the tip of her broomstick.'

Bert Travenar dismissed the claim. 'That was rubbish when Sir Eugene's barrister told the court he brought the pornography into the country because of threats ... As a matter of fact he [Goossens] told me privately that, 12 months or so before his arrest he'd destroyed his own collection of pornography as soon as he heard that Norton and her boyfriend had been arrested on pornography charges and charges of buggery and what-not ...'

In the last, lonely years of his life, said a friend, Sir Eugene was 'like a man encased in ice'. He looked like a lost soul, his daughter, Renee said. 'And whereas my father had always carried himself very well, rather grandly, rather like an actor, he now was slumped and had almost the equivalent of scoliosis.'

He found that he was boycotted by the international music world he had once been so much a part of and spent much of his time at his sister Sidonie's farmhouse in Sussex. We're all human ... to a certain extent, naturally,' she said, 'but, that it should become that ... Well, it killed him, really. One can say that.'

Officially, however, Sir Eugene Goossens died of a ruptured ulcer in 1960. Pamela Main told *Rewind* that 'If things had gone smoothly, which unfortunately they didn't, I would have married him in 1960. That was his plan. Things didn't go smoothly. But if he'd lived a few weeks longer, until the beginning of September, we would have been able to get married and would have done.'

It took 20 more years for Sydney to honour the man who was the impetus for the building that is today the city's symbol. A sculpture of him now meets visitors to the Opera House but the shameful treatment of Sir Eugene still embitters those who knew him. Sir Richard Bonynge, a student at the Conservatorium when Goossens headed it, said, 'They took a great influence away from Sydney, and then destroyed a human being. It really killed him. He was a great man, a great musician, and Sydney did him a great disservice.'

Renee Goossens lovingly recalled a kind father, a man who, despite his public autocratic and at times despotic image, in private had an offbeat sense of humour. 'He was a very funny man, funny like silly funny; he would have adored John Cleese.' But John Cleese and the entire creative crew of *Monty Python* would have been hard put to raise a smile at the despicable fall of Sir Eugene Goossens.

The spy who never was ... was he?

Was he the boy who cried wolf?
Or was he the wolf who cried boy?

Was he really just an amusing 'character' who pretended to be a spy? Or was he a spy who pretended to be just an amusing 'character' pretending to be a spy?

Whatever the truth there can be no doubt that Francis James was a remarkable ratbag: less an enigma, more an egotist, he succeeded in turning his long imprisonment by the Chinese into a spy story that had journalists around the globe in a frenzy. At its climax, when he was released from prison and stumbled, looking aged, weak and drained, into a battery of international film and press cameras and was carried away by stretcher to a Hong Kong hospital, Francis James had probably never been happier.

Although secretive – Rupert Murdoch's second wife Anna said, 'No-one will ever know the true Francis James' – and although he himself once claimed, 'I am a shy, nervous sort of person,' he loved the limelight, something that a good spy scrupulously avoids. Above all he lived to tweak the nose of life, and to do it in as public a way as possible.

Bob Ellis, a devotee of Francis James, described him as a man of many parts: fighter pilot, prisoner of war, churchman, double agent, political mischief-maker, teacher and adventurer. 'He was the boyhood hero Australians never had,' Ellis said.

Warming to his theme, Ellis said Francis had 'an infinite capacity to conjure magic out of the universe, poetry out of the past. He should occupy a position like Douglas Bader, Lawrence of Arabia or Lord Mountbatten.' And, Ellis concluded with rare understatement, 'He had a strong sense of mystery and gamesmanship that may have tiptoed over into fiction occasionally.'

Francis James was born in Queenstown, Tasmania, in 1918 and went to Canberra Grammar with Gough Whitlam and Sir John Kerr. The school magazine predicted that Whitlam would become Archbishop of Canterbury and Francis James Prime Minister and got it more than half right. James was the son of an Anglican minister who, perhaps significantly, was also a pug, a notable boxer known as the Fighting Parson of Cessnock. Francis James's passport described him as a theologian. He became editor of the *Anglican*, a church newspaper such as Australia had never known, and his obituary in the *Sydney Morning Herald*, his old newspaper, wrongly described him as a 'renaissance clergyman'. But he certainly never became the Archbishop of Canterbury.

He would have made a memorable Head of the Church of England, but instead of taking Holy Orders he joined the RAAF at Point Cook in 1936, the youngest cadet pilot in the Air Force's history. He failed to get his Wings because of his habit of arguing with senior officers (James claimed to have been expelled from five schools because of his frank opinions) but he went on to get his pilot's licence taking lessons privately, and when war came he joined the Royal Air Force in England.

Twice, flying his Spitfire with the famous Fighter Command, he was shot down over France. The first time he parachuted to safety and escaped back to England. Then, the second time, on Anzac Day 1942, his flaming Spitfire went spiralling into a death dive.

Francis James's handsome face was hideously burned in the crash. Temporarily blinded, his back broken, he was captured by the Germans. But his pluck and his profound impulse to cause mischief and to put himself in the centre of things, even as he was being dragged from the wreck of the Spitfire, led him, when asked who he was, to gasp: 'I'm Air Commodore Turtle Dove.'

Greatly impressed, the Germans gave Turtle Dove VIP treatment. The German army's leading ophthalmologist, General Lurlein, treated his badly burned eyes and plastic surgeons transplanted the skin from his buttocks to his face. (Forty years later, to his grandchildren's never failing glee, he would tell them that when they were looking at his face what they were really looking at was his bottom.)

He was, nevertheless, a prisoner and tried to escape five times from Stalag Luft III, eventually succeeding when a neutral Swiss Red Cross commission decided he was in such a bad way that he should be repatriated to Cairo and thence to England. The Germans didn't fight to hold him – they were clearly glad to see the last of Air Commodore Turtle Dove.

At the end of the war he was demobbed and went to Oxford on a special grant. He lasted three terms before he was inevitably sent down. He wouldn't have had it otherwise. He had taken part in the kidnapping of a fellow student who was held at gunpoint until he paid his bridge and poker debts. A year later he went back: 'The blighters forgave me.' Too late. In the meantime Francis James had discovered journalism and Fleet Street.

Generically, journalists have very little dress sense. Not Francis James. He wore a black coat, striped trousers and a homburg for his interviews and so impressed the management of *World Review* they made him editor. Back in Australia he went to work as the education and religious correspondent and occasional leader writer for the *Sydney Morning Herald*. On his first day he turned up for work in a 1926 Rolls-Royce Phantom I.

'Magnificent old bus,' he told Melbourne writer Keith Dunstan, 'I bought it for 800 quid and sold it – a mistake probably – and bought a 1936 Phantom II. It was faster, easier to drive and I put air-conditioning in it.' In it he also installed a desk, typewriter and a bar for entertaining, and blinds to shield him from the vulgar gaze. When his subeditor wanted to talk to him he would shower a handful of paper clips onto the car from his office window high above.

He was by this time also affecting a black hat with an enormous brim and a scarlet-lined cloak that he would swish elegantly whenever he felt the urge. The hat, he used to say, was necessary to protect his eyesight. 'My skin had to be shaded from the sun and my eyes were photophobic; couldn't stand direct light. The Ministry of Pensions in England decreed that I should wear a large-brimmed hat.

'The Department of Repatriation here sent an agent to me, told me I had to wear a wide-brimmed hat. Nobody could provide it and they had to go to Akubra and have a couple especially made. One day a Repat. bloke drove up with two large boxes, two splendid hats, one grey, one black. Not a bad effort.'

The cloak, he admitted, was purely for effect. It gave him entrée anywhere.

He was at the *Herald* for three years before, in 1952, the Archbishop of Brisbane and the bishops of Armidale and Newcastle, took him to dinner and told him the church newspaper, *The Church Standard* was ailing. It needed fresh blood.

Francis and an old Oxford friend bought the paper, re-christened it the *Anglican*, and took its circulation, in six months, from 1,700 to 90,000. The paper he and his wife Joyce produced was not quite what the bishops ordered. But it was compulsory reading for its mostly non-believer readers. The *Anglican* broke hard news stories about the big political issues of the day.

'We were able to tell in the *Anglican* that we were gong into Vietnam and so were the Americans,' he told Keith Dunstan. 'When the first battalion was going – and which battalion it was. All hell broke loose.

'Oh, Christ! The Prime Minister rang up the Archbishop. "Espionage! How does James get this information?"'

There was a simple explanation, he said, but the question that had puzzled Prime Minister Menzies was to puzzle the Russian and Chinese Governments not long after – and lead to Francis James's imprisonment. Where did he get his information? Was he a spy?

The solution to the puzzle, James said, was simple.

'You see' my background is really a service one.

'Inevitably I knew a lot of people who were contemporaries of mine. Half my family are Regular Duntroon [then the Army officer training camp]. My uncle Jimmy retired 2IC Duntroon. My dear friend General Pierre Rousselet, who lost a leg at Dien Bien Phu, was in Hanoi.'

His contacts also included members of the Communist party. So when, in 1966, Commonwealth security searched his house in the guise of looking for heroin, and he discovered his phone was being tapped, Francis decided to have some fun.

'President Lyndon B. Johnson was in town so I arranged a phone call [to his Communist friend]. I gave the impression to the listeners that a bomb was to be thrown and we could meet at the corner of Pitt and Market Streets and I would hand over the 'egg-timer' – code for the fuse and percussion device.

'So bloody funny. At precisely three minutes to eleven all traffic was brought to a stop and a half a dozen very large gentlemen in mufti closed in on us. They took us down to Central where they opened the box. A staff sergeant came up incredulous: 'Super! It *is* an egg-timer!'

Three years later, in 1969, the joke backfired badly.

At a time when tensions between the two Communist super powers, the USSR and China were at their height and each country was in readiness for war, Francis James wrote a series of articles for the prestigious and authoritative London *Sunday Times*. In them he claimed to have made a trip to the border between the two countries and visited the top-secret Chinese nuclear centre at Lop-Nor. He claimed to have interviewed scientists at the site who told him that China had the capacity to build hundreds of atomic bombs and its nuclear capacity was well ahead of the predictions in the West.

(He also described a wildly romantic and highly unlikely ride he had made with the Kazakh cavalry. More disturbingly the photographs that accompanied the *Sunday Times* articles looked very like those James had taken 14 years before in Manchuria on a junket with a delegation of Anglican bishops.)

The articles caused a furore in both countries. The Chinese, who had never allowed an outsider to visit Lop-Nor furiously denied the allegations, and the Russians reacted by arresting James at Moscow airport. He was taken to the KGB office at the airport. 'Now Mr James, do you deny you are a journalist, and not a theologian?' the KGB man demanded, waving a copy of the *Sunday Times*.

Francis James was more than a match for the Russians as he had been for the Germans and by the time he left he had a visa for Canton stamped on his passport. He got to China in October and according to westerners who saw him began to act in an extraordinary fashion. He seemed to be saying – 'Hey everybody! Over here, look at me! I'm a spy.'

'I detest publicity. I'm a simple student. I'm a very shy, quiet sort of person,' he had told Anna Murdoch. 'It happens that by sheer chance I've done things because I wanted to do them which people appear to find unusual. Well that's not my problem. Huh! I'm a very private person. Very private.'

But in China, a country whose dogma then, in the days of The Gang of Four, was strict conformity and utter predictably, he was very public, very eccentric and entirely unpredictable. They imprisoned him.

There he stayed for more than three years, while the Chinese tried to get him to admit he was a spy for the Russians. Or was he working for the CIA, MI5 or the Deuxieme Bureau in Paris? (The Chinese hadn't heard of ASIO, he said later.) Constantly interrogated and sometimes held in solitary confinement, he was told that if he signed a confession he would be freed. Years later he said he had signed 'five or six absurd fairytale confessions which would make good copy in a popular newspaper,' but the Chinese, not versed in the ways of the tabloids, clearly thought it was a case of crying wolf.

He admitted he could not understand the Chinese mind: 'It was all so incalculable,' he said of the attitude and motives of his captors. They, in turn, must have been totally perplexed by him. He held no bitterness towards them – 'The Chinese are mere tyros compared with Gerheime Staatspolizei, the Gestapo, at the techniques of interrogation, you see.'

Francis James, for all his Walter Mitty side, was a courageous man. But imprisonment was a tremendous strain. In March 1972 he was on the brink of freedom. His captors took him to the border with Hong Kong where one of his four children, Stephen, was waiting to take him to freedom. He would be able to join Stephen, the Chinese told him, if he would sign a confession. James refused.

He went back to jail while the espionage experts and 'China-watchers' on newspapers internationally pondered afresh the question: was this extraordinary man a spy – a new kind of espionage agent, highly extrovert and totally outrageous – and had he seen China's secret nuclear centre? Only Francis James really knew, and he was somewhere in China being held, likely as not, in solitary confinement.

Ten months later, on 15 January 1973, his old Canberra Grammar schoolmate, the Australian Prime Minister Gough Whitlam, announced that the Chinese government had found Francis James guilty of espionage but had decided to deport him. It was, the Chinese said, a friendly gesture following the establishment of diplomatic relations with Australia in the month before.

The next day newspapers around the world carried front-page stories and photographs of Francis James crossing the border. Swaying on his feet, leaning heavily on the Australian High Commissioner's arm, the once debonair James was dressed in black trousers, an ill-fitting blue Chinese coat and an incongruous red cap. His hair cropped and tousled, needing a shave, he looked, wrote one reporter, like an irritable Stanley Laurel of silent film days.

He was as indomitable as ever but clearly ill – a 54-year-old man who looked 10 years older.

Then he collapsed and was put on a stretcher and taken by ambulance to Hong Kong's Matilda Hospital. From the hospital bed, over a brandy and soda, he phoned his wife Joyce in Sydney, and then his Hong Kong tailor. He wanted to apologise for not having paid the man's last bill, now almost four years old.

'I have been unavoidably detained, old boy,' he said, 'for reasons beyond my control.'

Francis James had enjoyed life on the edge for most of his 54 years. At one time, when he was sending money to North Vietnam during the Vietnam war, he was branded a traitor to his country. He had been publicly denounced for his attitudes on China and Vietnam by three successive Australian prime ministers. And along the way he'd had an amusing skirmish with the law when, as religious editor of the very pagan *Oz Magazine*, he stood trial with its editors, Richard Walsh, Richard Neville and Martin Sharpe, on charges of issuing an obscene publication. They were given jail terms, overturned on appeal. He, as the magazine's printer, was fined £50.

He went home to Sydney and lived there for the rest of his life, another 20 years, writing as a freelance journalist and enjoying a kind of celebrity status (most people didn't know what to make of him). But he never told, and no-one ever really got to the bottom of, his China story. That was the way he wanted it, he claimed. 'Let me tell you something,' he said agitatedly to Anna Murdoch. 'My life is secret. Neither you nor anybody else will ever succeed in writing an article about the real James. I'm too shy to allow it to appear. Far too shy.'

Well, that was plainly not so. And to another journalist he said, 'I have done my best to eschew publicity ... I am not really a stirrer.'

He was wrong there, too.

10 Hats off to the unsung heroes

The man with the Nelson touch

The last the men in the water saw of their skipper he was standing alone on the bridge. Courageous and a navy man to the last, Captain Waller was going down with his ship, but not without the fight that had made him a legend. His cruiser and another had fought at least 60 Japanese warships and for 90 minutes had given more than they got. Between them the pair had damaged three cruisers and nine destroyers and sunk four transports and two minesweepers.

Yet Waller's heroism went relatively unnoticed by officialdom. It's hard to know why he was so snubbed. By any standards Captain Waller was an extraordinary seaman: a man with unorthodox but audacious skills that made him one of the outstanding naval commanders of the war. Had he been a fighter pilot he might have been remembered as one of Australia's most heroic and best-loved servicemen. The English certainly thought highly of him. He was twice awarded a DSO. But Australia, mystifyingly, confined him to a posthumous mention in despatches after his final, valiant, fight to the death.

Hector Macdonald Laws Waller was born in 1900 in Benalla, a town deep in northern Victoria, but in truth he was born to the sea. He was 13 when he joined the Royal Australian Navy and 17 when he graduated with the King's Medal, the best midshipman of the course. It was 1917, just too late for the teenager to go to war.

But by 1939, when World War Two broke out, Hec Waller was captain of the *Stuart*, one of five destroyers under his command. The five, HMAS

Stuart, Voyager, Vampire, Vendetta and *Waterhen*, were derisorily called the Scrap Iron Flotilla, a 'consignment of junk' by Goebbels, Hitler's propaganda chief, when they appeared in the Mediterranean just three months after Hitler invaded Poland.

Within that time, what had been the 'Phoney War' heated up with the capitulation of France and on 9 July 1940 Waller and the *Stuart* – a ship so decrepit it was laughingly said to be tied together with string – gave a dramatic glimpse of what a brilliant commander and a willing crew could do with a rust-bucket.

That day marked the first important naval engagement since the decisive Battle of Jutland in World War One when the British and the German navies engaged each other in battle that cost thousands of lives on both sides and ended with the German navy victorious, but fatally mauled.

The Battle of Calabria began when an Italian fleet of two battleships, 12 cruisers and 24 destroyers, sailing serenely 30 miles to the east of the 'toe' of Italy unexpectedly encountered a combined fleet of British and Australian warships. The Italians had the support of German fighter planes and shore batteries. Nevertheless, they ran for it, with the *Stuart* snapping at their heels. A lone Italian destroyer, the *Zeffiro*, put up a fight. When Admiral Sir William Cunningham's flagship, the *Warspite*, hit the *Cavour*, his opposite number, squarely amidships the *Zeffiro* came to its rescue, putting itself between the *Cavour* and the British. A broadside from the *Stuart* hit its quarterdeck and salvoes from three British cruisers saw it sink within seconds. The *Zeffiro*'s gallant and sacrificial action had given the Italians time for the fleet to scuttle for the protection of the shore batteries.

The role of the *Stuart*, with Waller throwing her into the action, was noted: there was a touch of the *Nelson* in the way he did things, they were saying in the wardrooms, and eight months later he again showed why. The Battle of Matapan, Winston Churchill said, was the most decisive naval victory since Trafalgar. And Captain Waller and the *Stuart* were so central to it that Admiral Cunningham called Matapan, *Stuart*'s Wild Night.

Once again it was the Italians who suffered. Off the coast of Greece on the night of 29 March, 1941 a dozen Italian cruisers and destroyers found themselves sailing into a British battle fleet waiting for them south of Greece. The first ship to do battle was the *Stuart*. The old destroyer was heading for the cruiser *Zara* when Waller saw the *Pola* coming to her aid. 'We'll get both of these!' Waller had the impertinence to shout exultantly. Waller brought the *Stuart*, dwarfed by the *Zara*, under the cruiser's big guns and fired all torpedoes. Two of them smashed into the *Zara* even as the *Stuart* was turning to come again. This time she hit the *Zara* with two salvoes and left it, helpless, to hare off after the *Pola*.

The *Pola* was waiting and fired on the *Stuart* point blank. The old destroyer took little damage and replied with two broadsides that set off a series of explosions and caused the cruiser to turn tail and run for it. She was finished off by other British ships. The *Stuart*, meanwhile, had taken on a third Italian, the destroyer *Vittoria Alfieri*, and left it on fire and out of control. The *Stuart*'s Wild Night was over, and also the Battle of Matapan.

Now the *Stuart* was needed to guard the transports taking the troops from Greece to Crete, and then getting them out again under heavy attack from the Germans and taking them to North Africa. In late 1941 Waller took the old girl back to Australia for a refit. Goebbels had been right. The Scrap-Iron Flotilla, was old – the five destroyers dated from World War One – and they were slow, but after two years fighting in the Middle Sea they left behind a trail of sunken submarines, battered cruisers and destroyers, downed Luftwaffe aircraft, and wiped the sneer from Goebbels' mouth.

Waller was given command of a cruiser, the *Perth*. On 26 February 1942 the *Perth* joined an Allied squadron of five cruisers and nine destroyers ordered to stop a Japanese fleet intent on invading the Dutch

East Indies. At Batavia the *Perth* beat off an attack of Japanese aircraft and two days later met the Japanese fleet in a tumultuous Battle of the Java Sea. Through the afternoon and into the night the ships fought at close range, and when Admiral Doorman was killed and his flagship blown up, Waller found himself in command of the only two Allied ships still afloat: the *Perth* and the *Houston*. The two fought their way to the safety of Batavia. Once there, hardly drawing breath, the crews refuelled and the following night, at 7 p.m., slipped away through the Sunda Strait hoping to reach Australia.

They ran straight into the Japanese invasion fleet.

Heavily outnumbered – they faced as many as 60 enemy warships – the *Perth* and the *Houston* went down fighting. For an hour they fought a running battle to force their way through the Sunda Strait. They gave much more than they got: they sank or damaged 18 enemy ships – but at the end of an hour, the *Perth* was hit by two torpedoes. She had been almost out of ammunition, her pom pom crew members killed or reduced to firing star shells, and Waller knew the moment had come. He ordered the men to abandon ship. The *Houston* too was done for.

On life rafts and in longboats on the dark oily waters lit by the flames of battle, the crews of the two ships saw the *Perth* slide into the darkness. The survivors were destined to spend the rest of the war in prison camps. Captain Waller was last seen standing alone on the deck, one of 453 offices and men of the *Perth*'s complement of 682 who were lost in action.

How Horrie the Wog Dog hoaxed us all

Horrie the Wog Dog's execution shocked a nation and became part of our folklore. A brave little dog, a hero to thousands of servicemen who had fought alongside him, 'destroyed' by the hands of a vicious and petty bureaucracy. That is what we have believed for six decades and that is why for many years wreaths were laid in his honour on Anzac Day.

But did Horrie really die? Or did he hoodwink the nation and live, in an identity switch that *A Tale of Two Cities*' Sidney Carton, who took another's place at the guillotine, would have understood and approved? The compelling evidence – and reading it defies you not to cheer – is that Horrie lived to fight and play another day and make love on many another night.

'He was whisked away to northern Victoria, where he lived out his days and sired many puppies,' Anthony Hill revealed in his book on animals who served with Australian forces, *Animal Heroes* (Penguin, 2005).

This new and improved happy ending to the story of the little dog now makes it suitable for a Hollywood feature film. Russell Crowe could be cast in the supporting role of Horrie's master, Jim, and as Horrie ... well, you could cast just about any Jack Russell with the head of the proverbial robber's dog: a Russell Crowe-type dog.

Horrie wasn't a robber's dog, as far as it's known. But he wasn't pretty. He was just a mongrel, a little runt of a dog with a big heart beating under his skinny ribs who saw action in some of the darkest days of World War Two. In Egypt, he trained with the Australian Infantry Force's 2/1st Australian Machine Gun battalion for the campaigns to come. In Greece, Horrie and his mates were relentlessly bombed by the invading Germans. In Crete, he was wounded when his ship went down. In Syria, he fought French troops who had gone over to the Germans. Through it all, Horrie's courage and fighting spirit never deserted him. He never wavered in his devotion to his mates. And in turn they were there when Horrie desperately needed them.

Horrie joined the AIF in Egypt in 1942 when Jim Moody and Don Gill, a couple of Aussie privates stationed in the Western Desert, noticed a pup chasing lizards among the rocks. He was hopping with fleas and rather comical looking with stumpy legs, a long body and not much of a tail to wag. But he was clearly in need of a good feed and Jim tucked him under his arm and took him back to the camp. He was, they reckoned, an Arab dog who had survived cruel treatment: he would bark furiously if Arabs came near the camp.

Within a week, Horrie the Wog Dog, as they called him, was everybody's mate, and a valued member of the battalion. No route march could start until Horrie was in the vanguard. The little dog took his place at the head of the column and proudly led it out. At night he guarded the camp against thieves. He was given a promotion, he was now Corporal Horrie, and wore a uniform, a khaki coat cut down from a regular army issue and complete with corporal ensigns.

Then, without notice, the days of training and route marches were over as the battalion was rushed to Greece to help stem the German invasion, Horrie went too. It was against regulations, but by now Jim had trained him to travel, keeping still and quiet, in his kitbag. Seasick on the way over, like many another Digger, Horrie was ready for action when he and his mates arrived in Athens. They were just in time to join what was to become one of the most disastrous retreats of the war. Day after day, the Luftwaffe were bombing and machine-gunning the retreating Allied columns. Horrie became an air raid siren – the best.

When the little dog suddenly sat to attention, his ears cocked, the men of the machine gun battalion knew he was hearing enemy planes on their way. Then Horrie's frenzied barking alerted the troops down the line to the imminent attack. British Tommies, Kiwis, Greeks, Yugoslavs and Australians scrambled off and away from the truck convoy and when the Stukas roared overhead the men had whatever cover they could find. Horrie saved hundreds of Allied troops. At night Horrie was on sentry duty, alert for saboteurs, as he had been in Egypt.

They were evacuated from Greece by night just as the Germans were about to invade. Horrie's ship, the *Costa Rica*, was hit by a torpedo and sunk but Moody held Horrie close and he and his mates jumped from it to the destroyer *Defender* that had swung to their rescue alongside. They were taken to Crete where Horrie was given new orders. He became a messenger. Men on patrol would tie despatches in a handkerchief around Horrie's collar and he'd race back to deliver them to Moody.

Once again they were ordered to be evacuated, this time back to Egypt, and once again the bombing was almost non-stop. Horrie was hit in the shoulder by a sliver of shrapnel and as Moody and Gill dug it out the little dog never whimpered.

In Tel Aviv, waiting to be shipped back to Australia and then to be sent to fight the Japanese in New Guinea, Moody and Gill took their mate to a vet. They'd been through a lot together and they had no intention of leaving him behind. The vet kept the little dog for a week, put him through tests and gave him a clean bill of health.

Now it was a matter of smuggling Horrie on to the boat to Australia. Moody had long before cut a hole in the back of his kitbag for Horrie to quickly pop into on command. When Moody had the pack on his back he'd wet his finger in his water bottle and Horrie would lick it through a ventilation hole. That was how Horrie boarded the ship. It was a risky business – a cat and a dog, smuggled aboard had been discovered and peremptorily thrown overboard. Moody was much more careful with Horrie. He was kept in a cabin where someone was with him at all times and if there was a knock on the door Horrie would jump into his smuggler's pack and his companion would toss some clothes over it.

He went ashore when the ship docked in Adelaide and from there was sent to Melbourne to live with Henry Moody, Jim's dad, until Jim got back from New Guinea.

And there the story should end, with Horrie living happily every after, an old soldier never dying, just fading away. Instead, three years after he had come into Australia, he was ordered to be put down. Horrie, said an officious bureaucracy, was an illegal immigrant who had evaded quarantine. He must be 'destroyed'.

Horrie's existence had been discovered when the Commonwealth Director of Veterinary Hygiene, Mr R.N. Wardle, saw an article about Horrie and how Jim had smuggled him into Australia. Mr R.N. Wardle saw red. He ordered his officers to seize Horrie. Jim Moody and Horrie were staying at Don Gill's Sydney home when the officials tracked them down, and Jim, distressed, asked them to give him one more week with his old mate.

A week later the officers returned for Horrie. They waited while Jim said a sad farewell, took the little dog, and, at 4 p.m. on Monday 12 March, gave him a dose of cyanide.

Horrie's death was front page news. The nation was outraged. Public meetings, questions in Parliament, the Prime Minister under fire, editorials thundering, abusive letters flooding in to Mr R.N. Wardle's office, a wreath was at the Cenotaph – all in vain. Horrie was gone.

But was he?

Canberra author Anthony Hill thought he was familiar with the story of Horrie until a friend suggested that he write a book about the gallant little dog. He picks up the story in the preface to *Animal Heroes*.

'"But Ion Idriess wrote that book in 1945," I said. "Horrie was destroyed by the quarantine authorities three years after he got here."

'"I mean," Norma replied, "that you should say what really happened."

'And for the first time in nearly 60 years, she broke her silence and told me the tale of the substitute dog – as Horrie's owner, Jim Moody, had told it to her ... I was able to confirm the main details of the story with two of Jim's children, Ian and Leonie Moody, and also with Brian and Betty Featherstone. Brian is probably the last surviving member of the signal platoon 'Rebels' of 2/1 Machine Gun Battalion ... Through them I learnt how Jim had the last laugh on bureaucratic authority: of the switch, and of the 'five bob dog.' He was a Horrie look-alike, who was bought for five shillings from a Sydney pound and given to the officials when they demanded Jim hand over his dog for destruction.'

Jim Moody was saddened to hand over the substitute look-alike dog he had found and bought for five shillings at the pound. But the sacrifice of the unwanted little dog, doomed in any case, allowed Horrie to happily live the rest of his life on a farm in northern Victoria.

Horrie's memorabilia is on exhibit at the Australian War Memorial in Canberra. There is Jim's ventilated kitbag, Horrie's khaki 'corporal's' jacket and his campaign medals. And up and down the east coast of Australia there are hundreds of little Horrie's and Horriettas, whose ancestor was the courageous little dog the Nazis and the bureaucrats couldn't kill.